Building Diaspora

Building Diaspora

Filipino Community Formation on the Internet

EMILY NOELLE IGNACIO

RUTGERS UNIVERSITY PRESS
New Brunswick, New Jersey, and London

Library of Congress Cataloging-in-Publication Data

Ignacio, Emily, 1970–
    Building diaspora : Filipino community formation on the Internet /
Emily Ignacio.
        p. cm.
    Includes bibliographical references (p.   ) and index.
    ISBN 0–8135–3513–1 (alk. paper) — ISBN 0–8135–3514–X (pbk. : alk.
paper)
        1. Filipino Americans—Social conditions. 2. Filipino Americans—
Ethnic identity. 3. Filipino Americans—Race identity. 4. Internet—Social
aspects. 5. Community life—United States. 6. Transnationalism.
7. Philippines—Relations—United States. 8. United States—Relations—
Philippines. I. Title.
    E184.F4I37   2005
    305.89'921073'090511—dc22

                                                                                2004011749

A British Cataloging-in-Publication record for this book is available from
the British Library

Manufactured in the United States of America

To my parents, Nolie G. Ignacio
and Corazon Sanchez-Ignacio

Contents

ACKNOWLEDGMENTS   ix

PREFACE: WHY FILIPINOS?   xvii

1 Introduction: Filipino Community Formation
  on the Internet   1

2 Problematizing Diaspora: If Nation, Culture, and
  Homeland Are Constructed, Why Bother with
  Diasporic Identity?   28

3 Selling Out One's Culture: The Imagined
  Homeland and Authenticity   53

4 "Ain't I a Filipino (Woman)?": Filipina as
  Gender Marker   78

5 Laughter in the Rain: Jokes as Membership
  and Resistance   113

6 E Pluribus or E Pluribus Unum?: Can There Be
  Unity in Diversity?   134

APPENDIX A: STUDYING THE DEFINITION OF "FILIPINO"   149
APPENDIX B: YOU MAY BE MARRIED TO A FILIPINA IF   150
APPENDIX C: ARE YOU REALLY FILIPINO?   152
NOTES   157
REFERENCES   163
INDEX   171

Acknowledgments

When I was in graduate school, crippled with writer's block, guilt-ridden (as any good Filipino Catholic girl would be for writing about her elders and her community in such a manner), and frozen with fear because I felt I did not have the right to write about the Filipino community with such an authoritative tone, one of my wise, sage advisors calmed me down by teaching me two things: (1) Every work is a work-in-progress and, thus, should be shared with others as soon as possible; and it's corollary, (2) the gift of academia is learning, not professing, and people cannot learn if they are under the impression that everything they produce must be perfect.

Another thing he taught all of us is that every work, whether it'd be a brownbag presentation given to one's department or a book complete with glossy, full-color cover, is inevitably written by more than just that person as ideas contained within those pages were generated through many conversations with trusted colleagues and friends.

This combination—"no one is perfect" and "the blame for this imperfect piece is shared anyway"—helped assuage my fears and allowed me to complete my research, defend my dissertation, and, after multiple rewrites, turn in this book. (I owe you many cookies, Norm.) To this end, I would like to acknowledge those friends and colleagues who helped me through the years; you are the ones I will be calling once one of my irate *titas* calls me and admonishes me for exposing Filipinos' dirty laundry!

At the University of Illinois at Urbana-Champaign, my Jedi council—John Lie, Susan Leigh Star, Norman K. Denzin, and Andrew Pickering—guided, advised, and encouraged me throughout graduate school and, especially, throughout this project. John's Zen master advice to his students (i.e., "Think thrice before picking a dissertation topic; you have to court your topic, as you're going to have to live with it for about ten years."), his pithy, yet strangely comforting, observations (i.e., "You know, there are some really bad books out there. So don't worry about yours; go talk to the publishers."), and his largely "invisible hand" (as I know he quietly made my work known to many scholars without saying a word to me) have been invaluable. He is an incredibly successful and renowned researcher and scholar; the best compliment I ever received from him was just two years ago at the annual conference for the American Sociological Association (ASA), when he said, "So, you're almost up for tenure, you've got articles out, your book is on its way, you're starting a new research project, and you're on the Asian and Asian American council at ASA. Is there anything you need from me?" Knowing full well that I could not have achieved any of this without John's help, I just thanked him for all his encouragement and told him that he could call on me if ever needed. (That offer stands, John.)

Susan Leigh Star's compassion for marginalized peoples, phenomenal ethnographic skills, vast knowledge of the impact of technology on societies, and innovative pedagogical skills (i.e., "Express in poetry the development of the relationships you've formed with people at your research site.") cultivated my interest in using sociological theories to explore the effects of technologies on the largely understudied Filipino community. In addition, her enthusiasm about the positive potentials of technology and her insistence that we understand better the intertwined relationship between late capitalism, technology, human beings, and our ideas of identity and community inspired this "nethnography." While I was collecting material for the dissertation, she took the time to talk through the emerging threads. Also, knowing that I had a problem with writing about my ethnic community with an authoritative, researcher's voice, she gently encouraged the use of that voice by consistently assuring me, "There's more to the debates than just that; you're treading on unchartered ground and I'd like for you to explain the contours of this territory." At trying times, whenever I had any doubts, Leigh quelled them by encouraging me to "talk out the links," and, when frustrations arose, she always had an abundant supply of Kleenex in her office.

Andrew Pickering may have seemed like an odd choice as a reader, as he is known for his expertise in examining practice in science and technology and, at the time, was studying the relationship between science, technology, war, and manufacturing during World War II. But, because of his love of learning about disparate subjects and his infinite patience in hearing me attempt to merge his theories about scientific practice with constructionist theories of race, I knew he would force me to look at theories of race, ethnicity, gender, nation, and diaspora from a different angle. As I struggled with explaining and applying much of the jargon associated with postcolonial, diasporic, and transnational theories, Andy helped me make sense of the collected posts by drawing the dynamics between theory and empirical material. Pulling out a large sketchpad and different colored pens, he asked me to draw the connections between various scholars' arguments and the bits of conversations I'd included in each chapter. Although what emerged looked like an abominable copy of a Jackson Pollock painting, he helped me organize my thoughts and urged me to explain the historical context which made these particular conversations about race, ethnicity, gender, and nation possible. Hopefully, that is reflected in this book.

Prolific and passionate about all the subjects he chooses to write about, Norman Denzin further encouraged all his students to write creatively and poignantly. Aware of the "culture wars" that ravaged the academy at the time I was in graduate school, he nonetheless encouraged all of us to engage ourselves in our studies, thereby developing our interpretive skills and our voices, while simultaneously teaching us the importance of systematically and rigorously collecting and analyzing our empirical material. Knowing how much importance I placed on keeping the soc.culture.filipino participants' voices and the debates' contexts intact, he encouraged me to look into various methods of conversational analysis that would reflect my concerns. But his most powerful piece of advice that I've since tried to implement in all areas of my life came at my dissertation defense when he said, "Emily, your dissertation is good. But you are most powerful when you allow your voice to be heard. Use your voice." John, Leigh, Norm, and Andy—thank you all for everything you have done and continue to do for me. I only hope that somehow I can be of some help to you.

Alice Ritscherle and Zine Magubane have served simultaneously as friends, coaches, and colleagues throughout the revisions of this book. Their brilliant minds and vast knowledge of the theories I leaned on helped me turn this dissertation into a book. Alice and I completed many of our chapters by writing steadily for monstrously long periods of time and barely sustaining ourselves over heart-attack food and gallons of coffee. Her determination to complete the tasks at hand and her abundant energy provided me the focus and discipline necessary to getting this manuscript completed. My best friend since high school, Alice is well aware of my ingrained Catholic guilt and fear of imagined moans of "ay! walang hiya ka" that often impeded my analyses. Her time around my family and the vibrant Filipino community in the southwest suburbs of Chicago gave her the skills to simultaneously thrust me back into the world of academia and make me use my personal experiences to better explain various nuances that were deeply imbedded in the empirical material.

Zine Magubane's wry sense of humor and quick wit, combined with her incredibly comprehensive knowledge of diaspora, transnationalism, and postcolonialism theories, helped me piece together often scattered analyses and add some coherence to this text. Her work on South Africa and the construction of race and racial imagery (Magubane 2003), as well as her willingness to talk about theories (and gaps within theories) for hours on end, gave me the confidence and fortitude to complete various revisions of the book.

But, more importantly, Alice and Zine instilled in me the importance of balancing the demands of academia with much needed laughter. Alice's penchant for wry and exceptionally irreverent British humor found only in *Father Ted* and *The Office* and her fondness of taking photos of "Creepy Chicago" provided much needed fun and laughter when we sorely needed to take a break and rest our brains from our marathon writing sessions. Similarly, the always calm, cool, and collected Zine insisted on remaining a "regular person" and encouraged me to achieve balance by switching the channel from pundit-laden "news" channels to endless repeats of BBC America's *What Not to Wear* and Bravo's *Queer Eye for the Straight Guy*. Shopping trips to the Nordstrom Rack and the procurement of good hand lotion and thick hair conditioners helped make my outward appearance marginally respectable during that harrowing tenure year.

Over the years, several students at Loyola University Chicago shaped this book. Fearful that I had used too much jargon, I often relied on their reactions to certain chapters to figure out what I needed to revise. Geoff Burkhart's, Tammy Smith's, and Emily Drew's readings of earlier pieces helped me prepare this text for publication. Geoff and Tammy have been exceptionally kind, reading numerous drafts and helping me clarify certain passages in exchange for dinners at Ethiopian Diamond, Gulliver's, and sometimes even Steak and Shake. Dennis Cooper's artistic eye helped turn my mundane touristy photo of my mom boarding a plane into the funky image which serves as the cover of this book. Also, three caring students (J. R. Lujan, Tuan Ngo, and Connor Schmedling) helped me out at a most trying time. Weeks before my last draft was due to my publishers, I had, unfortunately, been burglarized. Having lost both the computer and the backup disks, I faced the prospect of having to type the entire manuscript again, as no scanners translate the characters correctly. J. R., Tuan, and Connor generously offered their time and helped type in three chapters of this book. Thank you all so much; you have no idea how much I appreciate your generosity.

Without the help of my colleagues and undergraduate students at the University of Illinois at Urbana-Champaign and Loyola University Chicago, I would have drowned in a mountain of paper, Kleenex, and sorrow. Marlon Esguerra is responsible for sending me to cyberspace. His undying hope in educating Filipino Americans about our culture and his penchant for looking for anything Filipino everywhere sent him to soc.culture.filipino ten years ago. Hoping that I would have an interest in seeing what "real" Filipinos said about our culture and identity, he asked me to "check it out" and tell him if I found anything fruitful in there. Richard Cavendish was particularly a source of strength; he served as my sounding board from the time I began the preliminary analyses of the posts to the time I grumbled over the ridiculous formatting procedures demanded by the graduate school. Thanks also to Nancy Abelmann, Nancy Berns, Ann Bishop, Geoff Bowker, Philip and Jacquie Bowman, Cyd Crue, Aya Ezawa, Eri Fujieda, Serife and Emin Genis, Ann Herda-Rapp, Chris Hickey, David, Judith, and Xena Hopping, Gina Husting, Frances Jacobson, Elizabeth Jenner, Kirk Johnson, Naranjan Karnik, Leslie King, Cece Merkel, Laura Neumann, Kevin Powell, Bob Sandusky, David Schweingruber, Michael Twidale, Mike and Sue Tyler, Amit Verma, Chia-ling Wu, and Maryalice Wu for reading early drafts and convincing me that there's something there.

At Loyola, all my colleagues from the sociology and anthropology departments have been a source of strength. Encouraging and always supportive through the years, they made the tenure-track process bearable, which allowed for the completion of this work. Thanks especially to Kathleen Adams, Kevin Henson, Marilyn Krogh, Kathleen McCourt, Laura Miller, Peter Whalley, and Judith Wittner for serving as my sounding boards when I suffered from writer's block.

Outside Damen Hall, Martin F. Manalansan IV, Rick Bonus, and Linda Trinh Võ have been my loudest and most ardent cheerleaders, offering profuse amounts of support from the get-go. Martin's willingness to share his incomparable knowledge of transnational and diasporic Filipino communities strengthened my understanding of the Internet conversations in which I had been ensconced. Rick and Linda's insistence in including my work in their documentation of the emergence of disparate Asian communities (Võ and Bonus 2000) allowed me to smoothly enter into the Asian American studies community. In addition, Rick Baldoz, Esther Chow, Mary Yu Danico, Shilpa Davé, Melinda de Jesus, Pawan Dinghra, Michael Eric Dyson, Augusto Espiritu, Yen Le Espiritu, Evelyn Nakano Glenn, Ana Gonzalez, Theo Gonzalvez, Allan Isaac, Steve Jones, Nazli Kibria, Rebecca King, Yvonne Lau, Emily Lawsin, Rachel Lee, Judith Liu, Andrea Louie, Glen Mimura, Joane Nagel, Lisa Nakamura, Leilani Nishime, Jonathan Okamura, Michael Omi, Terri Pigott, Barbara Posadas, Vicente Rafael, Dylan Rodriguez, John Rosa, Leland Saito, Jiannbin Shiao, David Silver, Charlene Tung, and Morrison Wong provided much intellectual stimulation at various conferences, prompting me to think about my data in new ways. They also are a lot of fun and share my penchant for trying out new restaurants and balancing the sometimes-fatiguing conference activities by taking tours.

At Rutgers University Press, I must thank David Myers, Kristi Long, and all the supportive, helpful, and intelligent people for their patience and for their enthusiasm for the ideas contained in this book. Kristi, especially, was incredibly patient and understanding when the manuscript was delayed due to the burglary. As each chapter was completed, she methodically read it and gently prodded me to provide more descriptions or empirical material in key areas; as a result, the manuscript was eventually sent out to the final reviewer. In the last stretch, Karen Johnson and John and Sue Morris at Wordsworth Typing and Editing Services were invaluable. Having read, reread, and reread again this book, I could no longer discern whether any of my ideas were honed or obtuse. Meticulous and incredibly knowledgeable editors,

Karen, John, and Sue did a stupendous job of combing through this manuscript, dissecting my arguments, and, most importantly, helping me articulate my thoughts with more clarity. And Meghan Burke's insatiable enthusiasm for learning and her unfailing support helped me put the finishing touches—and the index—on this book.

In their insistence that I live a balanced life and eat what they believed to be a balanced diet, my friends and family provided much entertainment and generous amounts of home cooking through the years. Mimi dela Cruz-Galvez, Eileen Sulit Konopacki (thank God; it took you two long enough), Nat Hawkins, and my dear cousin Bernie Villanueva provided me with much needed balance, encouragement, and laughter. As I researched the posts about Filipinas, it was my "sistahs" anecdotes and furious reactions to the Web sites posted on soc.culture.filipino which helped me express the simultaneous sorrow and shock many Filipinas feel when they experience Orientalism. My parents, Lolo, Aunties Jan, Norma, Vi, Orphie, Uncles Ric and Jhun, Kuya Angie, Tita Mimi, and my cousins Bayani, Bernie, Kris, John, Ringo, Miko, Ritchie, and Nene were especially understanding as, on many occasions, they put up with my vampiric schedule and the vile coffee which allowed me to keep said schedule. Made of thick skin and light dispositions, they all rode with the storm and attempted to counter the intake of sludgy coffee by baking large portions of *ube, lecheflan,* and banana bread. Thanks also to Tito Joven, Manang Ponsa, Inday Dora, Manog Maing, and cousins Wellyn and Joy (R.I.P.) for their prayers and loving letters from the Philippines; they frequently offered gentle assurance that I have the intelligence and fortitude to complete this "tedious and laborious task" while cultivating my nostalgia of the Philippines by sending me updates about my favorite water buffalo.

Speaking of Filipinos, I must thank Kevin Buckley for indirectly offering a prime example of the difficulty of determining Filipinoness as, when comparing our biographies, it is unclear which one of us is more Filipino and which one is more American. To others, he may appear to be a white, Irish American male. But, his stories of growing up in Makati, his proficiency in Tagalog, his knowledge of Filipino customs, and his tales of actually eating *balut* (something I have not, nor ever will, attempt), compared with my story of being born in Canada, living in Illinois almost all my life, and merely understanding Tagalog and Bisaya, only reinforced two things I hope readers of this book will learn: Filipinoness is fluid and often performed, and one's degree of Filipinoness is frequently constructed in relation to another's identity. In addition to embodying *differánce,* Kevin has been a caring and supportive friend. His calm presence, kindness, and compassion helped me weather many storms through the past three years, and his unwavering faith in my ability to communicate ideas challenged me to quit leaning on cumbersome jargon and write with clarity. *Maraming salamat,* Kevin.

Alice Barkwell, Lauren Jonik, Megan Kanipe, Jenni Mehlenbacher, Theresa Needham, J. R. Richards and Dishwalla, and all the *wallawhacknuts* brought the world of rock and roll into my life in a surreal manner by occasionally whisking me out of the world of academia and into the world of (of all things) rock reviewers and photographers. Thank you so much for your friendship and this opportunity. The absurdity of this situation, strangely, honed my researching and writing skills as it forced me to watch shows with different eyes and then rigorously describe the context within short period of time to meet Lauren's strict deadlines for soundaffects.net. And, while I'm at it, I may as well publicly thank Pearl Jam for writing eloquent lyrics which cultivate my sociological imagination and enkindle my passion to work for the common good. If it weren't for *Ten,* I would never have become a sociologist, and all the blessings I have written about above would never have occurred.

Lastly, but most definitely not least, I thank my mom and dad for their steadfast love, patience, encouragement, and unwavering faith in me. You are my inspiration, and I thank God I have you for my parents.

Preface: Why Filipinos?

"Pilipino ka ba?" I never know what to say when I hear these words. Am I Filipino? "Um—yes, I am," I answered. "Ah—Kano, ha?" he said, confirming his suspicion that I'm an American. Okay, maybe I'm not a Filipino. . . . I always feel awkward whenever an older, first generation Filipino American asks me about my ethnicity. I never know what to say.

—Journal entry, November 1995

"Good—your mama raised you as a Filipino. My other niece shook my hand when she greeted me. That's [shaking one's hand] very American. And to think she was raised here in the Philippines! Cora—you raised Emily right!"

—Journal entry, June 1991, written during trip to the Philippines

I never understood what it meant to be Filipino. As I was growing up, I received so many conflicting definitions that by the time I reached high school I was sure that no one (not even my parents, who are first-generation immigrants) could sit down and tell me what it means. At first, I'd thought that, perhaps, this phenomenon was unique to my family. I'd grown up in what is often called an "extended family household"; that is, I lived in a house filled with aunts, uncles, grandparents, cousins, my mom and dad, and even, at one point, seven dogs and a turtle named Floppy. To many of my classmates, colleagues, and many others I have encountered throughout my life, this may seem like an extraordinary case. Yet, to many racial minority groups and immigrants of all races, especially within the United States, this is what we consider to be "family" (hooks 1994; Stacks 1996). At any rate, I attributed my confusion over what constitutes a "true" Filipino to my experience of living with several self-defined Filipinos who each had different ideas of what it means to be "Pinoy."[1]

But, as I met more Filipino Americans, particularly my students while I was a graduate student-teacher at the University of Illinois, I realized that my dilemma was not unique to my family. Indeed, the popularity of the grassroots film *The Debut* (2002)[2] is evidence that questions of identity among Filipinos are just as commonplace as with other races and/or ethnicities. Yet finding a singular, authentic Filipino identity is important to many Filipino Americans. Espiritu (1994) found that Filipino Americans feel as if they aren't completely regarded as Americans by their non-Filipino counterparts because of their racial characteristics. In other words, like other racially subjugated and racialized ethnic groups, Filipino Americans' brown skin and/or other physical characteristics, such as eye shape, hair color, and nose shape, preclude their ability to be recognized as "real" Americans. This project stems from understanding the importance of discovering and being able to articulate a singular sense of Filipino; but as a Filipino Canadian who grew up in the United States and as a sociologist, I know that finding a singular identity is akin to acquiring the Holy Grail.

Most Filipino Americans acknowledge diverse, sometimes contradictory definitions of Filipino (Bonus 1997, 2000; Espiritu 1995; Manalansan 1995). While some celebrate this diversity, some believe it is a weakness. The latter group believes that we lack a unifying definition because of our ignorance, erasure, or even rejection of authentic culture. This belief is most probably prevalent because scholars have erroneously described Filipinos as a "people without culture" because they had spent "three hundred years in a monastery [under Spanish colonial rule] and a half century in Hollywood [under American colonial rule]" (Rosaldo 1989, 77). Because many cultures in the Philippines seem to have embraced American culture, they have somehow lost any claims of authenticity;[3] hence, the Philippines and Filipino culture have not been studied as extensively as other cultures. This institutional erasure has not only devalued Filipino culture, it has made Filipinos feel somewhat invisible. Or worse, any problems or social issues we claim affect us are not "real." Yet, the Philippines and Filipinos are at the center of a very real history of colonialism and economic exploitation which still profoundly affect Filipinos all over the world and place us squarely within U.S. history and corresponding histories of resistance.

This presumed nonexistence of an authentic Filipino culture profoundly affects Filipinos outside academia. Many debates on soc. culture.filipino, the Internet newsgroup I studied, reflect most participants' goal of eradicating Filipinos' colonial mentality and teaching all Filipinos to learn about their "real" culture. Many of the participants argue that Filipinos can make themselves more visible through learning about culture. But achieving this goal is difficult because participants disagree on the description of Filipino culture. Some celebrate the different influences (such as Chinese, Spanish, Japanese, and American) that have shaped the Philippines and Filipinos: "You know, there are no 'real' Filipinos. We're all mixed up. And all those different cultures mixed together is what makes us unique." Others are more critical because they have seen Filipinos "embracing the influences and rejecting [their] culture. Filipinos are so Americanized now. They don't know their culture and they reject anything that's Filipino." Some participants remain confused about Filipino culture and identity and are doubtful whether Filipinos can ever achieve political visibility because of the apparent lack of a static, solid, homogenous culture. These sentiments are echoed by many ethnic, racial, and immigrant groups within the United States about their own cultures.

Similarly, many second-generation Filipino Americans have stated that to find information about our culture and identity, it is "best to go to the source"—to first-generation Filipino Americans or, better yet, to Filipinos who reside in the Philippines. This desire has led many of my students through the years to the Internet, specifically to the soc.culture.filipino newsgroup. This turn to the Internet for knowledge is what led me to this study.

No matter how large the network of aunts, uncles, *lolos, lolas*,[4] and godparents my students and I belonged to, the prospect of talking with twenty thousand or more Filipinos from all over the world was appealing in that we were able to "test" our ideas of what constitutes Filipino on people we had not actually met, but with whom we still felt a sense of kinship. The Internet is a medium in which people can be both intimately involved and anonymous; people in the newsgroup may get to know one another through their posts (and the tone of their posts), yet they may never actually see one another. In many ways, it is easier to post a question on the Internet than face a gaggle of aunts and uncles whose boisterous laughter could send an already timid second (or more) removed generation Filipino American further into the nebula of the Margins. Thus, on the surface, it appears that the Internet would help second- and later-generation Filipino Americans (as well as other diasporic Filipinos) efficiently and quickly obtain information about Filipino culture and identity from "the source," as "traveling" to and "talking" with "real" Filipinos from the homeland could be done more easily online than via traditional traveling methods.

Diary of a Cyborg: Reflections on Analysis

White, First World authors who are interested in studying works from Third World cultures are often told that they "can't understand other cultures until [they] understand their own" (Lippard 1990). On the flip side, because I am a Filipino American who grew up in an extended family household of first generation immigrants and "1.5ers" (i.e., people who immigrated at a young age), non-Filipino colleagues often assume that I have a complete understanding of both Filipino and American cultures and, therefore, can "look from the outside in and from the inside out" (hooks 1994).

However, the process of collecting and analyzing empirical material for this project has reinforced my feelings that I can neither look from the outside in nor from the inside out. Rather, I see things from a liminal space, neither Filipino nor American, but a unique combination of both. In addition, other factors have influenced the way we all understand the world: my race, citizenship (I am Canadian), gender, accent, as well as my physical appearance and my last name have all contributed to my experiences and given me a unique perspective.

For example, two weeks after I arrived as a graduate student in the sociology department at the University of Illinois, a woman approached me and said, "Okay, Em. Grace[5] and I have a bet here. I think you're Latino. She thinks you're Asian. So which one are you?" Having heard many variations of this question before, I gave them my standard answer: "I'm Canadian," I said as I walked away. Instead of playing the race game, I have chosen since grade school to annoy people by telling them about my citizenship rather than my race.

When I was younger, I used to answer "both" when asked if I was Asian or Latino because one of my grandmothers is Chinese and one of my grandfathers is Spanish. However, this conversation would often take too long, because being "mixed" warranted some explanation. When asked about my "mixed race," I couldn't give them an entire history lesson, although this was often what my curious peers wanted.

I didn't know anything about colonization when I was a kid, but my parents had explained their different ethnicities by telling me that the Spaniards, Chinese, and Malays visited the Philippines, liked it, and decided to stay. So, I opted for the shorter, pithier answer. "I'm Canadian (or worse, "I'm a Chicagoan"). What are you?"

Other Filipino Americans also have their own perspectives. For example, my cousin, a 1.5-generation immigrant with whom I grew up, assures me that she can look from the outside in and from the inside out. Because she was born in the Philippines and immigrated here when she was ten, she has the experience of living and studying in the Philippines as well as the United States. For the first few years in the United States, she had to assure our family that she was still Filipino while assuring her non-Filipino classmates that she knew how to be American. As a result, she vacillated back and forth on a daily, sometimes hourly basis, proving herself to both camps. While I was somewhat comfortable maneuvering in the nether areas, her struggles with our family and with non-Filipino classmates, as well as her marriage to a later generation Italian American, taught her, she argues, how to be both an American and a Filipino. Yet, she also tells me of her constant efforts to prove herself as either and both.

Although we grew up in the same small neighborhood, lived in the same household, and went to the same schools, what struck me most is the difference between our experiences and the outcomes. My "extended" family could never perceive me as a true Filipino, despite the fact that they taught me to understand both Filipino dialects spoken at home, despite the fact that I learned and followed the customs they taught me, and despite my attempts to learn about the Philippines and the culture. Never mind that until I went to college, they were more versed in American history and politics than I was or that when they immigrated here, they already knew and practiced many American customs. My being born and raised outside the Philippines, according to my family, is the determining factor for my ethnic identity. Like my cousins who were born and/or largely raised in the United States, my family continues to distinguish between their "Filipinoness" and my lack of it. Thus, my effort to learn about Filipinos and the Philippines is akin to a subject that I'm interested in, while for others it is "catching up with what's going on at home."

Yet, when relatives visited from the Philippines, they always commented on how "Americanized" my extended family had become while simultaneously praising my family for raising me as a "true Filipino."

And outside my home, in my classmates and teachers' eyes, I was the resident Filipino, often asked to translate words into Tagalog or to explain certain customs. They did not doubt that I was Filipino, even though I demonstrated through social interactions and academic ventures that I clearly understood the American way of life.

I have struggled with these issues since many members of my family immigrated to the United States, and I have recently concluded that all of them are right: I cannot be Filipino as they are Filipino, just as there is no one way to be white, black, Asian, Latino, Native American, Chinese, Ethiopian, Lakota, or other races or ethnicities.[6] This does not mean that I have no ethnic identity, nor do I consider myself a wandering, marginal person. Although some members of my family do not regard me as an authentic Filipino, I perceive this not as a rejection (although it is trying sometimes), but as an opportunity to question why they and others (especially second-generation Filipino Americans) believe there is only one way to be Filipino, as it has been so clear, even within our home, that there are several ways to be Filipino.

Because I have heard my family continually discuss whether I or other Filipino Americans are Filipino, I have sensed the fluidity of culture and identity as well as cultural syncretism and heterogeneity within the Filipino community for most of my life.

No need to hear your voice when I can talk about you better than you can speak about yourself. No need to hear your voice. Only tell me about your pain. I want to know your story. And then I will tell it back to you in a new way. Tell it back to you in such a way that it has become mine, my own. Re-writing you I write myself anew. I am still author, authority. I am still colonizer, the speaking subject and you are now at the center of my talk. (bell hooks 1994, 343)

My biggest fear in doing this project was that I would suppress instead of support the voices of Filipinos on the newsgroup. Even though I use each participant's own words, I know that the analysis of these words is mine; thus, "I am still author, authority."

Yet, I was an active participant on the newsgroup and a Filipino-American struggling with issues of identity. Although I did not post very often, I did follow each discussion very carefully for over two years. When I needed clarification (depending on the touchiness of the question), I posted an e-mail to the whole group or c mailed the person privately. If the posts concerned the contents of a Web page, I logged onto the Web and studied the page in question. Some threads lasted over a month, others only a few days. And I was there, an active participant and a researcher in this newsgroup. That said, I extend my hand and welcome you to my virtual home of two years.

Building Diaspora

1 Introduction

Filipino Community Formation on the Internet

Today we suffer the consequences not just of an 800-year-old crusading tradition but also an 80-year-old effect: the joint British-American dismantling of the Ottoman Empire after the First World War. We designed maps and invented states. We dreamt up national identities where none had existed before and attributed them to the new countries. And the states were designed to be feeble, for older ethnic identities both stretched across the boundaries and coexisted awkwardly within them. This was classic imperial "divide and rule" for oil's sake. In this horror we do truly stand "shoulder to shoulder with the United States."

—Hywel Williams, "Crusade Is a Dirty Word"

The discourse surrounding "America's New War" on terrorism has been confusing for some commentators, scholars, and the U.S. public because it illuminates the difficulties of and problems with the easy dichotomizations of the past. The events surrounding September 11, 2001, have shaken many people's sense of security and stability, but have also forced some people to question the stability of seemingly naturalized categories of nation, race, and culture, and openly scrutinize the use of religion for political gains. The above quote by Williams reminds (or informs) its readers that nations are indeed imagined and were often created to serve other established nations' agendas. According to Williams, in the case of Central Asia and the Middle East, oil was at the center of nation building. At the very least, the war against the elusive "enemy" reveals that the categories of nation, race, religion, culture, and ethnicity are no longer (or may never have been) sufficient in discerning who among us are the "righteous and the wicked": Who, exactly, are our enemies in this conflict? To which groups do they belong? Do they all profess the same religion? Do they share the same culture? Where do they reside? If members of the enemy are scattered across the globe, then with whom does a country wage war? Even Osama bin Laden himself exemplifies blurred boundaries: born in and exiled from Saudi Arabia, he is well versed in an extremist and—religious leaders and scholars remind us—a highly inaccurate reading of the Koran. Trained indirectly by the CIA through the Pakistani Intelligence Agency (ISI) to combat the Soviets during the USSR–Afghanistan War (Coll 1992) and once hailed as a "freedom fighter," he is now our public enemy number one. And news of the capture of John Walker, an "American Taliban," added much confusion for those who held onto deep-seated notions of absolutely distinct boundaries between "us" and "them" as it became clearer that, no matter how well policed, ideologies can easily travel across national and cultural borders.

As the months pass, it has become increasingly apparent that this notion of "getting the bad guy" or bombing "those who harbor terrorists" is not an easy task. This battle is not against any one person, one nation, one territory, or one religion. It is against a deterritorialized ideology that has spread throughout the world. Indeed, if we are to wreak havoc on all the places that have "harbored" suspected bin Laden followers, that would include sixty countries and hundreds of cities, including Justice, Illinois, Bradenton, Florida, and San Diego, California.

Yet, especially since September 11, 2001, our nation simultaneously needs (1) to have a clear sense of "unity" that is not based on one nation, race, class, creed, or gender; and (2) to establish that our new enemy is also not based on nation, race, class, creed, nor gender. Interestingly, although the mainstream media and governmental officials warned us against making false generalizations soon after the 9/11/01 attacks, the "us versus them" mentality still abounds. Within one month of the terrorists' attacks in New York City, Pennsylvania, and Washington, D.C., the FBI reported that they were investigating over ninety hate crimes against Arab Americans; and despite all the warnings against targeting those who practice Islam, some U.S. citizens across the nation still hurled firebombs at mosques and many people increasingly viewed their "Arab-looking" neighbors with suspicion.

Socially constructed or not, the concepts of "nation," "creed," "race," "ethnicity," and "culture" are divisive and, unfortunately, have overridden pleas for unity, even after these tragic events. We have encountered much trouble because we, as a society, haven't examined (or at least paid much attention to) the social practices and ideologies that underlie the creation and maintenance of these constructed categories. This deterritorialization of the enemy appears to be a new concept to the American public; however, when examining historical patterns sociologically, we see that this is not a new phenomenon at all. Nations, as Anderson (1991) and other pointed out are "imagined communities"; race, gender, ethnicity, and culture are socially constructed concepts. And, as Williams' (2001) quote shows, it is imperative that we begin to take seriously the sociopolitical, historical, and ideological reasons upon which these divisions were socially constructed before we can understand how and why wars and other atrocities are waged in the name of nation, race, ethnicity, creed, and/or culture. In other words, our present is highly dependent on understanding our past, and examining current occurrences of social construction is imperative for our future.

This book is not about the horrific events of 9/11/01, nor about Osama bin Laden and al-Qaeda, but it is in the spirit of understanding how larger sociopolitical issues and ideologies affect diasporic communities, particularly those that share a history of colonialism. Recent events demonstrate that race and cultural studies can no longer be confined to national contexts, especially in the age of the Internet. Nations, "always already" entities, have been constructed and maintained largely through technological breakthroughs like print capitalism, easily reproduced prints and photographs, TV and satellite images, and even museums and maps (Anderson 1991). In all these cases, the images of a nation often go through a gatekeeping process, whereby some authoritative figures uphold and approve the images that reflect current political alignments. But what happens when images of a nation—or even race, culture, and gender—don't just cross national boundaries, but are articulated in a transnational space by anyone, regardless of authority? Because the Internet is a transnational space where people from all over the world can converge, I argue it is a space where this kind of rearticulation and community building can occur in a more efficient manner. In this book, I examine how technology affects the construction of national, racial, ethnic, and gendered identities. And, I show how this technology can help create new coalitions which are based on an understanding of how these constructed categories served to divide and conquer.

We have seen how these kinds of technological advances can change the history of a nation. For example, in 2000 in the Philippines, demonstrators who pushed for then-President Estrada's resignation from office congregated and organized largely through the use of "texting" through cell phones.[1] Similarly, the anti-globalization and antiwar protests from Seattle to Quebec to Genoa in the late 1990s and early this century were also largely organized through alternative media sources on the Internet.[2] But, in conjunction with studying the impact of larger sociopolitical issues on diasporas, we need historical, sociological specificity in order to uncover and understand more fully how similar sociopolitical policies, processes, and tactics affect various races, nations, social classes, and genders differently. In other words, it is important to study the impacts of globalization, colonization, racism, and other sociopolitical processes on each group separately so as to illuminate the specific ways inequalities are maintained. In doing so, we can put pieces of the puzzle together and understand better how and why inequalities are maintained and exactly who benefits.

I have chosen to study debates within a Filipino Internet newsgroup against global and local historical backgrounds. In this transnational space, I was able to witness people struggle with establishing a cultural community in the face of seemingly divergent national histories, and, thus, I am able to show how sociopolitical issues and ideologies simultaneously tie these histories together and encourage divisions within the Filipino diaspora. This study is a documentation of the process of diasporic community formation on the Internet and developed from my attempts to show my students and colleagues that the experiences of Filipinos around the world can tell us much about larger issues of race, colonialism, gender, and nation.

Filipinos, though marked by over four hundred years of colonization, are not merely puppets in the global stage, nor are they plagued by an overwhelming "colonial mentality," as is often written. Specifically, I show how national, racial, and ethnic identity is articulated, reified, and re-created within the soc.culture.filipino newsgroup on the Internet. Through an extensive analysis of several debates, I focus largely on community and identity formation of a diaspora in relation to various political and polemical arguments—mainly neocolonialism, Eurocentrism, Orientalism, and patriarchy.

In these debates, we witness the constant articulation, re-articulation, and impacts of local and global political issues and social policies in the definition of "Filipino." Specifically, we are able to see how different articulations of real-life issues such as racism, multiculturalism, sexism, and colonialism traveled onto the supposedly neutral and parallel world of cyberspace and affected the participants' notion of identity as well as broadened their views on how oppression operates. In particular, I focus on how the members of the Filipino diaspora "submitted" to their ethnicity (Chow 1993), illustrate what clues (e.g., existing categories and stereotypes) they used to debate the definition of Filipino, and show the tactics they used to articulate a Filipino identity. Through these debates, we are able to witness social constructionism at work. Contrary to some scholars' concern that deconstructionism leads to the death of the Subject and flattens all identities, we are able to see how the Subject is maintained even in a decentered, transnational space because of prevailing policies and ideologies which maintain hierarchies. In witnessing this, we can see the importance of deconstructionist theories, as, in this space, we have the opportunity to watch participants struggling to uncover an "authentic history" while global and multiple local histories collide and render this a difficult project.

Finally, I show that regularly conversing with other members of a diaspora in this virtual homeland and being faced with divergent national histories and convergent global policies eventually created the need to transcend national or cultural boundaries when defining identity. Just as it is important to study the deconstruction of identities, it is also important to study their reconstructions. On this particular newsgroup, I was able to watch participants attempt to create an identity which transcended national, racial, and gendered boundaries. In doing so, I illustrate how computer-mediated communication can help members of a diaspora better understand their post- or neocolonial situation and serve as a possible site for broader organizing and community formation.

Because all diasporas, as well as other racial and ethnic communities, are affected by these ideologies, this discussion tells us much about the impact of politics on the personal lives of members in all diasporic communities, not just the Filipino community. As a result of seeing the impact of these oppressive practices on members of the

Filipino diaspora, hopefully, people of all races and ethnicities will see the commonalities each community faces, instead of just focusing on the differences among them.

National and Ethnic Identities in the Age of the Internet

The desire to find an authentic self by traveling to the homeland is not new. Although many studies concentrate on "external factors" such as the push and pull of immigration and the impact of the economy and governmental policies on assimilation (see Pido 1986, for example, for statistics on Filipino immigration), others have studied the relationship between the individual and society (see, for example, Boyarin 1994, 1996; Flores 1993; Radhakrishnan 1996) and the importance of finding one's ethnic and/or racial identity (see, for example, Espiritu 1995, 2003).

Bello and Reyes (1986) have shown that transnational, Filipino political communities have been formed in the past. In the 1970s, when President Ferdinand Marcos declared martial law, many Filipino Americans formed anti-Marcos political organizations and kept up with political developments by reading newspapers, watching the news, visiting the Philippines, and pressing relatives from the Philippines who came to the United States for a visit. As a result, "those in the Philippines acknowledged that their counterparts here knew more than they did about what was happening back home" (Bello and Reyes 1986, 76). Eventually, transnational anti-Marcos ties were formed which, Bello and Reyes argue, helped overthrow the Marcos government. The widespread dissemination of information regarding the Marcos dictatorship aggravated thousands of Filipinos worldwide and brought this political issue to the forefront. As a result, strong world powers (such as the United States) could no longer stand by Marcos in good faith; this relatively peaceful revolution succeeded.

The importance of identity differs in various contexts. Currently, because of increasing migration and transnational networks and the rise in nationalist and multicultural movements, studies on immigrants, racial, and ethnic groups have revealed that establishing identity is desired not for assimilation, but for differentiation (Espiritu 1994; Waters 1990). Many people wish to learn about their culture because they want to recapture the power to name themselves. That is, they need an identity, not only so that they know their own roots, but so that others can learn of their roots as well. And, in the aftermath of

September 11, 2001, as news spread of possible al-Qaeda members living within the United States, many wished for easily identifiable ways to draw boundaries between "real" and "fake" Americans, as legal immigration papers and even naturalized citizenship no longer seemed to be sufficient.[3]

However, as stated before, cultures, nations, races, and identities are constantly being redefined in both real and virtual life, actively constructed and maintained through various media and the sciences (Anderson 1991). But, in the age of the Internet, they have the potential to be redefined in different ways, as members of the diaspora have the opportunity to discover the global historical processes which underlie their local histories and personal experiences. As we will see, the Internet makes possible the sharing of identities about culture and politics—but it also makes possible fierce debate over information. In some circumstances, an Internet forum allows people to recreate a larger picture depending on the different information and/or experiences of the participants. Furthermore, in their attempt to "go to the source," participants have the unique opportunity to discover that the source itself is defined and redefined. In the case of a former colonial subject, that redefinition is often still in relation to the colonial power. While many scholars of computer-mediated communication have extensively studied how this technology changes gender identities, the link between postmodern subjectivities and the 'Net, and the prevalence of racial stereotypes on the 'Net (Jones 1995; Poster 1995; Kolko, Rodman, and Nakamura 1999; Nakamura 2002), we still have not yet systematically examined continued discussions online and their effects on an online community's ideas about national culture, race, gender, and/or ethnicity.

Merging Computer-Mediated Communication and Postcolonial Studies

Both computer-mediated communication (CMC) and postcolonial scholars analyze the creation and re-creation of identity. Yet, these discourses have not intersected with each other because their reasons for studying identity transformation are different.[4] Postcolonial theorists have been and still are focused on peeling away the "fixed shapes of historic ethnicity"; their studies often revolve around the fragmentation and (re)creation of ethnic (as well as racial and gender) identities. Many seminal works on postcoloniality explore the development, maintenance, and possible decentering of national, cultural, racial, gender, and/or ethnic identities through archival research on the colonial period (McClintock 1997; Rafael 1993; Stoler 1997). By studying the images of male and female colonizers/colonized, we learn how both patriarchy and ethnocentrism (and their intersection) are used to justify imperialism and colonialism. Deconstructing "embedded" stereotypes and grand narratives are two major goals of postcolonial writers (Hall 1990). Studies of construction in the present show us how racialized/gendered images of the colonizer and colonized continue to be maintained (Gilroy 1993; Hall 1990; Radhakrishnan 1996). But they also show the importance of imagination and shared experience in possibly re-creating images in such a way that they are antiracist, antisexist, and empowering to the colonized.

Still, postcolonial writers study the maintenance of racial, national, cultural, and/or gendered imagery outside cyberspace. This is not to say that postcolonial scholars have not written about the present impact of new global media on diasporic members. Paul Gilroy (1993), Rojagopalan Radhakrishnan (1996), Stuart Hall (1990), and Arjun Appadurai (1991) are among many scholars who have traced cultural (re)productions across national boundaries. However, postcolonial studies remain in the realm of "real life" and usually within the colonial period largely because most postcolonial scholars have been concerned with exposing the *origin* of the constructed images. I argue that Internet research can add to our understanding of postcoloniality (and postmodernity) in that it allows us to see the process of redefinition among self-defined members of diasporas in a decentered space. Because of this, there is the potential for more voices to be heard simultaneously (Poster 1995, 1998).

But although CMC scholars have extensively studied gender identities, the link between postmodern subjectivities and the 'Net (Jones 1995; Poster 1995), and the continuation of racialized discourse in cyberspace (Kolko, Rodman, and Nakamura 1999; Nakamura 2002), none have systematically studied over a long period of time how people online radically alter their own ideas of national cultures, race, and/or ethnicity after continued discussion within one transnational community. The CMC study that has come closest to engaging postcolonial studies is Mark Poster's (1998) research, "Virtual Ethnicities." Poster's analysis of a listserv whose members were predominantly Jewish and which dealt with subjects pertaining to Jews, however, showed him that, because of the changing nature of 'Net content, "individuals in cyberspace cannot attach to objects in the fixed shapes of historic ethnicity" (1998, 209). In other words, defining one authentic Jewish identity was extremely difficult because the listserv participants brought different experiences and information to the listserv and because the subjects discussed changed so rapidly. However, given the conversations prevalent within Internet studies at the time, Poster focused mostly on proving that virtual communities are real communities, not on examining or describing the *process* in which the participants articulate ethnicity.

Furthermore, some scholars have added to a utopian vision of the Internet by documenting instances within newsgroups and Multi-User Dimensions (MUDs or Multi-User Dungeons, a class of multi-player interactive games, accessible via the Internet or a modem) where peaceful communication and collaboration take place (Baym 1995a, 1995b; Correll 1995; Rheingold 1993). They found that the cultures' characteristics and identities on these newsgroups and MUDs were negotiated by the participants. Since most newsgroups are currently used by participants who have no particular offline ties to each other to discuss hobbies and personal interests, the participants on these newsgroups actively try to form communities because they believe that more meaningful discussions can occur when a community is established (Baym 1995b). Thus, Internet communities are not dependent on formal membership or geographical space (Stacey 1969; Strauss 1978). Instead, like other "social worlds" (Shibutani 1955; Strauss 1978), they are groups with commitments to at least one main activity.

Turkle (1994) described the communities she studied as "parallel worlds"; that is, they were separate from the "real world," and new communities and community practices emerged in these locations. But, many Internet communities are based on those within the real, nonvirtual world, including soc.culture Usenet groups. So even though the soc.culture newsgroups are located in a transnational space, they are still based on traditional, boundaried spaces (usually nations). Thus, I argue, these particular transnational locations are "perpendicular worlds" which computer-mediated communication theorists have not yet systematically analyzed.

Unlike perpendicular lines, however, each world is constantly changing. That is, the Internet world changes as each participant debates issues and as the participants themselves change. Similarly, the lines connecting the Internet to the real world change. Each person brings different experiences and bodies of knowledge to Internet discussions.

Methods: Doing Nethnography

"Wow!" You're doing your dissertation on a newsgroup! That is so great! You're tapping into some really new material and you're [sic] already have all of your data transcribed and dated for you! I bet that saves you a lot of time right there!"

—Journal entry of a conversation with Eric, a fellow sociologist, at the ASA meeting, 1995

When I first began my project, I thought that doing Internet research would be less time-consuming than traditional ethnographic research, as transcribing conversations takes twice as long (or longer) than the conversations themselves. However, other than this advantage, studying conversations on a newsgroup was filled with many unanticipated challenges. This section describes some of those obstacles and how I dealt with them.

Moving from Traditional Ethnography to Nethnography

Because I was interested in how members of a diaspora articulate concepts such as culture, race, and ethnicity (if they even talk about these concepts at all, as Internet researchers and race, diaspora, and identity theorists assumed), I chose to study conversations on a newsgroup which was created for members of the Filipino diaspora to talk about their culture: soc.culture.filipino. I chose to do a case study of this particular Internet community because this was the only place where diasporic Filipinos *could* meet for sustained periods of time. Hence, I had to become a participant-observer on the one place people from different locations around the world could interact for sustained periods of time.

Although this particular community does not reflect the demographics of the entire Filipino community, that does not mean it cannot or should not be studied. While it is true that the participants of this newsgroup were not representative of the entire Filipino diaspora, and it is true that the Internet is a relatively new form of communication, and while there is a serious digital divide, which means the demographics of Internet users do not reflect the world's population, scholars are still interested in studying the effects of the Internet on users, particularly in the areas of community building, identity formation, and creating meanings (Jones 1995; Poster 1995).

Methodologists have argued that the context within which the practitioner wishes to study must guide the researcher toward a particular method. If the context changes or various behaviors occur in a new place, then the researchers should either use a combination of methods (i.e., triangulation) or, in some cases, develop a new method to best answer their research question. C. Wright Mills, Pierre Bourdieu, and Loic Wacquant have warned against devotion to particular theories or methods as that may hinder the growth of the discipline and/ or keep us from studying other useful communities (Bourdieu and Wacquant 1993; Mills 1959).

Methodologists who had written about doing research online have argued that when studying meaning-making, researchers must be participant-observers so as to understand the context in which conversations develop (Kendall 1999). In addition, because communication is text-based, Hewson et al. have argued that linguistic observation must be used when studying Internet communities, particularly those who do research in newsgroups (as I had done) and in chat rooms.

Because I studied conversations between members of the Filipino diaspora on a newsgroup, the methods I used to study this community were participant observation and conversation analysis. In particular, I used the "method of instances," a method developed by symbolic interactionist George Psathas (Psathas 1995; Denzin 1998). The techniques for analyzing conversations mirror those of other ethnographic methods: coding, writing memos, discovering threads. The difference is that the units of analysis are the conversations, not the people themselves. So, those of us who are interested in meaning-making must rigorously analyze each conversation for lengthy periods of time, pick out recurring threads, and make note of the contexts in which those threads recur. Paula Saukko, who has written about studying online communities, argues, "Those discourse analytic studies, focusing on the social, political, and economic connections and implications of discourse, as well as the space-oriented approach, mapping the global context of its object of study, can help to locate identities more firmly in the world."

My Role as a Researcher, a Filipino, and a Participant of soc.culture.filipino

In the movie *Chan Is Missing* (Wang 1989), a cab driver (Jo) and his nephew (Rick) search for a man who has mysteriously disappeared (Chan Hung). As the film progresses, we soon realize that Chan Hung symbolizes Chinese identity and that this identity is never found. The director, Wayne Wang, illustrates this by showing the diversity of the Chinese American community. Every Chinese American whom Jo meets has different characteristics and describes Chan differently. At the end, Jo remarks that the more he looks for Chan/identity, the more confused he becomes. This exercise apparently led him to question his personal definition of identity. He recounts the many conflicting descriptions of Chan that he received from the people he met and concludes that the only way he could find identity is to "look into the puddle." In other words, he finds definitions of Chinese identity are unique to each person and that there is no one, unifying identity.

As a participant observer of the newsgroup, my role was similar to Jo's in that I kept track of what people have said about Filipino identity and how my own changed. Before I collected my empirical material, I explained to the newsgroup participants my intent. I told them that I was a Filipino American sociologist studying Filipino identity. I assured the participants that their responses would be kept confidential and their anonymity preserved. I also encouraged them to e-mail me if they had any questions and/or wished to tell me their definition of Filipino in private. I e-mailed this message once every four weeks to remind the participants of my project (see appendix 2 for the original message).

As in other sciences, the research questions one asks should guide the practitioner to the methods used, and no one method is superior over another. In other words, no one method is considered to be the "best" form of inquiry; however, scholars must carefully choose the method which will enable them to best answer their research questions. To study the production, maintenance, and reconceptualization of knowledge, sociologists have paid close attention to language and patterns of communication.

Discourse and conversation analyses have been used by sociologists since at least the 1920s. Some scholars have charged that focused studies on so-called micro-processes are apolitical and reflect a "postmodernism turn" or are "mere cultural studies, not sociology." The accusations that "interpretive" methods and social constructionist perspectives are anti-realist, relativistic, "mere cultural studies," and "a turn to post-modernism" are overly simplistic and show a serious misunderstanding of social constructionism, cultural studies, and postmodernism. Worse, this is a serious misunderstanding of the work done by interactionists, particularly sociologists who study race, ethnicity, and culture (Joas 1987; Denzin 1992).

While it is true that some cultural studies projects may not focus on the material effects of culture and ideology on economic or political policies, sociologists who study culture and knowledge production do take up that task. Sociologists who do cultural studies use modes of inquiry and methods we feel will allow us to closely scrutinize the knowledge that communities construct and then examine the material consequences (or origins) of that knowledge (Berger and Luckmann 1966; Cicourel 1968). We merge, expand, and sometimes contest others' theories of cultural formation, particularly if they seem ahistorical and apolitical, as we consider culture to be something that affects and is affected by economic and political consequences. This has been practiced even in the earliest days of the discipline via Max Weber, W.E.B. DuBois, and Alfred Schutz and continues on today (for some examples, see Hall 1996; Omi and Winant 1994; and Bonilla-Silva 2003). For those of us who study race, closely scrutinizing culture is absolutely imperative now in this age of "color-blind racism."

A close look at cultural studies of race also reflects the work that a number of symbolic interactionists value: to closely look at culture to understand the processes involved in maintaining race and racial inequality and, more importantly, to uncover issues sociologists have not yet studied or understood were important when researching race (Gerth and Mills 1946; DuBois 1978; Stonequist 1961). This kind of research allows us to verify or counter assumptions that scholars, activists, and policy makers may have about race and, thus, develop our understanding of race and ethnicity and racism within the United States and abroad. In other words, once we have established how people make meanings, sociologists of race can then use these findings to help us use other modes of inquiry (like surveys or interviews) which will help us understand race relations and the needs of immigrants better. Eduardo Bonilla-Silva (2003), for example, formulated surveys and interview questions based on Omi and Winant's (1994) findings regarding the racial formation process and the changing nature of racism.

The main difference between traditional ethnography and Internet ethnography, or nethnography, is the absence of face-to-face interaction. While studying text-based conversations does eliminate the need to transcribe, the lack of a physical meeting with the participants seemed daunting. First, conversations were different on the 'Net than they were during various focus groups that I conducted as a graduate student. As in many newsgroups, some participants were anonymous posters. Since I was not interested in studying how the participants on the newsgroup changed their identity, but rather in the conversations themselves, I treated anonymous posts the same as "authored" posts. After all, the study is, ultimately, about how this particular technological advance (i.e., computer-mediated communication) affects the process of identity and community formation. Since anonymous posting has been made possible through the use of Web-based e-mails, I had to include them in my study. If I needed to include an anonymous poster's letter in my chapters, I simply referred to this person by the pseudonym they used.

I made no inferences regarding any participants' racial, ethnic, gender, or sexual identity unless the participants disclosed their identities. Although the lack of face-to-face interaction could allow the participants to misinform the newsgroup, I believe that the trust between the members of this newsgroup was very high, especially during the years I researched the group. I logged onto the newsgroup when it was fairly new and when anonymous posting was at a minimum. Most of the participants used e-mail addresses provided to them by their place of work or school, and even those with commercial addresses used their real names as they hoped relatives or long lost friends would be able to find them in this "virtual homeland." We were very honest with each other in revealing the categories to which we belonged, as our agenda was to define Filipino culture from Filipinos' viewpoints. This study defined the participants as they defined themselves; however, to protect their anonymity, I changed their names and the names of the threads.

From 1995 to 1997, I logged onto the newsgroup at least once a week to see how the participants talked about, debated and/or defined Filipino identity. If anything within the post referred to identity, I saved and printed it. I lurked and just read the debates most of the time; however, if a person wrote anything that I felt needed clarification, I posted a response to the whole newsgroup and entered the discussion. As a participant-observer, my own stories and posts are included in the empirical material. If something within the discussions made me rethink my own identity, I either wrote it down in my memos or posted it on the newsgroup. Over twenty-one months, I printed and analyzed over two thousand of the posts I read.

I believe that the lack of face-to-face conversation also made participants comfortable enough to "flame" (i.e., to rant, to speak or write relentlessly about a subject with either hostility or sarcasm toward a person or group of people who had initially written about the subject) one another. This Internet format allowed participants to air their viewpoints in ways that they might not have during face-to-face conversations. There were major "flame wars" throughout the twenty-one months that I collected material from the newsgroup. Although many of the scathing posts did not contribute to the debate, others pushed it into different directions. Because of the importance of these posts, I included them in my data analysis. However, because these posts often prompted one conversation to morph into several, I had to devise a new system to file and categorize my empirical material and fieldnotes. The next section addresses this system.

Filing Empirical Material and Field Notes

From 1995 to 1996, I checked the newsgroup at least once a week using PINE (Program for Internet News and E-mail) a tool for reading, sending, and organizing e-mail. The messages in the newsgroup were arranged in chronological order, not by thread. But I needed to separate the empirical material by thread, since I was studying identity articulation and re-articulation in each thread. As such, separating the posts in any other way (e.g., by specific subjects discussed within the thread) would destroy the thread. For example, many participants discussed the definition of "Filipina" in terms of race while others focused on U.S. colonialism. Rather than separating these posts into two piles labeled "race" and "colonization," I saved them in a folder that contained all the posts in that thread group.

Saving posts by thread appears to be a straightforward task since threads are labeled in the subject line. However, various threads were often not reflected in the subject line. Participants frequently carried the same thread under a different subject heading. To keep up with the changes, I kept written notes of each thread as I read the newsgroup, including a summary of the argument and snippets of quotes. If a post appeared to continue the thread under a different subject heading, I wrote the new heading in my notes and saved that post in the appropriate folder. When the folder became too big or the snippets of quotes on my notepad too long, I printed the posts in the folder. I kept the hard copies next to me so I could better determine whether a post was the continuation of a thread or the beginning of a new one. Over almost two years, I printed the contents of these folders at least once a week.

To add to the confusion, threads often morphed into new ones. That is, posts frequently carried the same subject line as a thread I had been following, but contained new, unrelated material. Other participants then continued this new thread. At this point, I saved these posts into a new folder even if they had the same subject heading.

Organizing the individual posts within the threads was a challenge as well. Because the participants were located around the world, I had to quickly learn the various time zones. Most of the time, I could easily organize the posts. In addition, frequent printouts made the organization less time consuming.

Because threads were often continued under different subject headings and because they frequently morphed into new conversations but retained the same subject headings, I soon learned that I could not depend solely on the subject headings. As a result, I read each post very carefully. When I first began the project in April 1995, there were only 250–300 posts per week, so I only logged onto the newsgroup for three to four hours per week. By 1997, however, the posts increased to 1,050 per week. By then I had become used to my system of reading and collecting material, so I was not as overwhelmed. In addition, I also read the newsgroup using a Web browser, which organized the material by subject line. Even though I still had to read every post, having the conversations organized by subject heading was a great help, as most posts in the thread carried the original subject heading. The Web browser also organized the replies in hierarchical order so I could visualize the conversational posts to which participants responded. Being able to print these hierarchical trees helped me organize the posts more efficiently.

After a few weeks into the project, I had several folders sitting on my desks, a big note pad with descriptions and snippets of threads, and felt completely overwhelmed. At this point, I stopped logging onto the newsgroup and began to analyze my empirical material. As I stated before, I wanted to separate the posts by thread, so I could see how Filipino identity was negotiated, not by various subjects discussed within each post.

Analyzing Conversations

Mikhail Bakhtin (1986) has argued that, when studying conversations, scholars should study utterances and responses rather than analyzing structures of sentences. As far as context is concerned, each utterance has its own context and is in itself a rejoinder to another utterance. In addition, researchers should examine how others responded to the speaker's utterance.

Researchers study these utterances to understand "culture in practice" and to learn about their reciprocal systemic relationship, not just the effects of structure on practice. By studying culture this way, researchers can understand how structures change. The method of instances is based on the same premise: members understand and respond to each instance (in my case, each post) in a context. I chose this method because I wanted to see what people debated, how the debates played out, and if and how they articulated Filipino identity during these debates. Using the method of instances and the cultural studies perspective, this study analyzed threads in soc.culture.filipino to understand the process of identity formation. However, because the conversations about identity took place on the Internet, certain methodological modifications were required.

Picking which threads to include involved the cumbersome process of (1) grouping the posts by thread, (2) analyzing each thread to find out what the major debates were about, (3) grouping the threads by debate (similar to grouping instances into collections), (4) reanalyzing each thread from a cultural studies perspective, and (5) choosing which threads to present in my study. Although any of these debates would have facilitated my analysis of identity formation, I chose those threads that were most frequently discussed. In picking these particular threads, I do not wish to imply that the debates I picked are ideal types; every thread had its own flavor. Several threads discussed the Tagalog language and many discussed the imposition of English and Spanish words into the language; but, obviously, these topics were not debated exactly the same way. However, these particular threads allowed me to explore how a Filipino identity was debated, (re)configured, and (in)validated, what happened when members disagreed, and how debates were temporarily resolved. In addition to containing recurring topics and several analytic codes, the debates that I selected had personal relevance. They reminded me of things that happened to me. I wrote about these links in my memos and journal and I have included many of these memories in this study. I aimed to present threads with topics frequently discussed between 1995 and 1997 so the reader could experience the kinds of debates that faced the participants during this time.

While I collected the empirical material, I wrote memos to remind me of the overall context of the conversations that occurred during that day and how they fit into the conversations that occurred during that week and/or month. I also kept a journal that described how I felt about the debates. In addition, I stopped at least once a month to analyze the debate printouts. I first determined what the major topics of debate in each thread were and then I grouped them accordingly. Although subject headings are supposed to contain a description of the post, I could not rely on these as they often did not reflect the post's content. Instead, I did a cursory reading of each post to discover the topics discussed. Because the threads were differentiated by topic, I had several piles: Filipino jokes, the commodification and descriptions of Filipino women, language, Filipino history, cultural values, food and traditions, and the differences between Filipino Americans and Filipinos in the Philippines all went into separate bins.

After this grouping, I analyzed each thread again, this time paying attention to *how* the topics were discussed within each debate. What clues did they use to argue the debate? How were their arguments framed? What kinds of categories, definitions, and/or metaphors did they use? This involved a line-by-line analysis of each post. In this way, I created new categories such as "the Filipino/American dichotomy" and "racialized culture" and wrote these notes in a separate document, so I could keep in mind recurring themes.

After reanalyzing each thread in a collection, I separated them into two piles: "possibly present" and "don't present." The threads that immediately were placed in the "don't present" piles contained too many immature rejoinders and not enough debate about the definition of Filipino. Most threads ended up in these piles. Many threads started out with promising topics, but disintegrated into these kinds of flame wars. Flames that degenerated into immature rejoinders (e.g., "You totally suck!!!") were not presented as most did not pertain to my research questions. However, flames which addressed Filipino identity (see chapters 2 and 3 for examples) are included as they often pointed to the categories and characteristics the posters used to classify people.

Those that ended up in the "possibly present" piles were threads which (1) did not contain many immature rejoinders and (2) contained responses that contested and/or confirmed the original post. I regarded flames that did not degenerate into name-calling contests as critical responses; many threads that included these kinds of flame wars were included in this pile. Most but not all of the threads in this pile were rather lengthy. To choose from these threads, I reanalyzed the threads yet again.

Out of over two thousand posts and more than two hundred threads (I stopped counting after a while), I picked less than ten threads that contained many of the recurring topics. These threads lasted for weeks or sometimes months and contained the least amount of non-constructive flames and cross posts. Although I included excerpts of conversations I have had with several Filipino Americans and non-Filipino Americans, my study emphasizes the search for identity in a transnational location (i.e., the newsgroup). The vignettes that I included reflect the connection between the debates and my own experiences and memories outside of the Internet.

All the names except for "Mom" and "Dad" are pseudonyms. Since there are several easily searched archives of Usenet groups (e.g., DejaNews, www.dejanews.com), I did not include exact dates, real names, or the real subject headings of the threads to protect the participants' anonymity. Although the Institutional Review Board designated newsgroups as public spaces at the time I presented my proposal, I still assured the participants of their confidentiality and anonymity. To give readers some sense of context, this study does give the participants' location and general time period of the posts. Although I did not observe many anonymous posters, if I quoted any, I changed their pen names, as finding anonymous posters' real-life names is currently possible.

Filipinos and the Internet

Filipinos in the United States cannot escape the computer revolution because we are constantly inundated with advertisements about global communication and the Internet. MCI, AT&T, and Microsoft commercials shown every few minutes on major television networks and cable channels ensure more efficient, speedy communication across both state and national boundaries. They promise global yet tight-knit communities on the Web, herald the freedom of speech, and imply that the world on the Internet is egalitarian, without real-world structural barriers. It is ironic (or perhaps merely telling) that one commercial features a song by Steely Dan, whose lyrics assert, "What a wonderful world it could be. What a joyous time to be free," while another heralds the emergence of a universal language (read English) that the Internet makes possible. The 'Net may appear to shrink the world, but many gaps have been more clearly widened as well.

Although my students and the participants on the newsgroup knew of many Filipinos' access problems, we still felt we could begin a political revolution on the Internet and then let others in our respective areas join in. Soc.culture.filipino held the promise of allowing Filipinos worldwide to join into one united Filipino community. While the majority of those that post on soc.culture.filipino claim to live in the United States, between 1995 and 1997, self-defined Filipinos posted from the United States, Philippines, Canada, Singapore, Australia, Austria, Sweden, and Greece as well. This newsgroup has allowed Filipinos to "go back home" and see what's happening there. Although Internet communication is not synchronous, it does provide information at your doorstep and allows people to interact with potentially thousands around the world through the simple act of typing words on a keyboard. Efficiency and speed equals "nearness" on the Web; thus, in this newsgroup, the Filipino diaspora appeared to become more compacted. As one participant exclaimed, "It's a small world and the 'Net totally shrinks it!" We had, as Kling and Iacono (1995) wrote, believed the hype of the "computer revolution."

In late 1994, when I first started participating on soc.culture. filipino, members of the newsgroup were optimistic about the speed and efficiency of e-mail and newsgroups. People who joined soc.culture.filipino aimed to "help others to understand what our culture is really like and not what it is rumored to be" (soc.culture.filipino FAQ, 1994), and they hoped to use the Internet to meet Filipinos worldwide, learn about Filipino history and culture, and locate long-lost relatives. All also desired to understand the issues that impacted Filipinos worldwide. It appeared that soc.culture.filipino was a virtual homeland to which diasporic Filipinos could return.

In 1996, in the midst of this study, the estimated number of readers on soc.culture.filipino was twenty thousand, many of whom resided in the Philippines (Atkinson 1996). In the beginning of my study, most of the participants posted from the United States, Canada, Australia, and the Philippines. Almost all posted from either educational or business accounts. Because the Internet was fairly new and most accounts were given to the participants (as opposed to participants having the ability to sign up for and configure the accounts themselves), people's identities were out on the table. As we will see, the openness of people's identities helped create a familial community on soc.culture.filipino, as people could easily tell from one's e-mail address where they resided and either worked or went to school. In addition, gender identities were also, for the most part, out on the table.

Also, within one year of my arrival at soc.culture.filipino, people were posting from many other countries, including Singapore, Austria, Greece, Sweden, and Italy. However, there were also more participants who held more commercial and Web-based (such as AOL and hotmail) accounts which slightly changed the nature of communication, as people could hide, change, and/or morph their identities more easily. (We can see the impact of anonymous posts in chapter 4.)

Throughout this book, I show that participants often linked their posts to conversations both on and off the Internet. I focus primarily on the discourses that underlie the debates, the process by which the discussants work through these debates, and the conclusions to which they arrive. Although I do not systematically analyze how the real world has changed due to participants' virtual interactions, I give examples of discussions that emerged on the newsgroup and later moved into the real world (see chapter 6).

Filipinos' need to become visible and regain agency has often been expressed on the newsgroup soc.culture.filipino. In fact, in the 1994 charter document, the founders of soc.culture.filipino stressed the newsgroup's mission to provide an open discussion on issues concerning the Philippines; this includes the following topics:

—new technology in the Philippines
—"what's happening back home" information and passing this
    on to others unable to read news. PURPOSE: Would like to
    discuss relevant Filipino issues in a newsgroup that would
    single out Filipino culture. Currently, there are several
    other nations that have started their newsgroups. . . . I be-
    lieve that there will be a consistent flow of news, espe-
    cially with the state our country is in presently. This
    newsgroup may help others to understand what our cul-
    ture is really like and not what it is rumored to be.
    (soc.culture.filipino)

By separating Filipinos from "others" in the last sentence, the newsgroup's founders move Filipinos from the margin to the center, from the background to the forefront. This newsgroup offers information about "real" Filipinos and it serves as a "virtual homeland"—a place where people can receive information as if they are back home. Thus, it is also a place where Filipinos can form a virtual community with thousands of other Filipinos. This utopian notion of a newsgroup is based on the idea that computers will revolutionize the world.

People constantly rearticulate their identity in non-virtual locations; I had already witnessed this as I was growing up. Although these
events were sporadic, I saw my aunts rearticulate their identity as each
relative from the Philippines or as third-generation Filipino Americans visited our home. As stated in the preface, more recent immigrants or visitors from the Philippines highlighted the "Americanness"
of my first-generation family members, whereas third-generation
Filipino Americans reinforced their Filipinoness. However, these shifting identities were sporadic, occurring most frequently during summer barbecues or at weddings and ending once people went home. In
contrast, because soc.culture.filipino is centered upon the Filipino
community and culture, I was able to watch this articulation and rearticulation take place between people physically located in different
places on a daily basis. By watching the debates unfold, I could see
how members of the diaspora established what Filipino identity means
with people back home and how people at home forged an identity
with members of the diaspora, especially those in the old colonial country. This project examines how Filipino identity is articulated in this
virtual homeland. Given that Filipinos from different locations would
log onto this newsgroup, I suspected that they would articulate different experiences as Filipinos. I asked how these different images and
experiences would affect the articulation of a Filipino identity and
culture.

Direction and Scope of the Study

In the following chapters, I illustrate, through the
use of ethnographic data, the prevalence of polemical arguments about
community, race, and other identities central to identity, postcolonialism, and Internet studies. Through the participants' discussions and
debates, we can see how different nationalist paradigms for concep-
tualizing about race and other concepts fail when confronted by the
intercultural and transnational formation, particularly communities
formed on the Internet. While scholars have analyzed the creation and
re-creation of identity, few have shown how new technologies and the
ability to communicate in transnational locations (such as cyberspace)
have impacted the notions of race, nation, culture, and/or gender.

Chapter 2 was prompted by the debates surrounding the seemingly
simplistic, postmodern deconstructions of "race," "nation," "culture,"
and "homeland" and their effect on our discussions of community and
identity. I describe how the scholarly definitions of culture and na-

tion have changed and how these changes have affected theories of diaspora and diasporic identity. Then, focusing on the United States, I describe the importance of identity to various ethnic and racial communities. Although identity is not static, because of continuing racism as well as the current focus on cultural authenticity and multiculturalism in "Westernized" countries, people in the United States desire to articulate an authentic ethnic and/or racial identity.

With respect to the Filipino diaspora, many Filipino Americans state that they need a strong Filipino identity to be able to define themselves in relation to others (see Espiritu 1995, 2003). Posts on soc.culture.filipino written by Filipino Americans indicate their desire to learn more about Filipino culture through the newsgroup and/or to share their knowledge of being a Filipino American in the United States. In chapter 2, we can see the impact of racism and colonialism on the participants' definition of Filipino identity and the formation of group membership. When defining Filipinoness, participants first had to negotiate culture by drawing upon images of the Philippines and the United States, their common history, and lived and imagined experiences. I describe in detail how the participants used these images, their experiences, and history to define Filipino culture and identity and explain how these discussions enhance our knowledge about race, culture, diaspora, and nation.

Through these brief exchanges about citizenship and "authenticity" of Philippine-born, raised, and located Filipinos, we also see that definitions of the Filipino community (like other racial and/or ethnic communities) have in their origins Orientalism (rooted in racialized reason), Eurocentrism, capitalism, and white supremacy. It is here that we begin to witness the prominence of ideology in the maintenance and up-keeping of "traditional" identities.

Chapters 3 and 4 pursue these themes in conjunction with a historical commentary on the U.S.–Philippine colonial relationship and tie this relationship to racialization of culture (e.g., American equals white). I show that because of real-life political concerns, the participants on soc.culture.filipino dichotomized and reified the notions of culture, nation, race, and ethnicity despite the social constructedness of each concept. In particular, they articulated Filipino identity against the backdrop of the U.S.–Philippine colonial and economic relationship.

In chapter 3, we see how the participants describe homeland, homegrown values, and traditional language against this colonial relationship which affected the negotiation of Filipino. Participants from various locations brought images of America, the Philippines, American life and culture, and Philippine life and culture into the discussion. As a result of the desire to define a Filipino identity against American culture, Filipino participants who are not as critical of the United States and those who are located in the United States were often challenged and sometimes dismissed by those who wished to define Filipino in opposition to the former colonial power, the United States.

When images of locations were no longer sufficient, images of dichotomous cultures were used to establish who the real members of the diaspora were. In chapters 3 and 4, we see how the participants used notions of authentic cultures to create a strong national Filipino identity and to discredit other speakers. In addition, we can see how lived experience is used to establish the authenticity of Filipino experience. However, because experiences are also constructed by prevailing discourses (Scott 1995), the participants also reassessed the meanings of experiences. The discussions in chapters 3 and 4 demonstrate why essentialist theories of race, culture, ethnicity, gender, and nation impede communication between diasporic members. More importantly, this begins to show new common threads by which all members are connected—the most salient being the political process of globalization.

Chapter 3 revolves around the concept of "citizenship" and membership in the Filipino community. Here, we see how the ideologies of capitalism and Eurocentrism played a part in developing both the Philippine nation and Philippine identity. Specifically, I show how the topic of "benevolent assimilation," discussed on the newsgroup regarding the existence (or nonexistence) of "authenticity" and "colonial mentality," permeated discussions about membership within the Filipino community. Three debates are discussed: (1) oppositional identity versus colonial mentality; (2) the racialization of Americans (i.e., "Kanos" as white); and (3) Tagalog versus English as a national language. Some questions they debated include, Are Filipinos who have emigrated to other countries as Filipino as those who stayed? Or have they betrayed their homeland? I show how these discussions are directly tied in with the issues of global capitalism introduced in chapter 2 and show how their ideas of authenticity preclude the participants' understanding of how emigration policies have contributed to the diaspora in the first place. At the end of this chapter, we see how "homegrown values" had to be negotiated among participants on the newsgroup. This topic ties directly to the next two chapters, which demonstrate how females represent and are expected to carry the culture, as they serve as the "gender markers" of a nation.

In trying to create a Filipino community, the participants attempted to create what Kwame Appiah (1994) calls an ethnic "script." The ethnic script that the participants articulated, not surprisingly, treated Filipino women and men differently. Chapters 4 and 5 are key chapters because we see various discourses come to a head and realize the difficulty of engaging in coalition politics without first interrogating the underlying processes that created divisions in the first place.

In chapter 4, we see how the participants' anticolonialism and desires to define an essential Filipino identity affect their battle against negative stereotypes and the commodification of Filipino women. Debates over personal ads and "pen pal correspondences" and Asian female/white male relationships show that "Filipina" serves as a gender marker between cultures—that is, definitions of Filipino women are used to solidify the division between Filipino and American culture. As a result of the emphasis on culture, traditional patriarchy is not questioned. Some posts even perpetuated oppressive stereotypes. Hence, the drive to define an essential Filipino identity devoid of what participants perceive as American characteristics has marginalized Filipino women, especially those raised in the United States.

Furthermore, we see how stereotypes of people in Asian female/white male relationships highlight the effects of the struggle against anticolonialism and antiracism on the definition of "Filipina." Specifically, by privileging national identity, participants often referred to common derogatory stereotypes of Asian women to define "Filipina" (e.g., Filipinas are hypersexual, yet monogamous, wives). They are obedient, nurturing mothers—unlike Westernized (i.e., white) women. In addition, good Filipinas married other Filipinos (or at least other Asians). Filipinas who did not wish to be stereotyped were derided and told they were "selling out the race" and had a "colonial mentality." By focusing exclusively on building a national identity, Filipinas were merely treated as a gender marker between the United States and the Philippines, and the participants essentialized the boundaries between East and West, essentialized the boundaries between American and Filipino, and perpetuated traditional patriarchy.

All of the prior debates about culture, authenticity, racialization, and colonial mentality converge in a discussion about interracial relationships between Asian and/or Filipino women and white males. This chapter revolves around two cross-listed e-mails about "Asiaphiles" and "Whiggies"—derogatory terms for the white males and Asian women involved in these relationships. Through analyzing these threads and the soc.culture.filipino participants' reactions to these two threads, we can see how the boundaries between oppressed/oppressor and authentic/inauthentic become even more unclear. More so, in this chapter I show how the participants' reliance on creating community based on socially constructed categories of culture, race, gender, and nation backfires. And we can see why it is very important that scholars analyze the effects of cultural and economic colonialism so we can better understand various issues, including the commodification and stereotyping of Filipino women.

Despite the constant debates on Filipino identity, most participants were able to keep their sense of humor. In chapter 5, I analyzed jokes that participants used as tools to obtain the closure of heated debates and, more importantly, to determine membership within the Filipino community. I show that participants framed their jokes against commonly debated issues (introduced in chapters 2 through 4) and attempted to transcend the traditional boundaried groups such as race, gender, nation, and culture that they had earnestly debated for months at a time. At the same time, I also describe how cultural "roots" are determined and how particularities are both essentialized and abstracted. I argue that participants chose the "You might be Filipino if" genre as a tactical move to prove to everyone that Filipinos can and do share a common bond with one another.

With these jokes, participants were able to imagine a different, hybrid Filipino, one who re-articulates culture and uses this re-articulation as resistance. Instead of dichotomizing Filipino and American cultures, they attempted to collapse the hierarchy into syncretized, but strictly Filipino language and customs. By examining cultural artifacts and language very closely, they simultaneously articulated hybridity and Filipinoness. It is through these jokes that some participants learned that diversity is the root of Filipino identity.

In the concluding chapter, I return to the question of unity and diversity. Regardless of the tactical move to find common characteristics among all Filipinos, the participants knew that the Filipino diaspora is extremely diverse. The debates described in the previous chapters are just a few of the different ways this diversity was articulated on the newsgroup. In the concluding chapter, I include one regular participant's argument that attempting to find Filipino roots is futile; addressing not only colonization but also regionalism, he claims that the Philippines have no roots. Although "diversity can be a root," he says, "it is not a very stable one."

How then can Filipinos create a diasporic community? In this chapter, I analyze a debate about whether there are common roots that all Filipinos share. I show how the jokes in chapter 5 pertain to this discussion and analyze the similarities between this and other scholarly debates on identity politics and the politics of identity. I suggest that instead of trying to base a coalition on identity, this book shows us that we should attempt to coalesce in relation to the politics of identity. That is, the process of categorization—whether by race, ethnicity, culture, gender, and/or a combination of all concepts—is based on common political agendas. In the case of Filipinos, the common political agendas illuminated by members in this newsgroup are colonialism, capitalism, Orientalism, racialization, and patriarchy. This information is important because, if we are to put these conversations alongside other historical moments, we will see that the Filipinos' diasporic experiences, though different, have a common root. In other words, these conversations and historical accounts together show us "a changing same." I conclude the book with some personal reflections on my experience as a Filipino American and scholar on soc.culture.filipino.

2 Problematizing Diaspora

If Nation, Culture, and Homeland Are Constructed, Why Bother with Diasporic Identity?

Why do they always have to show that poor, dirty, shoeless Filipino child on this commercial [about alleviating global poverty]? Hypocrites! As if there aren't any poor people and dirty places in this country! There are many beautiful and modern places in the Philippines!

—Mom

There's No Place like Home

The fuzzy blue "Welcome home" mat in front of my mom and dad's house signals to me warmth, safety, and a place to escape. (I can practically hear that "Welcome home, to Maxwell House" jingle as I pull into the driveway.) To relatives from the Philippines and various acquaintances, however, this image is a bit disconcerting. The mat and the outside of my childhood home don't "fit" with what's inside. For some visitors, it signals the death of a culture and absorption into mainstream white American life. For others, the outside of the home masks the exotic foreignness of immigrant living—the smells, artifacts, and foreign tongues spoken inside the home. Though not articulated as such, assimilationist and pluralist paradigms dominate many visitors' characterizations of my family life and childhood home. More than that, however, is the imposition of boundaries between cultures—in this case between American and Filipino culture.

"Where Have All the Natives Gone?"

For example, last summer, Carla, a white second-generation Italian American acquaintance from college, remarked that the outside of my house and the "Welcome home mat look so very American! Kinda like the Brady Bunch. But when I walk into your house, it's like I'm in a totally different country! . . . It's like, so *not* American in so many ways. It's so Filipino; I just love your rice dispenser! . . . Even though you've got American things in it, it's like, so Oriental."

"Geez," I thought. "Should I show her where we keep the magic carpet?" Dismayed, I exchanged pleasantries with her (at mom's request, I gave her some coffee and cookies—American enough, dear?) and showed her toward the front door of our Americana-style home.

In contrast, relatives from the Philippines come and comment on how "Americanized" our family and family life has become. Curious, I asked one relative, Uncle Ernie, what made our house American. He pointed at the electronic equipment (TVs, VCRs, stereos, and, of course, a videotape rewinder), the velvety American couches, the carpets, the layout of the house, and most of all, chocolate chip cookies ("American food everywhere!"). Yet on returning from visiting Uncle Ernie and his family in the Philippines, my mom revealed that his house is equipped with the same machines and fuzzy couches and that the cupboards contained Nestle's Quik, Chocolate Chips Ahoy! cookies, and, unfortunately (for my uncle's heart and possibly for the reputation of the United States), an abundant supply of Spam.[1]

Finally, my friend Janice visited me at my parents' house over break and was distraught when she saw that my mom had replaced framed pictures of Filipino landscapes with Renoir prints. A white, American, feminist, comparative-lit grad student, she lamented that "home" was becoming too American: "Where the hell is everything?! It's not the same; it looks so foreign to me." (Her idealism, belief in a "United Colors of Benetton" or "Taste of Chicago" type of cultural pluralism, and her aversion to U.S. economic, political, and cultural hegemony is heightened whenever she comes over and sees my mom's acquisition of more American objects. Renoir prints were somewhat tolerated, but my dad's singing bass [fish] was too much to handle!) To assuage her feeling of loss, she focused on the new ways my mom displays bath beads. (Mom thinks they're too pretty to hide in the drawers, so she puts them in jars and places the jars on the shelves in the bathroom.) I didn't have the heart to tell Janice that I've seen bath beads displayed in similar ways by people of different ethnicities and races— this was not uniquely Filipino, nor do my mom's actions automatically make it a Filipino trait. Janice needed to hold on to her image of my home as "Filipino."

Why? These images strangely made *her* feel at home again; she felt comfortable because my non-white-American family was continuing to do what she believed to be non-white-American things. And most of all, it gave her hope, she said, that "the hegemonic forces haven't gotten your family." She saw the novel way of displaying bath beads as an appropriation of American culture. "No matter how hard Americans want people of color to assimilate and succumb to their ways, it just ain't going to happen!" she exclaimed proudly. She then attempted to engage me in a discussion about Fanon's *Black Skin, White Masks* (1967) and Bhabha's "Of Mimicry and Man" (1994) to assure me of the revolutionary undertones of mom's artistic bead venture. In her mind, removing bath beads from the bath reflects the potential of subjugated groups to resist assimilation or "colonial mentality" because it shows the oppressors that, no matter how hard they try to kill the Other's culture, the Other remains "almost, but not quite" (Bhabha 1994). Although I do believe in the power of sly civility and mimicry (see chapter 5 for details), I couldn't help but feel that Janice's reading of my mom's "revolutionary" bath-bead venture was almost, but not quite.

Nostalgia and History

All of these instances made me realize the power, potential, and possibilities of naming and renaming. In each of these cases, Carla, Uncle Ernie, and Janice insisted on relegating objects into one of two disjointed camps—Filipino and American. In addition, my own reluctance to accept any of these conceptualizations made me want to explore more how others in the diaspora negotiated their ethnic identities.

Confused, I went to the source: "So, what's it mean to be Filipino, Ma?" Interestingly, she made no reference to materials, artifacts, or the landscape. Instead, she described her carefree childhood, her best friends, and the freedom to walk around wherever and whenever she wanted. She spoke of a lifestyle divorced from the pressures of conspicuous consumerism, free from the impact of multinationals (like Pepsi, Nike, and AOL) that are ever so present in the Philippines today. At the same time, she acknowledged the impact of the Philippines' emigration policy and the corresponding U.S. offerings of H1 visas. In doing so, her answer represented the importance of nostalgia and an awareness of history and political economy that many people, perhaps unconsciously, use to define their culture. "Freedom is the Philippines," she said. "America is where we work."

Culture/Power/Place and Memory:
Is This a Great Time or What? :-)

My friends, Uncle, and Mom differentiate Filipino and American cultures in different ways. The focus depends on each person's intention: Carla was in the mode to discover the Other; Uncle Ernie in the mode to observe how my parents have adapted since they moved away from the homeland; and Janice wished to see the self-preservation of ethnic culture. All but my mother focused on objects within my parents' house. However, if we examine the objects that they used to differentiate American and Filipino cultures, it reinforces the idea that the boundaries between cultures are fuzzy and contingent upon one's images of both cultures.

More importantly, Carla's, Uncle Ernie's, and Janice's definitions of Filipino and American culture were contingent upon how they read certain objects in the house and which objects they thought symbolized each national culture. Carla focused on the rice dispenser, Uncle Ernie focused on chocolate chip cookies, and Janice, the disappearance of things. Each took these particular objects as evidence of an overarching culture rather than as part of a unique fusion of two or more cultures.

Each reading, of course, is also based on the reader's experience, lived and imagined. Interestingly, none examined their own households. If they had, they would have seen the same combinations within their homes. Uncle Ernie's collection of electronic devices could be read as an attempt to be American. James Bond and other action flicks abound. However, knowing Uncle Ernie, I believe that he owns these things more to satisfy his love of movies and music than to be American.

Janice has always read the objects in my house. As far back as I can remember, she has kept track of Western items, and she expresses concern whenever something she considers to be Asian is either replaced or no longer visible. Never mind the fact that my mother's collection of Japanese furniture adorned with inlaid mother of pearl is also an attempt to infuse/admire a different culture. To Janice, pan-Asian motifs are "closer to [my culture]" than kitschy, 1970s, Elvis's Graceland-type objects.

Like Janice, some people are concerned that transnationalism—the movement of people, labor, culture, and capital across national boundaries—is causing a homogenization of culture and an Americanization of the whole world (Madsen 1993). But the fact that national cultural boundaries are blurred by increasing migration, global capitalism, and transnational networks does not mean that we all live in a homogenous culture (Appadurai 1991; Burayidi 1997; Clifford 1992, 1994; Lowe and Floyd 1997). Transnational networks have created not homogeneity, but multiple contested identities.

Even though there has been a McDonaldization effect in the last fifty years, defining identities, particularly cultural identities, appears to be more important as globalization and transnational movements increase (Barber and Schulz 1996; Hall 1996; Waters 1990). Perhaps because of the easy movement of artifacts, information, and images, descriptions and definitions of ethnic identity and diasporas often portray a fixed picture of static cultures. Unfortunately, cultures have never been static—such descriptions have been used to create and maintain global and local inequalities (Anderson 1991; Gupta and Ferguson 1997; Narayan 1997).

In this chapter, I begin by discussing the constructedness of nation, culture, and homeland and how the racialization of culture affects the identity of American members of the Filipino diaspora. I explain how transnational movements, globalization, racial projects, and political policies such as multiculturalism influence people's desires to "go back to their roots," particularly those members of the diaspora who feel a need to connect to a homeland. I explain briefly the dilemma of trying to find a fixed culture in a moving target. Finally, I end by explaining how this project can help us better understand why these transnational movements have led to displacement and how transnational lines of communication have the potential to form larger, issue-based communities within both local and global Filipino communities.

The Imagined Communities of Nation, Culture, Homeland, and Diaspora

World maps portray nations as rigid, inflexible regions. In most world atlases, each nation is colored differently so the reader can clearly see the boundaries between nations. Even though maps are updated as new nations arise, each nation is still colored differently and separated by dark, bold lines. But nations are not natural or unchanging communities; they are imagined, negotiated, and policed political communities (Anderson 1991; Gilroy 1993). This does not mean that all people residing within the constructed borders are included in these political communities. Currently, the world is looking at the situations in Central Asia, the Middle East, and seeing evidence of this process. Multiple identities exist within nations, including the United States; yet, the state and media's description of a national identity often erases or vilifies identities that do not fit the dominant narrative (Anderson 1991; Anthias and Yuval-Davis 1994; Gilroy 1987). Thus, in constructing these imagined communities, groups must be marginalized or effaced by those who wish to create or maintain the status quo. For example, blacks in England are marginalized and excluded from the descriptions of English identity (Gilroy 1987); here in the United States, the mainstream media still largely portray "Americans" as white.

This exclusion has caused many marginalized residents within nations to advocate multicultural policies (Burayidi 1997). This is not a purely American phenomenon. In 1988, Canada instated the Multicultural Act, designed to promote cultural diversity and enrich many citizens' quality of life. The four major points of the act are "i) to assist cultural and language preservation, ii) to reduce ethnic/racial discrimination, iii) to promote intercultural awareness and understanding, and iv) to promote culturally sensitive institutional change at the federal level" (Frideres 1997). Similarly, Australia's government created the National Agenda for a Multicultural Australia in 1989. Many indigenous groups in Asia and Africa are demanding recognition by former colonial countries of the varied cultures that live within their national borders.

Here in the United States, simple multiculturalism or liberal pluralism is promoted in the media and through "diversity talk" in corporations (Burayidi 1997). This "pluralism" is counterproductive to the assumed goals when it commodifies difference—United Colors of

Benetton, Crayola's Multicultural Markers, ethnic food fairs—or ignores differences in power and resources between dominant and marginalized groups (Chicago Cultural Studies Group 1995; Lott 1995; Wallace 1995; Waters 1996). And yet this kind of multiculturalism is quite easy to swallow. The ability to identify the difference between *pad thai* and *pad prik* and the ability to master various "foreign" phrases substitute for serious analysis of global inequalities. Less than forty years after Dr. Martin Luther King Jr. delivered what is now called his "I Have a Dream" speech in Washington, D.C., people in the United States (and perhaps worldwide) have forgotten that the core of his speech was to illustrate the present nightmares of structural racist and classist social policies, not to merely celebrate diversity. Although many of the problems he mentioned are still present (i.e., the problems of police brutality, residential segregation, and unfair voting policies), we pay attention only to the last third of the speech and boldly and wrongly assert that his dream has been realized.

But the emphasis on cultural identity, Burayidi argues, provides a "safety net [for those who] feel threatened by the dominant ethnic group" (1997, 2). One way to regain recognition is to be able to represent oneself (Goldberg 1995; Lippard 1990). This includes regaining the power to name oneself as well as to characterize one's group. Thus, learning about one's cultural identity is one way to regain one's voice. Waters (1996) argues that it is also used to fill a void in a person's life. A young Filipino American's message on soc.culture.filipino stated, "I want to learn about [the Filipino culture] because it is your culture that makes you rich."

This desire to "go back to their roots," the nostalgia for one's culture, and the eagerness to learn about the homeland is not limited to racially marginalized people in the United States. The excitement of many Irish Americans over Michael Flatley (aka "Flatheads"), *Riverdance*, and *Lord of the Dance* is an indication of this desire to learn about their roots. One fan raved on the *Riverdance* homepage, "I loved this show since the very first time I saw it. I believe that it has brought Irish culture back to America. Since Riverdance has been around there is more and more Irish music and dance being heard around. My niece has started Irish dancing and watches the tape of Riverdance at least once a week. Keep up the good work. Also I wish all of you a very happy St. Patrick's Day" (*Riverdance* homepage, 1997).

The benefits of multiculturalism are that people are more willing to learn about diverse cultures. But divorced from a serious analysis of racism, this kind of liberal, blind faith in pluralism flattens all ethnicities, thereby rendering discontented citizens as mere malcontents (Waters 1990; Bonilla-Silva 2003). Because of states' and media's emphasis on "equal cultures," critics of multiculturalism argue that it ignores racial inequality and thus may aggravate racism (see, for example, Rorty 1995).

One way to foster a more complex understanding of this kind of multiculturalism and its effects is to study the creation of cultures, nations, and notions of homeland. It is in understanding this creation that we may be able to uncover the various uses of the creations of authenticity.

Racial Projects and How They Affect Filipinos

But the war goes on; and we will have to bind up for years to come the many, sometimes, ineffaceable, wounds that the colonialist onslaught has inflicted on our people. . . . Because it is a systematic negation of the other person and a furious determination to deny the other person all attributes of humanity, colonialism forces the people it dominates to ask themselves the question constantly: "In reality, who am I?"
—Frantz Fanon, *Black Skin, White Masks*

Many people in the United States are under the impression that because slavery has been abolished and many institutions have been integrated, racism no longer exists. After all, a national holiday celebrating the life of a popular black man was recently added, the key proponent against affirmative action is black, the best golfer in the world is black, and the most popular rapper in the world is white. All social programs designed to help racially subordinated groups should be dismantled, they argue, except those that will eliminate "reverse racism" (Magubane 2002). Furthermore, if racism is discussed, especially in the mainstream media, it is usually only in terms of blacks and whites. For example, the respected ABC news series *Nightline* runs periodic specials about racism, but entitles them "America in Black and White." Many of those who are aware that other races face racism believe that their lot is not as bad as how black Americans are treated because they were never enslaved and, therefore, their problems can be easily solved. Thanks to multiculturalism, the rampant racism in the United States is hidden by images of happy-go-lucky multiracial friendships, an overattentiveness to seemingly diverse organizations and institutions, and, of course, the erasure or dismissal of news sources that point to the continuing significance of race.

But racism does not operate that way. In contrast, all racial projects are intertwined and work with one another to create and maintain hierarchies and inequalities. A *racial project* is "simultaneously an interpretation, representation, or explanation of racial dynamics, and an effort to reorganize and redistribute resources along particular racial lines." (Omi and Winant 1994, 56). In the United States, severe racial projects include the justification of the assimilation, education policies, and "removal" of Native Americans from fertile land; the internment of Japanese Americans during World War II; the firebombing of mosques in Southwest Chicago directly after September 11, 2001; continuing anti-Semitism; police brutality; the unwanted imposition of Norplant implants on African American women (and the sterilization of other women of color); and even the vilification of white, southern "rednecks."[2] These and countless other racial projects and practices simultaneously maintain the racial hierarchy and give the impression that racism no longer exists. Frantz Fanon noted, "A Black man is not. And neither is a White man," which illuminates the fact that whites, too, belong to a race, and notions of their "inherent" superiority were masterfully constructed in relation to ideas of inherent inferiority of those they wish to subjugate.

These constructions of binary races and cultures—that which is civilized and that which is barbaric—are full of paradoxical moments. In the United States, for example, various racial projects were used to justify the government's takeover of what we now consider the USA's mainland as well as Hawaii and other various territories. To justify Manifest Destiny, Native Americans were vilified and characterized as uncivilized, brutal savages who worshipped gods inferior to the Christian God and who did not possess any knowledge of how to efficiently make use of the vast land.[3] By the nineteenth century, as the numbers of Native Americans sharply declined from an estimated 22 million to less than 200,000, scientists overlooked American policies of war and forced removal and blamed the death on "survival of the fittest." Even as the citizens of this new land sought to preserve and understand the ways of the noble savage in this age of rising industrialization, the destruction of the Indian way of life was used by those who wanted to maintain the status quo as evidence of the superiority of the white, Anglo Saxon, Protestant way.

Similarly, U.S. governmental officials, embracing the established racial characterizations of black Africans (i.e., mentally inferior, physically strong savages), entered the slave trade in 1619. The rise of the United States as an economic superpower was largely a result of this use of slave labor, as well as indentured servitude and immigrant labor. Later in the eighteenth century through the present century, racial projects were created by those in power to justify the domination of non–Anglo Saxon white immigrants, Asian immigrants, and, of course, Latinos. Yet, while the U.S. economy has been built on the backs of these indigenous peoples, slaves, and immigrants, many written histories still give most credit to the white, Anglo Saxon, Protestant leaders of the nation, four of whose images are carved in the sacred Black Hills of South Dakota. This racial project has, simultaneously, established the United States of America as a land of immigrants and created a white national image.

American Beats out Kwan for Figure Skating Title
(MSNBC scrolling marquee, February 20, 1998)

This headline is just one example of how Asian Americans are marginalized in the United States and are forever foreign (Tuan 1999). For months, many Asian Americans were ecstatic for the media attention lavished on an Asian American athlete before the 1998 Winter Olympics. Michelle Kwan, an American figure skater of Chinese descent and the favorite to win the gold medal that year appeared on numerous magazine covers and was interviewed by multiple television shows in the two years preceding the Olympics. Yet, the author of this online article somehow forgot that she is just as American as Tara Lipinski, the white figure skater who took the gold.[4] Although the marquee was quickly corrected, and despite the apology from the sports editor of MSNBC (Edmundo Macedo), Asian American groups around the country were deeply outraged. Brandon Sugiyama of the Asian American Journalists Association sarcastically suggested alternative headlines, including "Whitey beats out slant" and "U.S. beats out Red China." This "mistake" was not taken lightly among these Asian American organizations or Asian Americans in general because of our past and present history of exclusion. This small blunder echoes the same marginalizing practices used to justify racial projects that uphold white supremacy: Asians are not only unworthy of being seen as Americans because of their skin color, but they are also somehow unassimilable. In addition to the aforementioned World War II internment, the passing of the Anti-miscegenation and Exclusionary Acts in the late nineteenth and early twentieth centuries, the killing of Vincent Chin in 1982, the murder of a Filipino American postal worker in Los Angeles in 1998, the jailing of Wen Ho Lee, and a myriad of Orientalist discussions, discourses, and displays in the media all fall under this rubric.

As a result of this consistent Orientalism, many political activists and scholars within the Asian American community have attempted to counter discrimination by forming racial activist coalitions (Espiritu 1989; San Juan 1992); unfortunately, many of these alliances are based on an adherence to the notion that race and/or culture are "natural" or fixed. With respect to my project and soc.culture.filipino, many participants (particularly self-defined second-generation Filipino Americans) joined together for kinship purposes. "'Oi, mister! Indo-Aryans . . . it looks like I am Western after all! Maybe I should listen to Tina Turner, wear the itsy-bitsy leather skirts. Pah. It just goes to show,' said Alsana, revealing her English tongue, 'you go back and back and back an it's still easier to find the correct Hoover bag than to find one pure person, one pure faith, on the globe. Do you think anybody is English? Really English? It's a fairy tale!'" (Smith 2000, 196).

All these tactics and racial projects are common across colonial projects. With respect to racist colonial projects, Alsana (a fiery character in Zadie Smith's White Teeth, a fictional book which describes in painful detail how colonialism and racism affect people of color in England) proclaimed, "Do you think anybody is English? Really English? It's a fairy tale!" The Fanon quote at the beginning of this section refers to the French colonial project in Algiers. My mom's quote at the beginning of the chapter refers to the common perception within the United States of Third World countries, in this case, the Philippines. It is important to note that all three countries are technically independent nations, decolonized decades ago. Although people from the former colonies have emigrated and now reside within the former "Motherland," mere legal maneuvering cannot undo or eliminate negative characterizations of former colonized/subjugated peoples.

Though seemingly overwhelming and complicated, understanding the importance of the process of normalization in establishing and maintaining oppression opens up possibilities for social change as it destabilizes all levels of the hierarchy. No longer is there a "norm" against which the "problem race" should be measured. Instead, we understand that the characterization of the group in power as "normal" is one of the key elements in creating and maintaining these inequalities. In understanding how and why that norm is created and maintained, we understand that any effort to measure up against that norm perpetuates inequalities because there was never any neutral ground to begin with. With respect to soc.culture.filipino, I show the complications that arise when proponents try to construct an idea of Filipino in relation to a perceived norm. For Filipinos, when it comes to race, the norms are twofold.

Filipinos and Racial Projects

While the United States government characterized Filipinos as "little brown brothers" in the press to justify to the American people its presence in the Philippines for economic and military reasons, the various institutions they established (i.e., schools, governmental bodies, and media) both inside the Philippines and in the United States constantly pushed the American way, reminding Filipinos of their inferiority, of the necessity to attempt to assimilate them (though not *completely*) into Western (i.e., civilized) life, and of the thanks they should give their liberators.

Emilio Aguinaldo, once the U.S. ally during the last months of the Spanish American war, was vilified when he and the Katipunan forcefully resisted American occupation. Characterized as a pickney, this little brown brother and his supporters were "niggerized" in the American press and by the American public, even as they and their lands and their emigrants to Hawaii and the West Coast buttressed the U.S. sugar production and agricultural economy (see, for example, Pieterse 1995, 216).

Thus, racial projects, of course, affect everyone, including those who benefit from such projects. While the overall strategy of racial projects may be the same, each racial and/or racialized ethnic group has different histories and trajectories in the making of nations. It is important to note that, with respect to immigrants past and present, these basic characterizations hold true for *all* people of the diaspora, not just those who reside in either the colonized or colonizer's countries. In other words, transnationalism incorporates not only the movement of peoples between nations, but the movement of these images as well.

When discussing colonization and racial projects, many scholars focus on a colonial group's construction of the Other and how this construction justifies imperialism (for example, see Stoler 1997; Young 1995). These are incredibly important endeavors as, I believe, the unearthing of the process by which colonialization was successful is the first step in uncovering the origins of present inequalities. While I do touch on the various dominant discourses which affect subjugated groups, I focus on how the Other (i.e., Filipino participants on soc. culture.filipino) articulated identity and community against the backdrop of the U.S.–Philippine colonial relationship.

As stated before, this newsgroup was founded because of the perceived need to find an authentic Filipino identity. This quest for authenticity often meant both a clear separation from the colonizer's culture and survival in the midst of globalization. The emphasis on nontangible cultural artifacts such as values and motivations as well as race shows us that *Kano* is not just a reference to the United States, but encompasses cultural and racial oppression.

In this newsgroup, the participants, particularly those in the United States and Philippines, continually ask, "Who is Filipino? Who is Kano?" the latter being a racialized ethnic term in that it usually refers to white Americans, but in soc.culture.filipino it was shorthand for oppression and globalization: "'Kano' is taken to mean Americans, but has broadened in popular use to mean *all White Westerners* who visit this country. . . . I also use it to refer to the values, motivations and stereotypes that are rooted in Western culture and are all too often the motivation and perspective of Westerners, particularly Americans . . . who are interested in the Philippines" [my emphasis].

The above quote stood out because the poster stated this up front, while in others the connotations of Kano are more implicit: "Jeff [a white American male] told me that after he got divorced, he didn't want to marry a *puti* [white] again. . . . He said that he always wanted to be with Asian women, you know, because of our culture. We know how to treat our husbands, not like those *kanas* [American women] who don't know how to make marriages work. He likes that Asian women are good wives, you know, not like those *puti* who don't know how to please their men."

These quotations further show that "American" and "white" are inextricably linked, but also implicit in these posts is a complex set of racialized and gendered assumptions which the posters have used to characterize and categorize Filipinos and Americans. The point of the second poster's quote was to show members of the newsgroup that Filipino women know how to be women. What is interesting about this post, though, is that she doesn't do this by talking solely about what she believes to be some traditional values Filipinos hold. She establishes her points in relation to stereotypes of both white Westernized women and Asian/Filipino women. I talk about this complex combination and use of Orientalism, racism, and sexism by both self-defined Filipinos and non-Filipinos in detail in chapter 4.

Since Kanos are defined as white Westerners, it follows that any self-defined Filipino who appears to have the same values, motivations, and/or follows a "Western" way of life is a "wannabe white." Quite a few participants held this opinion on the newsgroup, and the negative effects of this association stand out when Filipino-American participants attempt to assert their Filipino identity. George, a Filipino-American male college student on the East Coast wrote this when he introduced himself to the group: "I am trying my damnedest to get back to my roots and learn more about my parent's culture. Similar to other US Born Filipinos/Filipinas I've met, my parents never taught me Tagalog [a Filipino dialect] for fear that I would have an accent and that other kids would make fun of me at school. They also neglected to teach me . . . about the culture or history of the Philippines, so now, at age 23, I feel very whitewashed and sad."

The tone of this and other Filipino Americans' introductory posts often was riddled with guilt and resembled a cleansing process, similar to confessing one's sins to a priest. To George and other American-born or -raised Filipinos who don't feel a part of the American community, the lack of knowing the Filipino culture, history, and the language means being whitewashed—not just being lost, assimilated, or even just American. Because they are not of the normalized race (i.e., white), yet know only the normalized culture, many non-whites in the United States feel doubly inauthentic and do not feel a sense of belonging in either culture.

We Filipinos even have our food metaphor. While "Oreos" refer to African Americans who are "black on the outside but white on the inside;" "apples" to Native Americans who are "red on the outside, but white on the inside;" and "bananas" to Asian Americans who are "yellow on the outside, but white on the inside;" Filipinos are coconuts: "Coconut: [those who are] brown on the outside but white inside. . . . these people deny their heritage and claim to be other ethnicities."

On the Internet, participants can create new words or redefine common words and make them common parlance in that particular space (i.e., a newsgroup) or in different Internet communities simply through continued use. In this newsgroup, the word "coconut" took on a specific connotation as an insult, similar to the terms "Kano" and "puti."

The Asian/Latino Question Revisited

As we have seen, Filipinos who reside in the United States are not considered to be nor can they consider themselves to be completely American because of the conflation of American with white. Within the United States, Filipinos are, technically, classified within the Asian American race. But, because of popular images of Asians as anything Chinese or Japanese, partially because of our genetic makeup, and, in some areas of the United States, because of the remnants of Spanish influence (particularly in our surnames), many Filipinos feel marginalized within that race as well. This has led some Filipinos in the United States to join "brown power" groups through the years, in an effort to make ties with Latinos who face similar problems because of skin color and, of course, because of the immediate assumption that those who have Spanish surnames are "illegal aliens." But, knowing the clout held by the model minority, some Filipinos hold steadfast to their position within the Asian race (Espiritu 1989). These complications are well noted in this newsgroup; in the following chapters, I show how racial projects affect the discussions of Filipinoness. And what is interesting is how these U.S.-based characterizations played out on the Internet. The Internet makes it possible to move a person's local definitions of ethnic identity into a transnational location, and in this particular case, we discover the power of U.S.-based stereotypes. What images we thought were confined to the United States, in fact, have traveled across the globe via globalization and are as powerful as the notion of the American Dream. Because of the perceived threat of homogenization, members of the newsgroup also heavily turn to the concepts of nation, culture, and homeland. And yet, these concepts are also subject to debate.

Why Bother with Identity?

The focus on the social constructedness of such categories as race and gender was a breakthrough of sorts. It allowed scholars to explain the societal characterizations of categories and, more importantly, the functions the categories play in maintaining the status quo. But, despite its value in uncovering how inequalities are maintained, social constructionist theory has often been simplified and misused to maintain the status quo.

Many people make two particularly egregious mistakes regarding the concepts of race, gender, identity, nation, and culture. First, they see concepts as based on "natural" and/or fixed characteristics. Second, if these concepts are not natural, but socially constructed, then one can simply will away the problems associated with them. Both of these simplistic ideas are often used to maintain inequalities. With respect to the first assumption, the creation and maintenance of inequalities are based on the notion that, within each of these categories, some groups are superior and others inferior. Even if one tries to be a cultural relativist and judge cultures on an equal plane, the notion of separateness but equalness often still abounds, which at best can lead to personal misunderstandings, at worst, isolationism and a belief that others' problems are not our problems. For example, many still believe that the mass carnage in the West Bank and the threat of nuclear war within the borders of India and Pakistan are merely due to "fundamental cultural or religious differences" and do not bother to think about the historical, political, social, and economic policies and practices which underlie the formation of all national boundaries in the last (at least) fifty years (Narayan 1997). How people are willing to accept the complexity of interpersonal relationships, evidenced in their ability to follow convoluted daytime and primetime soap operas, and still relegate the threat of nuclear war to "fundamental differences" is disheartening. Clearly, the world is much more complicated, more interesting, and of more importance than whether the very fictional Ross could be a good husband and father of the very fictional Rachel's baby on the very fictional sitcom *Friends*.

With respect to the second assumption, turning a blind eye to social problems by merely proclaiming one's membership in the "human race" is nothing but failure of our sense of humanity. To be fair, the notion of color-blindness (or any other kind of hyphenated blindness) sounds appealing, as its proponents deftly use language which sounds humanitarian. Presently, a most pernicious bill is being circulated around California. Calling it the Racial Privacy Act, Ward Connerly, a trustee of the University of California, is seeking to supplement his anti-affirmative action measure, Proposition 209, with an act that forbids any California state or local agency, with the exception of police departments, from collecting racial data on any person. Presumably, this act is to protect racial minorities from racial discrimination and whites from "reverse racism." However, antiracists contend that the Racial Privacy Act can exacerbate racism because it merely hides racial data while structural racist practices—for example, inferior schooling systems in impoverished neighborhoods, etc.—remain intact.

But the very nature of social constructedness is precisely the reason we cannot turn a blind eye toward any of these concepts and the myriad of issues associated with them. Instead, we *must* take into account diversity, multiple identities, and hybridity within social groups (such as race, gender, class, and culture) and stop reifying the notion of natural, essential identities because classification schemes and standards were created and reified by those who wish to maintain the status quo to marginalize and subjugate certain groups of people (Bowker and Star 2000; Butler 1995; Haraway 1991; Lorde 1984a; Scott 1995; C. West 1995). They warn that if we continue to address or analyze social problems in this manner, any attempt to fight domination by adhering to the same classification schemes and using the "master's tools to dismantle the master's house" will be futile because it will only maintain the status quo (Lorde 1984b, 112).

This does not mean we can or should ignore the very real impact of culture, race, gender, or nation. Socially constructed or not, "[i]f men define situations as real, then they are real in their consequences" (Thomas and Thomas 1928, 572). Social constructionism is neither turning a blind eye to categories nor hoping that if we ignore them or don't address them or no longer acknowledge them as real concepts, they'll go away and no one will face oppression anymore. Of course, most scholars concerned with the social constructedness of categories do not believe in turning a blind eye to social issues. Rather, they use social constructionist theories to show exactly how economic and political power struggles create and affect the characterizations of various communities (see, for example, Foucault 1990), particularly those that are subjugated by biological explanations or rigid cultural differences. One major area of categorization that affects people in the United States and other countries is race. In the United States racism and laws that are contingent on race are constant reminders that, although racial categories are constructed, race matters. And Filipinos, being neither black nor white, are affected in a very specific way.

The Importance of Imagination, Memory, and Experience in the Creation of a "Global Ethnoscape"

In studying culture and diaspora this way, it is easy to understand the utmost importance of imagery. Because global hierarchies were partially justified through the divisions between "civilized" and "uncivilized" and other dichotomies, images and/or memories of one's "culture" must be included in the notion of "homelands," as well as that of diasporic identity (Appadurai 1991; Boyarin 1994; Chow 1993; Radhakrishnan 1996). Identities are often not contingent upon a physical return (as many diasporic members cannot afford to go home) but on an imaginary return. Many second-generation immigrants define their ethnic identity against the memories of the homeland and against the images of the homeland and the stories of people who have traveled there (Abelmann and Lie 1995; Lie 1995). And as we will see, this return to the homeland is also desired by some people who reside within the homeland and who believe that globalization has destroyed their motherland and culture.

Since political struggles and personal experiences are intertwined, researchers argue that we must also examine the role of experience in the making of diasporic identity (Radhakrishnan 1996). Ethnicities are defined against lived and imagined experiences as well as against perceived notions of homelands and cultures (Appadurai 1991). Images of the host countries and homelands travel across boundaries through transnational networks that blur the boundaries between nations. These images also affect people's real lives. As an example, Appadurai describes the plight of the women involved in the sex tours in Asia. Here, women make money by catering to Western ideas of Asian women. These images of Asian women affect gender politics not only in these bars, but worldwide. Because images travel through these ethnoscapes so easily, he states that scholars must incorporate the links between imagination and social life into ethnographies.

A systematic analysis of experiences and these imaginary returns to either a home never seen or a home never experienced can provide insight into the workings of "global ethnoscapes" and the difficulties of forming communities based on an identification with static cultures.[5] In transnational cultural spaces, such as Internet newsgroups, we can see how diasporic members identify membership in the culture. As we will see, to define Filipinoness, the participants on soc.culture. filipino have to negotiate culture. As this negotiation occurs, I show that they draw mostly upon images of the Philippines and the United States, common history, and lived and imagined experience to construct Filipino identity.

From the Classroom to the Newsgroup: Second-Generation Filipinos Speak

Before I began my project, some of my Filipino American students told me that the reason they checked the newsgroup was because they wanted to be able to converse with "real" Filipinos (i.e., Filipinos who reside in the Philippines). They hoped that they could learn more about their real identity by talking to what they deemed authentic Filipinos (i.e., Filipinos in the Philippines). One Filipino American who posted on the newsgroup seemed apologetic for his previous attempts to mask the Filipino part of his Filipino American identity:

> I'm a second generation Filipino-American. I grew up [on the East Coast], since my father was in the U.S. Navy. Fortunately, there were other Filipino families around, so that I really didn't feel isolated and "different." I will admit having the stereo-typical American boyhood. I played baseball, was a Boy Scout, and loved steak and potatoes. I avoided rice, fish, and pancit [a Filipino dish] so much that my parents wrote home to the Philippines that I was their "American" son. When I visited the Philippines for my first and only time in 1983, my parents wanted to serve me hamburgers instead of anything Fili-pino.
>
> It wasn't until I got [to attend a University in the East Coast] that I have thrown myself into the task of searching [for my identity]. I joined the [Filipino Student Organization at the University] and have attended several community events. I even joined a Filipino Folk Dancing Troupe. . . . When I was growing up I never wanted to be a part of folk dancing whereas my brother and sister both participated.

The issues this person brings up in this first part of the quote are commonplace among many second-generation immigrants, not just Filipinos (Espiritu 1995; Waters 1996; Tuan 1999; Zhou and Bankston 1999). In the United States, this desire to go back to their roots occurs when members of racially subjugated groups, immigrants, and/or racialized ethnics are placed in situations where they are consistently treated as representatives of their race/culture instead of as individuals. In the past twenty years, the desire to establish multicultural activities has been prevalent in high schools, colleges, and universities in the United States, and the burden is largely placed on those in marginalized groups to "bring culture" into each institution or student group. With respect to Filipino Americans, a recent movie (*The Debut*) was based on this process of Filipino identity formation. The success of the movie is largely due to the fact that many immigrants of all races can identify with this dilemma of being either/or/both and vacillating between each identity. In the newsgroup, many of the second-generation and/or non-Tagalog-speaking Filipino immigrants' initial posts contained explanations of why they joined the group, but what is interesting about this part of the quote is the tone. Simultaneously expressing the authors' pride in being Filipino and the guilt for not being proud all along, many of these posts were imbued with shame and resembled a public confession healed only by the welcoming replies of other real Filipinos. This type of expression is a political move—an admission of past sins—and many participants (particularly those who consider themselves to be "sinners") believed that this admission was central to gaining membership in the community.

In addition, it is interesting to note what cultural activities this participant considered to be "stereotypical American" activities (e.g., playing baseball, eating steak and potatoes). His characterization of American points to the fact that, even though we, as Americans, are proud of "E Pluribus Unum" and the Ellis Island stories, we still understand that we, as a society, impose certain characteristics on each person and culture. This national project is not unique to the United States, of course, nor is it confined within the United States (Gilroy 1993). But it does play a major part in the discourses throughout the book, as it points to the notion of distinct boundaries between cultures. Like other second-generation ethnic Americans, once in college, the poster above chose to emphasize his ethnic identity (Waters 1990). The reason for this change is revealed here: "A very important resource has been my parents. I reached that age where I was curious about my roots that I started asking questions. I guess I went through the ordinary rebellious attitude of a teenager, and kind of shut my mind to anything they had to say. *But in college, I think, people start relating to more and more different people and need to come up with a definition for themselves in order to share it with others.* [my emphasis] Best to start with the SOURCE!"

"The source" is often not questioned by any member of a diaspora. Voluntary or involuntary, diasporic members are constantly attempting or wishing to somehow make the pilgrimage to the homeland. This idea of deep-seated roots within nations and the accompanying levels of authenticity attributed to people who are closest in proximity to the homeland, or sometimes via birthright, is rooted in notions of static, boundaried nations, the kind of world that maps, atlases, and globes suggest. These boundaries are the same kind our political leaders and policy makers still suggest, even as we all bear witness to a level of organizing based on ideologies across multiple borders.

And yet, this need for a strong subject-position led many of the participants to essentialize "Filipino" because they felt they must have some formal representation of their group's identity before they could identify with that group. In this newsgroup, participants discovered that the Filipino is not as easy to define as it appears. In addition, there is a powerful relationship between images and/or memories of homelands and political issues (especially U.S. colonialism) in the articulation and negotiation of a Filipino diasporic identity. Despite participants' keen awareness of transnational networks and the permeability of national and regional borders, they actively chose to define themselves using notions of fixed cultures rooted within particular national borders. They make this choice largely because naming is always done against the perceived rigidity of ethnic, racial, and cultural classification systems and in reference to local political issues (Clifford 1994; Lippard 1990; Haraway 1991). So while the participants wanted to clarify their common group identity, they still often defined themselves against the current classification systems that were present because of the necessity to create a strong, political subject position.

The "Filipino"/"American" Dichotomy: The Economic, Political, and Cultural Impact of Spanish and U.S. Colonialism on the Philippines

The bourgeoisie, historically, has played a most revolutionary part. . . . The bourgeoisie, by the rapid improvement of all instruments of production, by the immensely facilitated means of communication, draws all, even the most barbarian, nations into civilization. . . . It compels all nations, on pain of extinction, to adopt the bourgeois mode of production; it compels them to introduce what it calls civilization into their midst, i.e., to become bourgeoisie themselves. In one word, it creates a world after its own image.
—Karl Marx and Frederick Engels,
The Communist Manifesto

A little English education can be a very dangerous thing.
—Zadie Smith, *White Teeth*

The erasure of Filipinos from American history and so-called world history (as if they can be separated) textbooks is unfortunate (at the very least) as Filipinos have been at the center of global political and economic movements over the past five hundred or so years. The history of the Philippines stands parallel with the development of both Spain and the United States as economic powers through agricultural capitalism from the fifteenth to twentieth centuries and through the presence of multinational corporations currently. Thus, the history of Filipinos, past and present, parallels the histories of Puerto Ricans, Mexicans, Cubans, Hawaiians, and the people of Guam, Samoa, and countless other former and current Spanish and U.S. commonwealths. In terms of capital, economic, and emigration policies, Filipinos have more than a one-hundred-year history of transnational movements,[6] and, thus, are an excellent source for studying the topics discussed above: the fluidity of culture, transnational ties, diasporic organization, etc.

Yet, many believe that because of years of colonial rule, Filipino history and culture are not good subjects of study because we no longer have a unique culture and authentic identity. Therefore, they claim, there is no use in studying Filipino culture. An unfortunate result of this belief is that, although Filipino studies have been growing in the past fifteen years,[7] there are still relatively few articles and books in the social sciences about the Filipino diaspora (Rosaldo 1989). This dearth of scholarship has negatively affected Filipinos worldwide, particularly those who reside in areas where multiculturalism abounds.

Many of the participants on the newsgroup felt the impact of erasure in historical accounts. They stated that characterizing the Philippines as "Americanized" and "Westernized" delegitimizes Philippine culture. It is partially because of the paucity of resources on Filipino history and culture that two Filipino Americans established soc.culture.filipino. In the introductory frequently asked questions list (FAQ) to the newsgroup, the founders wrote that they hoped the newsgroup would help all "understand what our culture is and not what it is rumored to be" (soc.culture.filipino FAQ, 1994). When I first logged onto the newsgroup, I had assumed that the posts would center primarily around the different regions and languages within the Philippines, as I entered with my own memories of how the Filipinos I came into contact with defined Filipino cultures. The American/Filipino dichotomy, I assumed, would not translate onto the newsgroup as, I wrongly believed, this dichotomy was used primarily within the Filipino American community due to fear that Filipino traditions will fade in the United States. However, in the following chapters, we will see that the colonial relationships (between the United States and the Philippines, primarily) are at the core of identity debates. As stated before, to establish Filipino culture and identity, the participants on the newsgroup referred to the colonization of the Philippines. Because of the importance of this relationship, I give a brief history of the colonization of the Philippines and its economic, political, and cultural ties with the United States and people around the world.

The participants on the newsgroup are well aware of U.S. colonialism and the continuing U.S. cultural and economic presence in the Philippines. In fact, participants have actively tried to construct a Filipino identity in opposition to what they perceive as American. In particular, participants consistently remind each other that American "help" amounts to American imperialism, and that Filipinos should not trust Americans. The following exchange in a thread about the negative influence of Americans typifies the discussion of the colonial relationship of the United States and the Philippines. Cecilia states, "[What did Americans do wrong?] Saved Philippines from the Spaniards and the Japanese and taught us what freedom is. If they did not commit this wrong-doing, then we should be enjoying still to this date, being called as Indiyos [*sic*] and watching our babies be pricked after being tossed into the air with bayonets."

Here Cecilia acknowledges the power of naming as she considers being called "Indios" by the Spaniards as one form of oppression. This reflects Lippard's (1990) argument that naming is one way to gain control over a group. She argues that this source of power is why many marginalized groups fight for the right to re-name their groups. Cecilia's discomfort with the name "Indios," however, is somewhat ironic, as she does not contest (and presumably accepts) the name "Filipinos," which the Spanish also created. Even though the Spanish referred to themselves as Filipinos during occupation and the indigenous peoples of the Philippines as Indios, the mere appropriation of the once-privileged term "Filipino" does not empower colonized peoples (Lippard 1990). But, this move does not seem to bother Cecilia.

Cecilia also mentions war atrocities committed by Japanese soldiers during Japanese occupation in the Philippines (1941–1945). By referring to the power of naming and the power of fear brought on by the Spaniards and Japanese and juxtaposing an image of the United States as savior, Cecilia incurred the wrath of at least two regular participants on the newsgroup. Here are Inez's and Joven's responses: Inez writes, "I think the U.S. robbed us [of] our freedom at gunpoint. We had been fighting for our freedom hundreds of years before the Americans came to our shores. Diego Silang, Andres Bonafacio, and Jose Rizal will rise from their graves if FREEDOM was alien to us and first taught by Americans at the end of the century. They will all dispute your thesis." Joven agrees with Inez, stating, "The United States did not come as liberators, but as colonizers. They did not come in peace, but attempted, in vain to wipe out the inhabitants of the islands. When that failed, they tried cultural genocide, and again, they failed."

By referring to Filipino nationalist leaders José Rizal and Andres Bonifacio, Inez points out that the Filipinos resisted both military and cultural colonization; as such, she refutes the notion that Filipinos were helpless people who needed to be saved from the Spanish. In doing so, she and Joven resurrect a different kind of Philippine history which moves Filipinos to the center stage, as active participants in the preservation of their freedom and culture. Interestingly, neither participant addresses the images of Spanish and Japanese occupation that Cecilia used to highlight the benevolence of the Americans. This focus on American imperialism more than Spanish colonization or Japanese occupation occurred quite frequently on the newsgroup. The myth of American benevolence was focused upon and torn apart, and threads that addressed the atrocities committed during Spanish and Japanese occupation were not only scarce, but rarely responded to. And, on newsgroups, non-response to a thread ensures its death. Thus, the history of Spanish colonization and Japanese occupation was often killed and buried by members of this newsgroup.

The conversations on soc.culture.filipino all fall within this rubric—self-defined Filipinos on the newsgroup were eager to peel away the layers of Western influence in order to find the authentic Filipino culture. Participants also frequently talked about the ill effects of the U.S.-sponsored Marcos dictatorship and about how the military bases in the Philippines supported militarized prostitution. As a result of participants' anticolonialism stance, the posts often reflect the desire to create a Filipino identity that differentiates (and dichotomizes) American and Filipino cultures. Anyone who brought up problems within the Philippines, or who seemed to support Marcos, or who lamented over the closing of the bases was usually accused of being a "traitor" or, more frequently, "whitewashed." In this transnational space, the participants realize the difficulty in this venture—finding

one's identity is not the same as unearthing untouched, preserved cultural artifacts on an archaeological dig. Because opposition to a strong
anticolonialism stance was often presented using racial terminology,
in the next chapter I address the participants' tendency to racialize
Filipino and American cultures. I also introduce a discussion of a seemingly cut-and-dry, undebatable topic—language—and begin to uncover
the continuing significance of colonialism on the diasporic Filipino
community.

3

Selling Out
One's Culture

The Imagined Homeland and Authenticity

Hughes ([1948] 1971) argued that knowing and/or living by one's cultural values is what differentiates "authentic" members of the ethnic community from others. However, he warned that cultural artifacts don't *identify* a culture; they are used to *form* a culture. In this chapter, I analyze participants' discussion and construction of Filipino cultural values and artifacts, such as language. As we will see, in these interchanges, the division between Filipino and American is highlighted through participants' articulation of cultural values and location.

Learning about the shared meanings of cultures includes learning about cultural values. As stated in the last chapter, liberal pluralists assume that people bring their own cultures to the host country. Multiculturalism, in this view, involves merely learning about cultural differences within the host country and does not focus on the construction of values. And yet, the construction of cultural values is often done in relation to other countries; for immigrants or decolonized peoples, it is often constructed in relation to the host and/or the colonizer's land. Not surprisingly, Filipino cultural values are associated with the "homeland" as the following sections attest.

As we will see, instead of unearthing authentic values and language patterns, while discussing these topics, participants become more aware that they are tied to "real life" political and social issues. In particular, as we will see, cultural values and language are heavily contingent upon the effects of colonialism, globalization, their images of the homeland, and the fear of colonial mentality.

The Construction of Culture

Like racial projects, culture is created with respect to political, economic, and national projects. Images and memories are often used to solidify boundaries; cultures have traditionally been defined as distinct systems of shared meaning (Clifford 1986; Gupta and Ferguson 1997). The world, according to this view, is comprised of separate, diverse cultures. In the late nineteenth and early twentieth centuries, social scientists were encouraged to learn about other cultures by collecting data through living among "the natives," objectively studying each culture and drawing generalizations from multiple cases. This differs from current studies in that, in the past, cultures were "naturally" associated with a specific place and practiced by a specific group of people. Even though anthropologists have long abandoned these notions of rigid, natural, boundaried cultures, both cross-cultural studies (Clifford 1992; Gupta and Ferguson 1997) and multicultural policies (Scott 1995; C. West 1995) are based on this definition of culture.

This is why it is important to study the creation of culture in relation to both space and power.[1] In addition to political and economic policies, we also must study the use of images and memories of cultures in the construction of culture (Appadurai 1991; Boyarin 1994; Gupta 1994; Radhakrishnan 1996). By emphasizing the authenticity of a culture, proponents of the politics of difference ignore the diversity within cultural groups and write scripts that marginalize individuals who choose not to follow the scripts (Appiah 1994). As stated before, articulating authentic cultures, whether from an institutional or grassroots level, is also a form of essentialism that can contribute to oppression (Appiah 1994; Taylor 1994). This is why it is imperative to analyze how (and in what context) differences are created, intertwined, and hierarchically organized and to explore the possibilities of recreating communities and identities based on non-static, fluid images of social categories, including cultures (Scott 1995).

Transnationalism and the Changing Definitions of "Diaspora"

The study of movements across national boundaries—whether for economic, political, or personal reasons—can illuminate the potential of creating such communities. The literature on transnationalism—which reflects increasing migration, global capitalism, and the technological advances that make transnational networks possible—captures the permeability of national boundaries and the possibility of re-forming networks and understandings of political organizing (see Schiller and Blanc 1993). A key concept is the notion of diaspora, which attempts to capture the constant flow of information, people, and/or cultural artifacts across nation-states and which simultaneously acts as a category or marker for a certain group of people. Some earlier definitions of diaspora are still dependent upon traditional definitions of culture and nation.[2]

Other authors try to rediscover the hidden histories that link members of a diaspora. The move away from an essence toward history is closer to Gupta and Ferguson's (1997) project of historicizing the creation of culture. However, Hall (1990) warns against fixing identity only on the past because we may ignore how it is changing in the present and will change in the future. For example, Hall cites the work of Armet Francis, who offers photographs of people in the Caribbean, USA, and Africa who are linked by "the underlying unity of the black people" through "colonisation and slavery" (Armet, quoted in Hall 1990, 224). Hall cautions that we must not characterize identity like this, one that is fixed in a common history. Identity is an ongoing project. By focusing only on the past, we miss how identity constantly changes.

But more recent definitions of diaspora also emphasize the creation of unique local identities in relation to the context of displacement (Clifford 1994; Hall 1990). That is, diaspora is always contingent upon a relationship to a homeland, but because there are multiple images of homeland and because the homeland itself is always changing, diaspora and diasporic identity are often constantly contested. This diasporic identity is not only a personal struggle, but also a political one: heterogeneity and change, not essence or purity. "[Diaspora is] the recognition of necessary heterogeneity and diversity by a conception of 'identity' which lives with and through, not despite, difference" (Hall 1990, 235). In other words, diasporic identities constantly change and are grounded not in tradition, but in patterns of political, economic, and other social changes. Cultural identities are continually being transformed; that is, they are not fixed but are "subject to the continual play of history, culture, and power" (Hall 1990, 225). Redefining diasporic identity in this way challenges us to view difference not as an endpoint (as liberal pluralists do), but as a tactic used to create and reify unequal power relations. This is why we should not just study difference, but how and why differences are produced.[3]

This emphasis on fluidity and change does not mean that people of a diaspora cannot be unified. An emphasis on common history can unify people, but "it does not constitute a common *origin*, since it was, metaphorically as well as literally, a translation" (Hall, 1990, 228). Thus, the alternative definition of diasporic identity that focuses on representation that unifies the people of a diaspora is never stable because the people who constitute its definition are all differently positioned. In this book, we will see that U.S. colonialism is ever present in the participants' discussion of past and present social issues and in their discussions about what constitutes a Filipino. The dialogue of power and resistance is contained in every element of the participants' discussions. This dialogue includes not only knowledge and experience of social inequalities, but images, memories, and nostalgia for the homeland.

Homelands and Filipino Identity, Location, and Authenticity

As many definitions of diasporas evoke the notion of a homeland, to define who fits into the Filipino diaspora, one needs to first define homeland. Like nations and cultures, homeland is "imagined" (Radhakrishnan 1996; Boyarin 1994; Rouse 1991). That is, the images of homeland that newly arriving immigrants carry and those images held by immigrants who have not gone home since they arrived as well as people who have never visited the homeland all contribute to the definitions of THE homeland.

Although most members of soc.culture.filipino did not believe that knowing one's heritage was dependent upon a physical return to the homeland, the soc.culture.filipino newsgroup offered, for many participants, a virtual return. That is, this transnational network formed through the Internet a space where members of the Filipino diaspora could "go home."

However, as in real life, there were tensions between those who left home (particularly for the United States) and those who never left (see Rafael 1995b on the feelings people hold of *balikbayans*, or those who come back home to visit). And when talking about values, this tension often showed through in the discussions.

The discussion about Filipino values started with this exchange between a Filipino in the Philippines (Eddie) and a Filipino who immigrated to the United States (Ray). Eddie wrote, "I've read that parents of Fil-Am gangmembers often send their kids to the Philippines to straighten them out. Perhaps the barkadas [gangs] here do exert a healthier influence." Ray replied, "Nothing beats home grown values."

In this post, Eddie began the conversation by alluding to the fact that there are many Filipinos in the United States who have sent their children to the Philippines during their formative years to learn the Filipino way of life (for some very interesting narratives, see Espiritu 1995). In the past fifteen years, the struggles many teenagers face (i.e., alcoholism, drug use, teen pregnancy, gang activity) have, predictably, also affected Filipino American youth (Wolf 1997). However, within the Filipino community, there is some discussion about whether these "problem" behaviors are due to too strict parenting (as claimed by many second-generation Filipino Americans) or whether the behaviors are because the children are "exposed" to amoral values and behavioral patterns here in the United States (a fear many parents hold) (Wolf 1997). In many cases, the parents have opted to send their kids back home to live with relatives in hopes that the kids will learn traditional values: respect for elders, love for family, obedience to authority, good morals, and the value of education.

Here, we see that Eddie and Ray also contend that values are not just associated with a person's culture and heritage, but are grounded within the homeland. Even more telling is the assertion that even associating with *barkadas* in the Philippines is healthier than raising children in the United States, particularly since Eddie chose to define *barkadas* here not just as a group of friends (as it is often defined), but as a "gang." In asserting and agreeing that Filipino gangs are a healthier influence than being around American children, both Eddie and Ray placed Filipino culture and values on a morally superior plane.

This poses some interesting questions. For one, if knowing and following cultural values points to a person's sense of culture, but those values are rooted in the homeland and can never emigrate, then how "Filipino" are people outside the Philippines? In the following thread about why Filipinos immigrate to the United States, participants debated whether Filipinos could retain their cultural values if they left the Philippines. Both participants (Rick and Peter) are Filipino American males who have immigrated and raised children in the United States.

Rick wrote, "[I came to the United States to] 1) Prevent my children from growing up confused about what is right and what is wrong (community values and standards); 2) have my children grow up respecting the law and learning to work within a stable (not necessarily perfect) political and judicial system."

Rick's references to not knowing right from wrong and not having respect for the law reflects how many Filipinos (especially those who emigrated from the Philippines during Martial Law, as did Rick) feel about the political climate in the Philippines. This distrust is aimed not only at political leaders, but at the military and police officers (especially after popular expatriate Benigno Aquino's assassination) as well as the judicial system. Aquino (1987) argues that the strong distrust of the Philippine government is reflected in Filipinos' common political vocabulary.

When challenged by another Filipino American (Peter), who doubted that the values Rick spoke of were particular to the United States, Rick replied, "Do you really have to come here [to the United States] to instill these values in your children? I seriously doubt." He continued,

> You can doubt it, since I assume you are dealing with this issue from a theoretical point of view, while I have had to deal with it as reality. I have compared the values of my children who are now over 20 yrs. (yes, I was talking of the Philippines of 25+ years ago, I failed to mention that in my post) and who have grown up here in the Silicon Valley with the values of my friends' children, nephews, and nieces who have grown up in Manila. BIG, BIG difference! Mind you, I used to have second thoughts about having migrated to the U.S. and leaving behind the family support group and laid-back life I grew up with in Makati. Today, as I watch my grown up children tackle the challenges of young adulthood, I am "convinced" that migrating to the U.S. was one of the smartest things I have done in my life.
>
> Let me know how your children turn out . . .

In this post, we can see very clearly that Rick wishes to associate values with specific locations. In this case, he obviously is implying that the United States culture emphasizes obedience to authority figures and, more generally, good morals more so than the Philippine culture.

However, within this post, we can also see that Rick believes that there was a shift in value systems that possibly occurred because of a change in the political and economic climate. His reference to "the

Philippines of 25+ years ago" reveals much about his distrust of Filipino political figures. In 1972, then President Ferdinand Marcos declared martial law, thereby making it illegal for anyone to question his authority. Those who did (such as much-beloved expatriate Benigno Aquino, husband of Cory Aquino (Marcos's successor) were often either thrown out of the country, jailed, or, worse, killed.

But, Rick also refers to a laid-back life in Makati. Like my mom, who declared, "Freedom is the Philippines. America is where we work," Rick hearkens back to a leisurely lifestyle enjoyed by many Filipinos who come from prominent families. Makati, the place in Manila in which he grew up, is one of the wealthier spots in the country. American consumerism in the form of the preponderant mega-malls and the old Spanish tradition of employing live-in servants abounds in this part of Manila. Of course, this particular lifestyle has its origins in both Spanish and American colonialism, particularly in the intertwined histories of agricultural capitalism, globalization, and militarization. What is interesting about Rick's and his retractor's statements, however, is that though they are willing to concede that the social climate in the Philippines changed because of various political events, they still have a tendency to frame their responses in dichotomous and more importantly *natural* American versus Filipino values. I argue that this tendency to essentialize values is partially due to the tense relationship between those who emigrated to the former colonizer's country and those who stayed in the homeland. In this newsgroup, the participants are intent on ridding Filipinos of "colonial mentality" and unearthing a "Filipino" untouched by colonial powers. And in doing so, they often defined Filipino in relation to and in contrast with the American way.

This becomes more apparent as more people enter into the conversation. A third person (Manuel) entered the conversation at this point, stating, "Of my relatives in the Philippines, none of them got into trouble as youths with the law. However, here in the States in and around San Francisco, I have a number of them who have been sent to juvenile hall or camps. Three of them who had to be sent back to the Philippines by their families to graduate high school because of all the trouble they were getting into. Many of them got into trouble carrying or even firing guns. Some of these guys came here as young teenagers who never got into trouble in the RP or touched a gun there. After arriving here they soon built up personal arsenals."

Here is an interesting switch. Manuel implies that Filipino youths who grow up in the United States are more prone to engage in violent behavior than those who grow up in the Philippines because of the different the values that are taught in each country. Although he mentions the importance of parental influence, Manuel's bringing up the fact that many of his troubled relatives had to be "sent back to the Philippines," presumably to be straightened out and learn how to be responsible adults, clearly suggests that the cultural environment enforces values.

What is missing from this assessment, however, are other factors which lead youths to engage in gang behavior. Some male Filipino youths enter into gangs because this protects them from violent, racist behaviors aimed at them, as well as because of the high ideals of the model minority stereotype which the society expects them and their families to live up to (see, for example, Espiritu 1995). Others may enter into these highly masculinized organizations because it also offers them a chance to forcefully counter the stereotype of the emasculated Asian male, an image I talk about in chapter 4 (see also Malabon 2001). In fact, the wide range of so-called aberrant behavior of Filipino American youths is not solely due to "natural" cultural differences (as many Filipino American parents and, indeed, American policy makers would have us believe about all immigrant populations) but also deals with gendered and raced images endemic in the United States.

Rick then responded to the suggestion that the values are "better" in the Philippines:

> After arriving here they soon built up personal arsenals.
>
> You raise a very good point [but] it does not mean that just because you do not hear about the youth being in trouble with the law in the Phil. that the laws are not being broken.
>
> Many of the kids I grew up with in Makati [in Manila] did the same things you mention back during our teen years (guns, drugs, traffic code violations, alcohol abuse, cheating, bribery, etc.) But, you would hardly hear about it because there was zero education and hardly any enforcement of the laws. We did it for katuwaan [fun], kursunada [to prove one's bravery], or simply because everyone else was doing it. Those that were caught with their fingers in the cookie jar were *quickly spirited by their parents out of the country* to avoid publicity or having to deal with what little of the law there was.

While Rick concedes that there are rebellious individual Filipinos everywhere, he buttresses his argument about the superior value system in the United States by institutionalizing negative behavior. With this move, however, Rick also succeeded in naturalizing the values even more so than when he began the discussion. While in his last post, he implied he left the Philippines because the Philippine government and other institutions "of 25+ years ago" were morally bankrupt and hid the youths' misdeeds, he now extends those misdeeds to when he was still growing up in the Philippines. To institutionalize negative behavior without offering any context as to why he believes some officials turned their cheek to illegal behaviors unfortunately makes it seem as if the value system in the homeland is inherently flawed. It is the enforcement of laws, Rick argues, that differentiates the Philippines from the United States:

> Here in the U.S., you break the law, you pay for it (in most cases). Here, the system makes you accountable for your actions. That is one of the lessons I wanted my children to learn and I figured they could best learn it in a society that practices it. Sure, you can learn it in Manila too, but it is all theoretical.
>
> The difference is that in Manila, the youth learn how to get away with breaking the law, while here in the U.S. the youth learn about the law (and what happens when you break the law). IMO many people here in the U.S. learn it as juveniles and that sets the tone for the rest of their lives. BTW, as a parent of 4, I have been through everything you mentioned above (and more) and I still stand by my decisions 25 years ago to bring up my children here in the U.S. I believe they are well on their way to becoming good citizens of this world.

Although their definitions of "Filipino values" conflict, the preceding quotations illustrate that Manuel and Rick both *want* to associate values with a specific culture and that they are tied to a specific location (United States versus the Philippines).

One participant disputed the idea that values are attached to a territory. Interestingly, he did not equally berate Rick and Manuel for making this assumption. He only addressed Rick's attribution of "good" values to being in the United States by stating, "I am 'convinced' that migrating to the U.S. was one of the smartest things I have done in my life. Sometimes, Americocentrism can work for you. But if you can get it off your back, maybe you will come up with a better reason why your kids grew up the way you want them to be. Needless to say, I'm happy for you that you have good kids."

The rest of the letters were similar to the above. Most participants only replied to Rick (some even repeated the "Americocentric" accusation), but no one attacked Manuel. I believe that this is because criticizing the Philippines (say, by calling someone Filipinocentric) was seen as attacking the homeland and betraying the Filipino people, as will become more evident in the following section. However, criticizing the Philippines was not the only form of betrayal: leaving the Philippines for the United States was worse.

Authenticity and Location

Newsgroup participants not only spoke of a binary Filipino identity; they spoke about the degree of Filipinoness. Interestingly, only Filipinos who immigrated to the United States were viewed with suspicion. This can be explained by the fact that some of the most active participants resented the U.S. influence in the Philippines (and elsewhere) and thus attributed any criticisms of the Philippines made by Filipino Americans, particularly those who *left* the Philippines for the United States, as evidence of "colonial mentality," "Americocentrism," and, most of all, a betrayal of the homeland.

In the following exchange between Norma, a woman who immigrated with her parents to the United States when she was eight years old, and Jhun, a Filipino male in the Philippines, the debate over whether Filipino Americans are "real" Filipinos is most apparent. Norma had earlier claimed that although she is a naturalized American, her family still has strong social ties to the Philippines and continues to keep up with Filipino news. This, she implied, made her qualified to give her opinions about the Philippines. Jhun wrote, "America is BANKRUPT. And the Philippines is booming!" Norma replied, "Here's another one that will have everyone shaking their heads. Just heard from my mother, who has been visiting my older brother in Manila. No sign of the 'boom' as far as they are concerned. Some progress, yes. Sent my brother to the town where General Aguinaldo was captured by Americans to check out some research. Other than some mechanized transport now, and a telegraph line, NO BASIC CHANGES IN THE QUALITY OF LIFE IN ALMOST 100 YEARS! Send a fax to the people there breaking the news of the 'boom' to them!"

This debate began with a post about the possibility of economic recovery and the hope of a stronger Philippine presence and influence in the world economy. It is interesting to note that before Norma posted her opinion, she felt the need to establish her authority in Filipino matters. To do this, she tells us (1) of her mother's recent visit to the Philippines, which allows her to report what is "actually" going on at home; (2) that her brother lives in the Philippines, which establishes that she has a close tie to the homeland; and (3) that she does original research on the Philippines and knows people at the homeland that can give her reliable news; and (4) she shows her knowledge of Philippine history by referring to General Aguinaldo, the first president of the Republic of the Philippines. Thus, she suggests, despite her physical location in the United States, that she still can authoritatively comment on what is happening in the Philippines.

She proceeds to remark on the economic state of the Philippines, in a somewhat demeaning manner. Jhun, a Filipino male in Manila, picked up on this negative tone and responded within twenty-four hours. I have left the note in its original state (like the other posts), as I did not want to interrupt the ease in which Jhun was able to weave between English, Taglish (a combination of English and Tagalog), and Tagalog. I translate this post in the analysis that follows the post: "Kanino mo ba ikukumpara! . . . Mas ok na kami rito kesa diyan . . . ikaw iha . . . naturalized ka lang eh akala mo kung sino ka na . . . eh di diyan ka na!? Di ba nung na-naturalized ka eh you pledged your allegiance to the United States of MERIKA!? And that you dropped your allegiance to the country you belong to before you STOOD there in court of naturalization together with the BROWN MONKEYS who wants to be called MERKANO at MERKANA?! Excited pa!"

Translated Tagalog: "Who are you comparing? We're better here than you are over there. You, child. . . . You're naturalized, so you think you're something else huh? Well, then stay there! Isn't it true that when you were naturalized, you pledged your allegiance to the United States of America?" Here, Jhun establishes his authority over Norma's by using several tactics, his use of Tagalog and his focus on Norma's U.S. citizenship, and he assumes her arrogance is directly tied to her being a naturalized American ("ikaw iha . . . naturalized ka lang eh akala mo kung sino ka na."). Jhun then accentuates the division between Filipinos in the Philippines and those in the United States. First, he states that she should just stay out of the Philippines ("eh di diyan ka na!") and then challenges her by asking, "Isn't it true that when you were naturalized you pledged your allegiance to America?" He also berates her for pledging her allegiance to the United States (along with the other "brown monkeys," a reference to the derogatory way the American people viewed Filipinos at the turn of the twentieth century) and makes fun of her for being excited about being a citizen of a country which, historically, has not considered Filipinos to be equals. This is a significant move; it is here that Jhun firmly establishes a division between American Filipinos and Philippine Filipinos. He privileges Filipinos in the Philippines and establishes that they are more authentic than other Filipinos. In doing these things, he is able to push her to the margins of the Filipino community. Jhun then states. "Changes here in the Philippines are very significant . . . at least for *US Filipinos living here* . . . who actually lives here. And that's what keeps us strong . . . that TINY and PROBABLY NON-EXISTENT LIGHT as you and your MOM told us here . . . NOW NORMA! PUWEDE BA HUWAG MO NANG PATAYIN ANG HOPE NAMIN NA IYAN . . . OO MERKANA ka na . . . pero ang dugo mo ay mananatiling kulay pula . . . hindi mababago . . . tulad ng lahi mo! Hindi mo puwedeng itapon . . . at isa pa, . . . di namin kailangan ang tulad mo . . . ang klase mo na Pilipino. Buti na lang at naisipan mong lumayas dito." Translated Tagalog: "Now Norma! Is it possible for you to not lose hope in us? Yes, you're an American now. But your blood remains the same . . . you're still the same [Filipino]. You can't throw that away . . . and one more thing. We don't need your kind, your class of Filipino. It's good that you thought about leaving here!"

After suggesting that everything is fine for the Filipinos who stayed in the Philippines, Jhun lectures Norma again and reminds her that, although she may think she's an American, she, deep down, is always going to be a Filipino. In doing so, he stresses that because of her heritage, she can never be fully American, either. But, simultaneously, Jhun tells her that she is not a "good" Filipino anyway and is glad she's not at "home." Regardless of whether she actually *was* insulted or not, Jhun assumes that relegating Norma to a liminal space—she is neither one or the other—is insulting. And, by saying all this, Jhun effectively labeled her neither American nor Filipino. Norma then goes on the defensive: "Okay, the Philippines has made progress and is a good place to stay and has opportunities for everybody. People don't have to go anywhere else because a poor boy can make it just like a rich boy. This thread has degenerated into a U.S. Pinoy vs. Philippine Pinoy due to oversensitivity on the part of some people."

Very sarcastically, Norma pretends to give in to Jhun, but at the same time she reiterates what she believes to be the major problem in the Philippines: the maintenance of the wide gap between the rich and poor. She then dismisses the whole thread because she perceives that it is only dividing the community and not coming up with any constructive ideas on how to effectively help the Philippines, which was one of the reasons the newsgroup was started in the first place. In emphasizing the "pinoy" after U.S. and Philippines, she attempts to realign herself in the Filipino community. To which Jhun answers, "Sorry . . . if I have offended thee m'lord . . . it's just that, a lot of Filipino turn Americans, seemed to have forgotten that they won't be there if not for the simple fact that they have, at least, been nurtured in some way, by the PHILIPPINE LAND. . . . Will she have grown that big, up to the state wherein she's able to bash back at the country where she once belonged to, if not because of that same land and country? Talk about ingrata at ingrato (is there such a word?) <grin>."

Jhun again refers to the Filipino/American dichotomy and questions particularly the loyalty held by American emigrants to the Philippines by emphasizing that Norma and her mother are "Filipino *turned* American." In contrast to his last post, where he states that she is neither American nor Filipino, she is now just American, an ingrate who has forgotten her roots and the values which allowed Filipinos to learn how to succeed. Jhun then suggests that Filipinos outside the Philippines are not as Filipino as those who stayed, and because of this, their criticisms of the Philippines are less valid. Although Jhun does not explicitly refer to his distrust of Americans in his responses to Norma, he does so in other threads, especially the following, which centers on what diasporic Filipinos can do to help the Philippines.

Jhun writes, "Let's see. . . . How would we change our position right now: from worse to better . . . first, kick out the very very naughty politicians . . . most especially the pawns of America. For example, J. De Venecia . . . Hohummm."

Thomas, a Filipino American participant, disagrees: "Pawns of america did you say? I think the worst politicians are those pseudo-patriots who proclaim to wear their ultranationalism on their sleeve. Those are the ones that should be kicked out!"

Although the focus shifts to politics in this exchange, it still reflects the Philippine-American dichotomy. Jhun's political standpoint resembles that of the dependency school: peripheral countries should try to sever ties with core countries (So 1990). Thomas, on the other hand, denounces the nationalists. This turned out to be a very bad move, because several people from the Philippines berated Thomas (and other

Filipino Americans, especially Norma) for being condescending toward Philippine Filipinos and more loyal to the States than to the homeland. Robert writes, "It's sad that we have Filipinos like this one. Very sad. A person like this is a good example of why Philippine condition is not improving. I encourage this person to continue posting so that readers here in the SCF will have a clearer picture of a true nationalist—a nationalist to the American flag."

Instead of asking Thomas to explain what he meant or taking a criticism as a mere criticism, Robert immediately denounces him and attributes his comments about pseudonationalists to his loyalty to the United States. Robert tries to diminish Thomas's authority on the Philippines by characterizing Thomas as pro-American. In response, Thomas defends himself, saying, "I've been observing Philippine politics for many years and I have seen a lot of so called Pro-Filipinos wrap themselves in the flag and proclaim that they know what is good for the country when in reality, they have no good ideas! What these pseudonationalists should first do is swallow THEIR pride and acknowledge that they are largely to blame for the mess their country is in! Does being pro-American mean being anti-Filipino? Absolutely not! When you seen a country wrecked by decades of economic and government mismanagement, you have to put the blame squarely on those in power."

Here, Thomas tries to establish his authority by stating that he has been following Filipino politics for many years, and then by stating that many nationalists do not have any good ideas. Like Norma, he wants people in the Philippines to be self-critical. He then dismisses Jhun's use of the Filipino/American dichotomy by insisting that it is possible for Filipinos to be loyal to both. A month later, one Filipino American (Rodney), tired of reading American Pinoy versus Philippine Pinoy posts, states, "You don't have to be physically in the Philippines to help both the country and the people. And it is probably better not to be a hero to help; most heroes, after all, are dead. I am still in contact with many former classmates, who are now in positions of responsibility in the Philippine's economic sphere; I see what and how they are doing. I do go back every now and then, but the vast majority of work I do in the avenue I have chosen to help is done here in the US."

This post closes the thread. Here, the participant gives an example of and describes the potential of transnational ties. He states that his knowledge of the Philippines comes from keeping in regular touch with

people in the Philippines (something Norma and Thomas also said they do) and by visiting the Philippines (something Norma and Thomas did not say they do). While Rodney tries to downplay the importance of location by explaining that he contributes to the Philippines from his position in the Unites States, he also emphasizes the importance of location by stating that he has gone back to the homeland.

This does not mean that all participants assumed that people who return to the homeland are more Filipino than those who do not. In chapter 5, I show how *balikbayans* (those who return home for a visit) highlight the division between Filipinos in the Philippines and those overseas. However, in this particular context, the fact that Rodney went home was received more favorably than in other threads.

The participants also tried to maintain Filipino culture and identity through preserving cultural artifacts such as language. In the next section, I show how participants debated whether the use of English and the Westernization of the Tagalog alphabet was detrimental to establishing a strong Filipino identity.

The English Language and Colonial Mentality

"Wall Street English" and Colonial Mentality

The resistance to colonialism is frequently expressed in the arguments about the use of English and the English alphabet in the Philippines. Associating the control of one's language with resisting the dominant group is not unique to Filipinos on this newsgroup. Many scholars argue that retaining one's language is fundamental to retaining one's identity (Anzaldúa 1987; Radhakrishnan 1996). On this newsgroup, some participants believe that instruction in English will only foster colonial mentality. Others argue that Filipinos should be pragmatic and put their nationalism aside because knowing English can only help the Philippines. As Jeff stated, "Many Filipinos equate instruction in English as a throwback to colonial days. Were English not the international language of business and industry, I might agree. The great advantage Filipinos enjoy over many is their ability in English. This has unfortunately been eroded in the past two decades by those who oppose English language education for nationalistic purposes. Nationalism and pride in one's country and culture is GOOD, but being fluent in the 'International' language (which happens to be English but could be anything) is also a great advantage in an ever shrinking world."

In this part of the post, Jeff's argument parallels those of the classical modernization school; that is, that for nations to become more advanced, they should emulate the more advanced nations in the world like western European countries and the United States (So 1990). Jeff then alludes to American colonization, but, in contrast to some participants, states that it has helped Filipinos (at least in their ability to speak English). He goes on to say, "The fact that Filipinos are fluent in Pilipino/Tagalog, their native dialect, and English is something to be proud of. Nationalism aside, I believe President Ramos policy of English comprehension in education and government is a positive step towards allowing the RP to take their rightful place among the ranks of the Economic Tigers of Asia."

Chris, a Filipino in the Philippines, completely disagrees and states that knowing English is not necessary for progress: "What we need for sustained progress is a language that will unite our people. And it doesn't have to be english. Again, look at Japan, Korea, France, Italy, and more. In China our company signed a 4150M communication contract. In Korea another $80M for network and computer outsourcing deals. On both cases we needed local interpreters to win the projects."

Chris's post is interesting for a number of reasons, the first being that he downplays the importance of doing business in English. Yet even in France, a country which Chris uses as an example, there are signs in many public spaces which advertise agencies that can teach business people how to speak "Wall Street English." I argue that the reason it was important to downplay Western, particularly American, influences is because the participants believed that one of the major weaknesses of Filipinos is "colonial mentality." It was believed that Filipinos could not form a strong, national community without first stripping the culture of American influences and then articulating a united national culture.

Ironically, the majority of debates on this newsgroup were written in English because the participants were aware that all members of soc.culture.filipino were not versed in the official national language, Pilipino.[4] Yet, Chris maintains that Filipinos have a need for their own national language and consequently need to conduct business using that language. This led to a discussion about the authenticity of Tagalog. The most interesting debate about English and the authenticity of Tagalog occurred when participants discussed the (relatively) new Filipino alphabet and the authenticity of Tagalog.

Debates about Grammar and Vocabulary: Mind Your P's and F's

In 1987, the Department of Education, Culture, and Sports of the Philippines issued a memorandum stating that the Philippine alphabet had been changed from the Pilipino/Tagalog Abakada version (twenty letters, excluding *c, f, j, q, v,* and *z*) to a new alphabet (twenty-eight letters).[5] For many Filipinos (inside and outside the newsgroup), the point of contention has been the letter *f.* In the preface of her book, *Asian Americans: An Interpretive History* (1991), Sucheng Chan justified her use of the term "Filipino" instead of "Pilipino." She reported that some Filipinos and Filipino scholars prefer to use the term "Pilipino." However, others argue that not acknowledging *f* might reinforce the stereotype that Filipinos are unable to pronounce the letter *f* and thus make them appear less educated than other ethnic groups. To avoid negative stereotyping, she chose to spell Filipino with an *f.* This debate continues today and has recently been a topic on the soc.culture.filipino newsgroup. Two threads highlight this debate: "Should there be an *f* in our language?" and, more recently, "Flipbonics."

Should There Be an F in Our Language?

The arguments that the participants had on this thread echoed the arguments that Filipino scholars have been enmeshed in for the last two decades. Some argue that since the original Tagalog alphabet does not contain the letter *f,* Filipinos should technically be called "Pilipinos." Proponents of the old alphabet state that the reason we should not have an *f* in our language is because it isn't authentic. More specifically, the letters *c, f, j, q,* and *v* should not be in the alphabet because they signify both American and Spanish colonialism. They argue that one of the ways to show independence from the colonial powers is to control one's culture and language; thus, keeping the traditional Abakada is one way of asserting the Filipinos' control over their culture and identity. Others argue that because *f* is not in the traditional language, it is difficult for many Filipinos to pronounce the *f* sound. Thus, rather than forcing Filipinos to use the *f,* it should be eliminated.

However, others argue that not having the letter *f* in the alphabet is a form of "dumbing down" Filipinos. Claiming that many Filipinos cannot pronounce the letter *f,* they argue, makes it appear as if Filipinos cannot speak "good" English and are less educated than other groups, which thus reinforces negative stereotypes. Another argument is that many Filipinos could not spell their own names using the traditional alphabet. Thus, the new alphabet was adopted for practical reasons. The debate by Allan and Brian contains almost all of the arguments that I have presented above.

> *Brian:* Dear Allan, . . . An impressive post, especially the sections written in "old tagalog spelling."
>
> *Allan:* Thank you. I always make sure that certain relevant facts that haven't surfaced are made known so that all of us could arrive at appropriate opinions which aren't based on ignorance or plain gut-feel.
>
> *Brian:* I'd like to point out, however, that the adoption of the Spanish alphabet was during the time when Pilipinos still had no concept of themselves as a nation.
>
> *Allan:* I also wanted to point out that the proper term now is "Filipinos," and not "Pilipinos." About the concept of nation . . . Even until now, culturally speaking, the Philippines still isn't a single nation. We aren't homogeneous like the Japanese and the Germans whose countries are prime examples of Nation-States.

In this first part of the debate, Allan (aware that his post could reach thousands of participants) attacks the authenticity of the use of the Filipino Abakada (and the idea of a static culture in general) by relying on words that symbolize legitimacy, such as "facts" and "proper." Although there was much information within Brian's original post, Allan uses this omission to his advantage, as any good debater does. In addition, he invokes the *f* versus *p* debate immediately by correcting Brian's spelling of Filipinos. This sets up his stance as one who rejects the idea of an authentic, unchangeable language and culture. Interestingly, his assertion that the Japanese and Germans are homogenous was never debated among any of the participants, although this, too, is a contested point.

> *Brian:* The "ridiculous ABAKADA" was part of an attempt to foster the nascent national identity of a newly supposedly independent state. An independent nation is hoped to be independent in thought and identity as well.
>
> *Allan:* But I thought you said (in your earlier posts) that you didn't like the government departments who took matters into their

own hands like what DECS did when it chose to use the complete Roman-Latin alphabet . . . The adoption of the ABAKADA was itself an arbitrary decision by the Institute of National Language and didn't hold a plebiscite or a Congressional hearing in order to arrive at that decision. I'm sure you didn't mean to contradict yourself, but really, that's what you've already done. . . . As it turns out, the ABAKADA was a mistake because Filipinos can't spell their names using it . . . so the government has the right to rectify it by adopting the more practical complete Roman-Latin alphabet.

This section of the debate mirrors a debate between those who purport that the incorporation of colonial culture signifies "colonial mentality" (e.g., the belief that colonized peoples who have embraced elements of the colonizer's culture have "sold out" and lost their heritage) and those who believe that cultures are fluid and constantly evolving and changing. Brian's insistence on retaining the original alphabet, the Abakada, reflects his anticolonial stance. By giving a historical account about the simultaneous development of the nation and language, Brian attempted to reify the authenticity of Tagalog. However, Allan used the idea that Tagalog was created (especially by a governmental body) to delegitimize the authenticity of Tagalog. In his view, whether it is imposed by a colonial body or an anticolonialist body does not matter. The fact that it is created and imposed only shows that culture and language are constantly in flux. Interestingly, Brian cannot spell his last name without letters in the new alphabet. Allan eventually pointed that out to the newsgroup to support his position that the new alphabet should stand. Allan then asserted that the incorporation of English words is pragmatic.

> *Brian:* As to gov't decrees, well my recent post covers my thoughts on that. The main reason we use so many English words is that our whole education system is based in English.
>
> I'm not saying this is a bad thing—it gives us an edge in the international level.
>
> But one has to admit that it has been to the detriment of our native languages. Since no attempt is made to translate curricula in Math, Science, Psychology, Computer Science, Engineering, etc. into Pilipino, the words don't exist. . . .
>
> Japan, Malaysia, etc etc don't have the same problem.

> *Allan:* Sure they don't. . . . The Japanese are trying to learn English
> left and right, and still feel they always lag in terms of in-
> formation, since most new books are in English. . . . They
> make up for this lag with their DISCIPLINE in whatever they
> do. (In many universities, there are student-apprentices who
> do duty as English to Japanese book translators, and do it
> out of a sense of Samurai-like feudal loyalty to their "Ni-
> hon." The translations aren't always very good, but many
> say that it's better than nothing . . .) Oh, and be aware of
> the fact that so many hi-tech words and even non-hightech
> words in modern Japanese come from English. . . . ZAITEK
> means "high-tech." . . . And "Merikurisumasu" means
> "Merry Christmas" just to show a few of the so many ex-
> amples.

Allan's response is interesting because he simultaneously asserts
evidence of cultural syncretism and cultural essence. He shows that
the Japanese have not only incorporated English words into their language, they have also changed them so they are distinctly Japanese
(i.e., merikurisumasu). He implies that the desire to improve techno-
logically and economically leads to the incorporation of English
words—in other words, that linguistic syncretism is embraced in the
interest of competing in the global market. Yet Allan still essentializes
Japanese culture when he refers to the strict discipline and sense of
"feudal loyalty."

> *Brian:* Anyway, it may be, as both of you say, inevitable. That does
> not make it good. My objection stands.
> *Allan:* Well, I'm sure that you'd agree with us that the ABAKADA is
> ridiculous anyway, since you won't be able to write your
> name using an ABAKADA typewriter.

In short, two intertwined issues were debated in this exchange: the
authenticity of the Abakada and whether the new alphabet and the
use of English constitute "colonial mentality." The use of *f* (among other
letters not present in the Abakada alphabet) is seen by some as selling out to imperialist powers.

In addition, the issue of language authenticity was debated. Brian
believed that the inclusion of English-sounding words signified the
loss of Filipino culture. Brian also argued that the use of English in

several academic disciplines indicated that Tagalog was being replaced, and thus U.S. cultural imperialism continues in the Philippines. He then derided Allan (and others who responded to him), saying that people think the incorporation of English words is inevitable: "That doesn't make it good." Allan tried to argue that other (seemingly) homogenous cultures were much stronger than the Philippines in part because they didn't allow other languages to seep in. However, Brian showed Allan that his assertion was untrue by either giving examples of English words that were appropriated (e.g., ZAITECH) or by showing the failure of countries to control language.

Here, the agency of Filipinos is at stake. Brian fears that the use of English will take away Filipinos' agency; that is, if Filipinos don't use their authentic language, they will eventually lose their culture and once again become colonial subjects. In contrast, Allan believes that the inclusion of English words (and letters) does not signify "colonial mentality," but "progress." To him, the use of English words is a practicality, not a denial of one's culture. He also indirectly shows that English can be harnessed and appropriated by the non-American culture. Other Filipinos also emphasize that the use of English does not necessarily imply a loss of culture; instead, "word-play" can be empowering. I will elaborate on how word-play is used as a means of attaining agency in the following sections.

To stop the argument between f's and p's, one person posted the following: "As long as we frounounce our f's froferly, I think here's no froblem with that." The conversation about f's and p's then shifted and revolved around this post. Specifically, participants ended the debate by intentionally misusing p's and f's to lighten the mood. In chapter 5, I further analyze how humor was used by the participants to end fiery debates and to contribute to Filipino identity. Of course, what is intended to be humorous is not always perceived as humor, especially if it resembles negative stereotypes commonly attributed to the marginalized group, as the next thread demonstrates.

Flipbonics

Nine months after the p's and f's debate and following the recent Ebonics controversy fought by school boards in California, some Filipinos started a "Flipbonics" thread that highlighted what they considered to be the Filipino way of speaking English. The thread was intended to be humorous, so most of the participants framed their responses as jokes. For example:

> I think they ought to teach FLIPbonics in schools. I'll give you an example . . .
>
> "Today I went to the store driving my behicle and bought some fancake mix and then saw a fregnant lady there."
>
> LOL
>
> Well actually it would be like this:
>
> "Today I went to da estore dribing my bicycle and bought some fancake mix and I saw a fregnant lady dere."
>
> If you're gonna go FOB, then do it right. . . . =)

Despite the smiley face at the end of the message, one participant was deeply offended by the thread, arguing that the messages made fun of recent immigrants to the United States and saying that those who posted should be ashamed of themselves. Other participants defended those who posted the "FLIPbonic" sentences, arguing that the dissenter should "lighten up" and be able to appreciate jokes. One participant even argues that "true" Filipinos have the ability to laugh at themselves and not take everything so seriously. Here is a piece of the debate between Paul and Roberto, both Filipino Americans: Paul wrote, "See, this is another problem with Filipinos here in the States. THEY MAKE FUN OF FILIPINOS WHO JUST RECENTLY CAME OVER. And you think this flipbonics thing is so funny, huh? You ought to take some american ethnic studies class so as to appreciate your own kind regardless of their background."

Here Paul invokes the U.S./Philippine dichotomy mentioned in the previous sections. By saying that these Filipino Americans need to take ethnic studies classes, he indirectly refers to the notion that Filipino Americans are too assimilated and do not appreciate their own heritage. But other Filipino Americans on the newsgroup (e.g., the Filipino American college student who lamented that he felt "whitewashed and sad") and many of my Filipino American students as well logged onto the newsgroup in the first place to learn about their heritage because of the lack of resources in libraries or ethnic studies classes. In addition, as I have stated before, this lack of resources is due to scholars not studying the Philippines because they feel the country is "too Westernized." Therefore, I read Paul's suggestion to Filipino Americans to take ethnic studies class as somewhat ironic: "I'm sick and tired of people making fun of people who speak with accent. Who the Hell do you think you are, those who are american born who consistently make fun of what you call 'fresh off the boat'? have some respect for

those individuals and stop these childish jokes. And if you are philippine born and do joke this way, you should be so ashamed of the way you are acting."

Paul then differentiates the Philippine/American dichotomy in a different way. He does not focus on location (as Jhun did), but on birthplace. Though both are reprimanded for being childish, Paul states that Filipino Americans born in the Philippines should be especially ashamed of making fun of people with accents. While Paul seems to believe that any Filipino who makes fun of those with accents should be ashamed he also thinks that Philippine-born Filipinos have a higher burden to protect those who speak with accents: "It's already too much that whites and blacks make fun of filipino immigrants and assuming all the time that we are 'foreigners' in this damn country. . . . Do you really have to add insult to the problem?"

He then appeals to those he perceives as common adversaries—whites and blacks, specifically—to show people that Filipinos cannot afford to be divisive. In addition, he reminds the participants that Filipinos in the United States, even those who have been here for generations, are perceived as "foreigners" and are the targets of discrimination. In addition to discrimination by skin color, Filipinos face the problem of "Orientalism" (i.e., the erroneous belief that Asians are unassimilable and are inherently loyal to their "Asian heritage"). Thus, they are perceived as less American than some Filipinos in the Philippines imagine. By invoking these common adversaries, Paul reminds the participants of their goal of unity: "Remember that your parents were in the same situation as these recent immigrants. You deserve to be smack by your own parents for disrespecting your culture!!!! For your info, FLIP and FOB are both derogatory . . . cut it out!!!"

Paul then attempts to draw commonalities between American-born Filipinos, first- and 1.5-generation Filipino immigrants by invoking the notion of family. Embedded in this reference is the accusation that participants who disrespect recent immigrants are shameless and arrogant (*walang hiya*). One trait that Filipinos attribute to their culture is a deep respect for elders, a trait even embedded in the language. *Ho* or *po*, respectful references to elders, must be added to each sentence spoken to elders. Not adding one of these words indicates *walang hiya*. Paul's post invokes the state of shamelessness, or *walang hiya*, by equating recent immigrants with their parents. At the end, Paul reminds Filipinos that FLIP and FOB have been used by non-Filipinos as slurs, and thus should not be used by Filipinos to describe themselves.

Instead of apologizing, Robert implied that the ability to laugh at oneself is Filipino:

> I have always believed that if there's one thing about Filipinos (or Pinoys or Flips), is that they have an incredible sense of humor. That, plus their love of music, which makes them quite unique.
>
> Filipinos seem to be renowned as a very jolly people, finding things to laugh about even in the worst situations. Call it a racial coping mechanism, but I believe it helps us to be strong in the face of adversity. And one of the things that Pinoys love is a joke based on word-play, specifically, word-play based on how we pronounce words, how english words sound if taken in a filipino context, etc.

In an interesting twist, Robert stated that the Flipbonics thread is not an indication of internalized racism, as Paul suggested, but very Filipino. Instead, the ability to laugh at the word play in the Flipbonics threads was not only a racial coping mechanism, but a redirected resistance to continued colonialism. After suggesting the association of humor with Filipinoness, Robert critiqued Paul:

> With that said, I believe you should lighten up and take the thread for what it is—a thread of jokes. And do not take our ability to laugh at our own account (which, I have been told, can *sound quite bizarre to some native English speakers*) [my emphasis] as an inability to appreciate our own culture. Far from it, our ability to laugh at it indicates how much we appreciate it. I mean, let's face it: our unique accent when talking in English is part of our culture, as well as our sense of humor!
>
> Bottom line is, I believe the thread never sought to denigrate recently-arrived Filipinos, and in my opinion never has. So lighten up, appreciate the humor, and share in the laughs.

In this post, Robert also alluded to another division between Filipinos: native English speakers and non-native English speakers. By claiming that Filipinos who are native English speakers cannot understand this type of humor, he implied that "real" Filipinos would have been able to appreciate this kind of humor. In addition, he also maintained that joking about different pronunciations of English words is not an indication of "disrespecting the culture," but highlights the

Filipinos' uniqueness. Thus, he argued, the Flipbonics thread and the Filipino way of speaking English actually showed an appreciation of and pride in Filipino culture. I discuss the significance of pride in the Filipino way of pronouncing English words in chapter 5.

Conclusion

In this chapter, I showed how the participants of soc.culture.filipino defined Filipino identity by referring to the U.S.-Philippine relationship. I argued that because U.S. cultural and economic influences are still prevalent, the construction of Filipino identity, culture, and values often involves dichotomizing "American" and "Filipino." Although many Filipinos in the United States perpetuate this dichotomy, differentiating these two groups has the potential to alienate those who live in the United States. For example, Norma, the Filipino American woman who commented on the state of the Filipino economy, had to defend her membership in the Filipino community. The articulation of a U.S.-Philippine dichotomy allowed other participants to consider their statements about Filipinos and Filipino culture as "inauthentic" because they were made outside the homeland and they were made in a hegemonic space. Jhun's response to Norma illustrates this point. But the difference between Filipino and American was often gendered as well, as the next chapter suggests.

4

"Ain't I a Filipino (Woman)?"

Filipina as Gender Marker

Single, White male ... is in search of a nice, attractive, honest single filipina for possible marriage. I'm a nice/normal guy. I have a college degree and a good job. I prefer a filipina because of the old fashion honest way they were raised. I believe marriage to be a 50–50 relationship.
—Personal ad posted on soc.culture.filipino

Filipino Women as Gender Markers

The development of racial and cultural differences often justifies an unequal, hierarchical power relationship (Gupta and Ferguson 1997; Michaels 1995) and is, unfortunately, articulated by the very people who are most hurt by these characterizations. With respect to colonialism, the constructions of cultural differences to validate the reorganization and redistribution of resources are also ensconced within a complex combination of national, gendered, sexual, and racial projects. I argue that gender and sexuality are similarly and simultaneously constructed for the same reasons.

In the two years I studied soc.culture.filipino, posts about Filipino women dominated the conversations,[1] accounting for one-third of the daily posts.[2] Of the more than two thousand posts I collected, roughly eight hundred centered around Filipino women. Many of these posts came within a month after Flor Contemplacion was executed for a murder that she may not have committed.[3] Because I did not actively collect and analyze threads at the time of Contemplacion's execution, I cannot be sure that it generated the discussions about Filipino women.

Regardless of the motivating factor, I can say that during the time I studied the newsgroup, the topic of Filipino women was constantly being discussed and debated. These discussions often revolved around "Wanna Filipina" personal ads. Between 1995 and 1997, posts that stereotyped Filipino women as "traditional, yet sexually adept" and as desirable spouses were prevalent. Moreover, news stories of abused mail-order brides and numerous Web pages extolling the "virtuousness" and "good morals" of Filipino women were ubiquitous.

Of course, the plight of female overseas contract workers such as Flor Contemplacion, the prevalence of personal ads, and the treatment of mail-order brides are three different issues. But the participants on the newsgroup closely associated these issues with each other (as well as the "problem" of white male/Asian female relationships). As we will see, participants saw all these issues as evidence of the weakness of Filipino nationalism and American dominance and attempted to fight back.

In this chapter, I show that participants wished to actively protect Filipino women in order to preserve Filipino culture. Preserving one's culture through protecting women is common among oppressed racial or ethnic groups both within and between nations (see Riggs 1995; Lorde 1984a). However, this narrow focus on protecting racial and/or national boundaries often maintains gender inequality within the group as well as exacerbates patriarchy (Anthias and Yuval-Davis 1994). In the case of the Filipinos on this newsgroup, the participants' anticolonialism stance and the drive to articulate an essential Filipino identity devoid of what they perceived as American characteristics further marginalized Filipino women and took agency away from them, especially those raised in the United States.

As we have seen in previous chapters, the notion of "agency" often leads to a slippery slope. To reestablish the agency of Filipinos worldwide, the participants on soc.culture.filipino attempted to use the concepts of culture, values, citizenship, language, race, and gender to demarcate boundaries—between Filipino and Other, oppressed and oppressor, resistance groups and colonial subjects. And yet, in each of these discussions, intense debates ensued, especially in their discussions of the roles of "Filipinas" as they discovered that none of these "variables" is as solid as it appears.

A large part of this chapter revolves around two cross-posted messages about "Asiaphiles" and "Whiggies"—derogatory terms for the white males and Asian women involved in these relationships. By

analyzing these threads and the soc.culture.filipino participants' reactions to these two threads, I show that the boundaries between oppressed and oppressor and between authentic and inauthentic become
even more unclear. Furthermore, it is in this chapter that the participants' reliance on creating community based on socially constructed
categories of culture, race, gender, and nation backfire.

I focus here on three main points. First, the newsgroup participants continue to define Filipino in *opposition* to American to
strengthen Filipino nationalism. "Filipino woman" is, in the words
of Yuval-Davis and Anthias (1989), a "gender marker" between the two
nations. In particular, as is evident in participants' discussions of the
commodification and stereotyping of Filipino women, many male and
female participants wanted not to fight for Filipino women's rights,
but rather to protect Filipino women from other races and to show
the difference between American and Filipino.

The second point is about how this dichotomy actually affected
female Filipino participants, especially those who were raised in the
United States. Because of participants' desire to differentiate and di-
chotomize Filipino and American, Filipino women who rejected the
sanctioned stereotypes of Filipino women were perceived as sellouts
and often ostracized. This caused at least one Filipino American to
change her identity from "Filipina" to "woman [of Filipino heritage]
born and raised in the United Slates" By doing this, she actively moved
herself from the center to the margin.

Third, an analysis of these interchanges identifies what approaches
concerned people can and cannot use to fight against the stereotyping and commodification of Filipino women without losing sight of
other issues. This community of interest cannot use "simple identity
politics" (i.e., the formation of distinctive identities) to fight against
oppression,[4] but must try to use other tactics, such as those Bernice
Reagon (1992) calls "coalition politics." However, as we will see, de-
ciding how to form the coalition is difficult, as members must also
negotiate how to articulate the issue itself.

Current Stereotypes

Writing this chapter was extremely difficult. Even
though I know that I cannot remove myself from my writing entirely,
as an ethnographer I tried very hard to distance myself from the posts.
But, of course, I could not, especially since I was also surrounded by
stories of stereotyping from my friends and in the media. In the two

years I studied soc.culture.filipino, I became even more aware of my identity as a Filipino American woman and, quite unexpectedly, felt a pain and anguish that I had never experienced before.

The desire to differentiate Filipino culture from American culture complicates strategies for fighting the commodification of Filipino women. While it is important to analyze and dismantle the hierarchical, colonial relationship between the United States and the Philippines, I will show that describing Filipino women through the American/Filipino dichotomy may actually maintain this hierarchical relationship instead of destroy it. Because the discussions of Filipino women did not move beyond the dichotomy, nothing was resolved. Before I describe how this dichotomy affected the newsgroup discussions, I will briefly identify current stereotypes of Asian women and men, as these stereotypes were used by many participants in speaking about "Filipinas."

Asian Women and Men

Asian women have been portrayed by the Western media as "superfeminine"—subservient, dependent women who know how to please their men sexually (Espiritu 1997; Kim 1982; Lai 1992; Mura 1998). In contrast to Asian women, white Western women have recently been stereotyped as "calculating, suffocating, and thoroughly undesirable" and as too concerned with independence to adequately take care of their families (Espiritu 1997). Through these contrasting stereotypes, scholars argue, the Western media protects white males from the feminist "threat" (Enloe 1989; Espiritu 1997; Marchetti 1993) and maintains hierarchical gender relations. In addition, these stereotypes culturally essentialize Western and Asian women, thus reifying Orientalism.

Simultaneously, Asian males have been stereotyped as "hypermasculine" (for example, "Yellow Peril" overly abusive to women) and "emasculated" (Espiritu 1997; Kim 1982; Mura 1996). Although contradictory, they both were formed in relation to white males. The stereotypes of Asian men as "hypermasculine," "lascivious," and a threat to white women were especially acute among Americans at the turn of the century, when there was a drastic disparity between Asian men and women in the United States, and a corresponding fear of miscegenation between Asian men and white females (Chan 1991; Espiritu 1997). In response, several anti-miscegenation laws barring "Oriental"/ white or "Mongolian"/white relationships were instated (Chan 1991).

This fear of interracial relationships cannot be divorced from Western colonists' views that nonwhite, male "natives" lusted after white, female colonists and thus threatened the imperial order (Enloe 1989) or from middle-class white men's projection of their own desires for the exotic Other. The middle-class, white male colonists concluded that it was the role of white males to protect their white females (Stoler 1997).

More recently, the Western media has portrayed white men rescuing weak Asian women from abusive Asian men, as in many American martial arts films (Mura 1996; Kim 1982). In these films, Asian males are "too controlling" toward their female partners, while the white heroes are sensitive to Asian women's needs. Through these images, Asian patriarchy skillfully showcases the "liberalness" of Western patriarchy: Western men are not so bad after all. Thus, white men are portrayed as the guardians of both white and Asian women (Espiritu 1997; Kim 1982).

Asian males are cast—literally and figuratively—as eunuchs, asexual beings who lust after both white and Asian women, but who, compared to other males, lack virility in many films, ranging from the Fu Manchu series to *Year of the Dragon* (see Lee 2000 and Eng 2000 for excellent analyses of the demasculinization of Asian men). Through these stereotypes, white males' virility is safeguarded (Espiritu 1997). Yet at the same time, the portrayal of white men as sensitive to women's needs impairs the Western feminist movement. By showing the difference between Western and Eastern men, these films insist that gender relations in Western countries aren't as bad as Western feminists claim. In short, these images of white women and men and Asian women and men preserve the current racial and gendered hierarchies as well as essentialize the boundaries between East and West.

Filipino Women

Hey, a neat postscript and possible fodder for further research: That sick-o from my not-nearly-distant-enough past just returned from a trip to the "Orient." He now has himself his very own mail-order fiancée. From Mindanao.
—letter from Eileen, March 1998

Where I come from (Norway) all we ever hear about is prostitution, child prostitution and poverty. . . . In addition to that, "all" (most) Filipinas we see, are relatively young Filipinas

*that have come here to marry an old Norwegian
man. . . . I think we just have to admit that
Filipinas . . . are viewed as "cheap."*

—From a white, male participant in
Norway who wants to fight against
stereotyping Filipino women

As Filipino American females, Eileen, Mimi,
Bernie, and I have endured many lewd comments from both non-Filipino and Filipino males about the supposed sexual prowess of Filipino women; we have also felt the effects of and have been subjected to many media images of Filipino women (and Asian women) as hypersexual: *"Hey! Are you Vietnamese? Filipina? Are you guys as good in bed as that chick in 9$^1/_2$ weeks? Me so horny!"* In addition, my friends' frequent stories about American males actively searching for Filipino women as lovers and wives reinforce this stereotype.

Their sordid stories and the numerous debates about Filipino women on soc.culture.filipino have made me suspicious of all men's intentions. Why are they paying attention to me? Is it because of me or because of the stereotypes of my race? Filipino women around the world have had to endure these stereotypes. But because of political and economic instability in the Philippines and the economic and political relationship between the Philippines and the United States, women in the Philippines have had to fight against another stereotype: that they are cunning women who would do anything to make money, including prostitute themselves or trap wealthy men into marriage (Chang and Groves 1997).

Cynthia Enloe argues that prostitution in the Philippines must be analyzed in relation to "nationalism, land reform, demilitarization and Filipino migration overseas" (1989, 39). Until the early 1990s, the United States operated several military bases in the Philippines. The three bases employing the most people were Clark, Subic Bay, and Wallace. Brothels around these bases were subsidized by both the U.S. and Philippine governments to provide soldiers with "necessary R and R" (Sturdevant and Stolzfus 1992). Cynthia Enloe has argued that when Filipino nationalists discuss prostitution in the Philippines, they usually point to the bases, arguing that militarized prostitution is not only a women's issue but a threat to the integrity of the Philippines and Filipinos in general (Enloe 1989). That is, they frame prostitution in anticolonialist, antimilitary terms.

Yet Enloe (1989) shows that in the mid–1980s there were more brothels around tourist spots in the Philippines, such as Manila or Cebu City, than near the military bases. During this decade, the Marcos government developed the sex tourist industry as a short-term strategy to bring in international currency and minimize the nation's deficit (Chang and Groves 1997; Enloe 1989). Ferdinand Marcos simultaneously capitalized on stereotypes of Asian women, stereotypes of Eastern and Western culture, and the growing feminist movements in Western countries to promote the sex tourist industry. By pitting the images of exotic "beautiful Filipino girls" against "emancipated" Western women, Marcos (along with many other southeast Asian leaders) sold Filipino women as "natural resources" to foreign men who believed that "Oriental" women were more available and subservient than women in their own countries (Enloe 1989, 38).

Lisa Law (1997) has found that most women "willingly" enter the sex tourism business. However, she warns, we should not accept their stated motivation at face value. Instead, we should look at their political and economic situation (Law 1997), as well as the idyllic images of life in America and other Western countries that bombard Filipinos (Ordoñez 1997). In fact, many scholars and Filipino feminist nationalists emphasize the structural factors that push Filipino women into the sex tourist industry (Azarcon de la Cruz 1985; L. West 1992). These Filipino women face high levels of unemployment and underemployment; thus, the attractiveness of high wages offered at "bikini bars." Many of these Filipino women are also drawn to the image of liberating, modern Western countries and often marry Western men in hopes of attaining that lifestyle.

Many Filipino nationalists draw attention to issues of prostitution, overseas workers, and the sex tourist industry to expose the shortsightedness of the Philippine government's economic policies, focusing on the fact that Filipino women are treated as commodities (Chang and Groves 1997). Unfortunately, many people worldwide have conflated the commodification of Filipino women with the stereotype of Filipino women as prostitutes (Chang and Groves 1997). Thus, some people (including participants on the newsgroup) characterize all Filipino mail-order brides and entertainers as selfish gold diggers and dismiss the argument that some of these women were forced into these situations. In addition, many generalize this sexually adept, prostitute stereotype to Filipino women worldwide.

Stereotypes on the Newsgroup

These stereotypes of Filipino and Asian women are ubiquitous in the soc.culture.filipino newsgroup and on the Web. The quote of the Norwegian participant indicates that the stereotypes are not restricted to the United States but have spread worldwide. With respect to the newsgroup, one particularly offensive discussant called upon participants to list reasons "Why Filipinas Need to Be Loved." In this thread, respondents reinforced the stereotypes that Filipino women are hypersexual and are good (e.g., monogamous) wives. The fact that the initial poster's main concern was that "bad words" should not be used shows that he considered these stereotypes of Filipino women as normal, not degrading. This became particularly apparent when the discussant stated that the contributions were meant to "honor Filipino women, not slander them":

> Please add your comment.
> Why are Filipina women great lover.
> (please no bad words, remember your kids might read this)
> No. 10 She wash her flower everyday
> No. 9 She eats eggplant in the dark[5]
> No. 8 She love lollipops
> No. 7 She loves to ride horsey-horsey
> No. 6 She is a mother, friend, and lover
> No. 5 She is monogamous
> No. 4 She always comes back (for more)
> No. 3 Her donut-hole is small

This post serves a variety of functions. First, it idealizes women who are both monogamous and sexually adept. Second, it differentiates Filipino women from (white) U.S. women. Third, it establishes a singular identity for all Filipino women. Though this piece may seem like just a list of stereotypes, this particular definition of Filipino women was sanctioned because it was written by self-defined Filipinos who presented contributions as facts rather than as expressions of desire. And when stereotypes become "facts," they assume a certain legitimacy that is sited and deployed for diverse and sometimes conflicting arguments. For example, some respondents who seek Filipino empowerment embraced this thread because it differentiated Filipino women from (white) U.S. women. However, in embracing these characteristics, they (perhaps unwittingly) sanction the commodification of Filipino women.

Newsgroup participants began to write posts, ostensibly to protect Filipino women when news of abused overseas contract workers and mail-order brides began hitting the newspapers and the Internet, and these posts increased after the newsgroup was inundated with personal ads and URLs for Web pages that advertise for "pen pal" correspondence pages.

The following is an example of one of the offending posts and the responses to it. As we will see, both posts—the original post describing the buying and selling of *Cebuanas* and the responses of those attempting to "protect" Filipinas—illustrate how stereotypes serve as gender markers. "I have a guy in Cebu City, Philippines. He's the father of a girl who married an American. This guy now makes his living by introducing visiting American guys to local girls. We are talking late-teen, young–20's virgins from (what over there passes for) lower-middle class families."

This post reflects the demand for Filipino women as wives and, like other mail-order bride catalogs, panders to U.S. men. Its author, a frequent poster on the newsgroup, knew by the plethora of personal ads and ads for online mail-order bride catalogs that he had an audience. He continues:

> This is not about getting laid. You most certainly can get laid any evening in Cebu for very little money (he can show you the ropes on that, as well). It's about getting one of those incredibly gorgeous girls in the dept stores or restaurants or whenever-you-saw-her, to go out on a date with you. The girl will bring along a friend. It's done that way. She will not get in the way of private talking—my man makes sure of that.
>
> You can be married within a week of your arrival in Cebu, if you're not one of these guys who keeps seeing an even more gorgeous babe when he went to pick up some toothpaste. Kid-in-the-candystore syndrome. It doesn't bother him.

Here the participant acknowledges the common stereotypes of Filipino women as hypersexual yet "good" wives, as well as the image of rampant prostitution in the Philippines. Though there are prostitutes and good wives in any culture or nation, what makes this part of the post stand out is that this author puts all Filipino women up for sale. Therefore, the assumption underlying this letter is worse than those underlying ads for mail-order bride companies or the sex tourist industry, as it does not differentiate between Filipino women who wish to be pen pals or prostitutes and those who do not. *All* Cebuanas are commodities, mere candy, at the disposal of pimps and their U.S. customers. The poster also assumes that all Filipino women desire the company of U.S. men. By rendering Filipino women commodities, desirable objects of exchange, he has completely stripped Filipino women of their agency.

In the next paragraph, the poster even provides specific descriptions of interactions, so customers know exactly what to expect when they arrive in Cebu. He assures potential customers that they will have access to his friend, a local pimp, and reassures customers that the entire exchange will be inexpensive: "Your cost is $50/day when you have him to yourself all day. $35 for a whole morning or a whole afternoon, nothing for the little stuff (phone consultations etc, when he otherwise isn't spending time with you). Out-of-pocket costs (taxi fares, bribes, meals he eats with you, etc) are from your pocket. It's not going to amount to a lot of money—the economy is set up to accommodate people who consider $100 to be two months salary. . . . I am a pimp—you pay me, I pay him."

Thus, even on a newsgroup created to discuss "what Filipino culture is and not what it is rumored to be," characterizations of Filipino women as hypersexualized commodities and an asset to the economy are rampant and are perpetuated by Filipinos and non-Filipinos alike.

Combating Colonialism with Stereotypes

How did male participants react to these posts? While many participants resisted negative stereotypes of Filipino women, they did not do so in the interest of Filipino women's rights. Instead, since their reactions are framed against the background of U.S. colonialism, Filipino women are caught in the middle of the nation-building and Filipino-identity-building process. That is, Filipina is used merely as a gender marker between nations, and the stereotypes used to characterize Filipina are not critically evaluated.

Yuval-Davis and Anthias (1989), among other scholars, have shown that (male) nationalists often treat women as property, not as human beings with rights. News of Filipino women in relationships with non-Filipino men is often described as "losing our women" and, therefore, a threat to Filipino integrity. Responses to the above post parallel this argument. The first post below was from a Filipino male (Ray) in response to "the pimp," but, as we will see, he was more angry that Filipino males were left "out of the loop" than about the stereotype or the commodification of Filipinos: "As Filipinos on SCF, we don't try to exclude Whites from the conversation or the enjoyment of it all. However, Whites are constantly trying to discriminate us and exclude us from our own newsgroup! Look at this thread. This guy is offering to connect Whites (American guys) with Filipinas from Cebu. He wants to cut us Filipinos out of the loop and, frankly, I've had enough of this."

Another thing that makes this post stand out is that Ray (1) assumed that the pimp is white and (2) conflated white and American. The normalization of American as white is not an uncommon move; W.E.B. DuBois's ([1903] 1990) explanation of the "double consciousness" exposes this normalizing stance, and Michael Omi and Howard Winant (1994) show that U.S. whites are not normally thought of as a race. However, as we will see in the next part of Ray's post, the conflation of white and American is utilized to highlight twin evils of colonialism and racism: "If anyone is going to get a sexy, 19yo, Cebuana to take out and have sex with—it damn better be me! Taking our women and cutting us out of the picture, it's time for a real race war."

Scholars have shown that being able to control one's women is perceived as reflecting the strength of the nation and/or culture (L. West 1992). This is one of the major reasons that so many participants were angry about the stereotypes and the selling of Filipino women to Western men. Many of the participants were aware that many Filipino women were dating and marrying white (U.S.) males. In addition, many believed that white males posted the personal ads and URLs for mail-order bride Web sites. Ray's wish to keep Filipino women "safe" from whites reflected his desire to preserve the cultural integrity of Filipinos and the race. Thus, the opposition to the commodification of Filipino women is not necessarily about Filipino women's rights, but about Filipino men's rights as Filipinos.

Here is a quote from Bill, a frequent poster on the newsgroup, in response to the earlier post about buying brides. His arguments are similar to other posts leveled against mail-order bride recruiters and posters of personal ads: "[The pimp] is a long time participant here at SCF. The fact that he is pimping here for 'wanna Filipina' wife shoppers is a sad statement . . . that SCF is NOT a Filipino news group as much as it is a magnet for Kanos with 'yellow fever'—Kanos who's interest in the RP and Filipino culture is limited to 'wanna/have a Filipina.'"

These responses (and other responses like it) all referred to the Kano/Filipino dichotomy. "Kano" is technically short for "Amerikano" or "American." In the United States, often, Kano refers to whites, whether they are Americans or not, again reflecting the normalization of whites as Americans. In the newsgroup, Americans are the "enemy" and Filipinos are the "victim." In addition, when participants other than Ray used the terms "Kano" or "American," U.S. ideas of race were often brought into the picture in that they assumed that all Kanos are white. This did not happen for just this thread; in all of the responses to these types of ads that I collected, only five (of about eight hundred), implicated nonwhite males. Again, the emphasis on white (American) males "taking our women" away from members of our race is related to the stereotyping of white males as virile and desirable and Asian females as hypersexual and good wives. And we will see that some of the participants attribute the fact that whites take Filipino women away from Filipinos to the fact that Filipino national identity is so weak. The feeling is that Filipino identity could be strengthened if Filipino women could be protected from white males.

Although it is true that Bill guessed the race of the pimp correctly, there is no evidence that only white U.S. males are involved in pimping/prostituting. In fact, many pen-pal correspondence Web sites are maintained by white male/Filipino woman teams. U.S. males (especially white U.S. males) are held suspect because, although scholars have shown that many women have willingly entered mail-order bride relationships out of economic need or for personal reasons, these relationships have been historically linked to the continued economic and cultural colonization of the Philippines (Chang and Groves 1997; Espiritu 1997; Law 1997; Ordoñez 1997). This will be apparent later, when I discuss the subsequent redefinitions of Filipino females and white males.

Lois West (1992) and others have shown that to combat this stereotype yet another stereotype was constructed: that of the Maria Clara, or the proper, marriage-minded Filipino Catholic woman with good morals. This has emerged simultaneously with the prostitute stereotype and parallels discussions of the Madonna/whore dichotomy prevalent in the discussion of other groups of women, such as Latinas

(Anzaldúa 1987). As stated before, many (but not all) Filipino feminist nationalists point to prostitution as a reflection of anti-U.S. imperialism. This argument associates promiscuity and prostitution with Americanization and Western values. Filipino values, on the other hand, center around the family. Traditional patriarchy is not fought against but embraced. In this way, the Spanish influence, despite being a colonial influence, is welcomed, while the U.S. influence is rejected.

Scholars have shown that the Maria Clara stereotype is used not only by certain Filipino feminist nationalists, but also by first-generation Filipino immigrants to the United States and by overseas contract workers in Hong Kong (Chang and Groves 1997; Espiritu 1997). K. A. Chang and Julian Groves (1997) explain that Filipino overseas contract workers in Hong Kong actively embrace the Maria Clara stereotype to control their sexual reputation. Because images of Filipino women as sexually available are pervasive in both public and private discourse in Hong Kong, Filipino women must "'take control of the situation' by adopting appropriate behaviors and appearances" (Chang and Groves 1997, 17). They show that Filipino women join all-female groups, distinguish "good" and "bad" places (church versus discos) and activities (choir versus dancing), and become closely affiliated with the local Catholic church.

Members of soc.culture.filipino held the Maria Clara stereotype in the sense that they characterized Filipino women as traditional wives and mothers. However, participants fused this with the sexually adept stereotype, which parallels the stereotypes of Asian women in general. Despite these stereotypes' basis in U.S. military intervention throughout Asia and despite the U.S. media's deployment of these stereotypes, participants on soc.culture.filipino nevertheless invoke these images. Various postings on soc.culture.filipino indicate that such deployments complement the definition of an authentic, unadulterated Filipino culture. References to this history of U.S. colonialism, which was never explicitly talked about, shaped the conversations about identity, including "Filipina" identity.[6] Because the stereotypes of Asian and white women have been consistently invoked to demarcate the difference between colonized and colonizer, it is particularly difficult for participants to isolate and challenge these stereotypes. Validated by their association with anticolonial politics, these stereotypes have become common currency on soc.culture.filipino.

The Problem with Binaries: Discovering Filipino Women's Agency

Mail-Order Brides and Interracial Relationships

As we saw in the last section, discussions about mail-order brides were extremely heated, especially when the topics centered on the men who subscribe to these catalogs. The participants tended to assume that women who submitted their pictures and descriptions to the catalogs had no agency, that they were poor, lowly women who entered into these relationships out of sheer desperation, and that they entered into these arrangements solely to support their families back in the Philippines. In addition, many newsgroup participants assumed that mail-order brides are uneducated women who married foreigners for no other reason but to send money back home to their families. Moreover, they assumed that men who perused the catalogs were white sex maniacs with "yellow fever" who preyed on poor, helpless Filipino women. Since news reports worldwide often focus on the divorce rates of and domestic abuse within mail-order bride marriages, people within and outside the newsgroup assume these kinds of marriages are doomed from the start (Ordoñez 1997).

But, as the discussion ensued and as more news reports and personal experiences of "mail-order brides" were posted on the newsgroup, the participants learned that many mail-order brides are college educated; some are even professionals who earn decent wages (Chang and Groves 1997; Law 1997; Ordoñez 1997). When this "alternative" information came out, their confusion was magnified. One member wrote, "At first I suspected that someone was preying on poor women, but when I looked at some of the personals I realized that many of the women were educated and professional. Is the mail order bride exploitation or a worthwhile service, or both?"

Since some women are economically secure, the argument that women place entries in mail-order catalogs to escape extreme poverty and help their families fell apart. Because oppression has been measured in large part by very sterile measures, such as a person's individual economic worth, the participants did not discuss (nor even appear to care about) sexism and patriarchy, much less the sex tourist industry. This opened the door to a discussion of exploitation and the link between the economy and sex. Fred, a Filipino American male, answered, "The word 'exploitation' is of course the key to understanding why the mail order brides phenomena exists. However allow me to humbly submit that the culprit isn't as much the old Kano sitting in the Ermita area compiling a list of naive Filipinas, but the structure of the Philippine economic system. Ferdinand Marcos candidly described the Philippines once as an 'economic oligarchy.'"

Instead of defining all this against a rich/poor, Western/Philippine dichotomy, in which rich Western individuals exploit Third World women and children, Fred introduces the effect of the Marcos regime on the Philippine economy. Unfortunately, Fred does not connect the Marcos regime or the economic oligarchy to the American government, as many participants did in other, random posts. Instead, he focused solely on the Philippine economy and how it affects the people within it: "This simply means that virtually all the wealth is controlled by a very small elite group. . . . The economic opportunities afforded by the 'economic oligarchy' leave virtually all Filipinas who define success in life in terms of material acquisition and some economic security for themselves and their families with only about 2 realistic options. The 1st is immigration, explaining why the mail order bride list exists and why young girls (even professionals) will marry foreigners from industrialized nations who are often double or triple their age and the 2nd option is foreign employment via the 'employment agencies.'"

In the rest of the post, Fred describes how difficult it is to become economically successful, and attributes emigration to the lack of resources within the Philippines. According to Law (1997) and Ordoñez (1997), this assessment is partially true. Ordoñez (1997) has shown that the high underemployment rate in the Philippines is one major reason why Filipino women seek work elsewhere, which mirrors Fred's assessment that Filipino women leave the Philippines in search of economic security.

With this post, Fred attempted to focus on the nation's economic plight so that the participants would blame neither the women nor the families involved in the mail-order bride industry. However, missing from this discussion is how the emigration policies of the Philippine government are also gendered (Enloe 1989). The sex tourist industry—which includes the proliferation of brothels in all the major Philippine city centers, the emigration of "dancers," and mail-order brides—is marketed using derogatory stereotypes of Filipino women as hypersexual yet traditional (i.e., non-divorcing) wives. In addition, without a full understanding of how the economy affects women's decisions, and with a growing number of stories of Filipino women as whitewashed opportunists infiltrating local and global news, inevitably the participants' image of mail-order brides began to change. Where participants once saw the mail-order bride as a martyr in that they placed an emphasis on the sacrifice that the mail-order brides made to feed their families in the Philippines, the absence of economic need led members to question the women's loyalty to their country and race.

To complicate matters, in the United States, interracial relationships between Asian American women and white men are increasing. Some scholars have shown that Asian American females are marrying outside the race more rapidly than the males (Espiritu 1997). This affects Asian men's perceptions of themselves, Asian women, and their own sexuality (Espiritu 1997). In addition, reports of out-marriage among Filipino women have circulated in Filipino newspapers inside and outside of the Philippines and through various transnational sources such as satellite TV (the Filipino Channel), newspapers (Bonus 2000; Ordoñez 1997), and, most recently, the Internet.

Because of the continued economic and cultural colonization of the Philippines by the United States and the rise in white male/Filipino female relationships, American males (especially white U.S. males) are held suspect by many male Filipino members on the newsgroup. In the newsgroup, the discussion quickly switched from mail-order brides to *all* women involved in interracial relationships. When economic need was eliminated as the sole reason for women to participate in the mail-order industry or to marry any Western foreigner, the participants needed to find another reason. But, like most people, they returned the discussion to individual motives, instead of looking broadly at the relationship between the United States and Philippines, much less gendered policies, and their effect on Filipino women and men. The reason that surfaced was that these women are weakened by their lack of "authentic culture," are ashamed of their culture, and, thus, have no problem "selling out the race":

> Since filipinos lack national identity and culture, I wonder if they are a liability to the asian race. filipinos have been raped by the spaniards, japanese, and americans. they don't have their own national identity and filipino women will marry anyone who is not asian. I see filipino women marrying white men who are social outcast, like the guy who killed his mail order filipino wife in seattle, washington.

Everywhere I look I see Asian women trying to sell them-

selves to any white man they can get and I also see Asian parents selling their daughters to any white men who will pay
the most (about 3 dollars for white skin). Since the females
are the most valuable asset a race can have, therefore Asian
are losing out to the white race when it comes to the racial
competition.

Colonial mentality, again, resurfaces as the social problem. It becomes clear here that the topic of interracial relationships is not just
about race, but is intertwined with the need to establish a strong national Filipino identity, independent from American hegemony. In this
post, Jonathan also suggested that forming a strong racial identity depends on the control of their own women. Asian women are "gender
markers" between races.

This phenomenon is not unique to the Asian community. Lorde
(1984a), C. West (1995), and many others have shown that some African American male community leaders also use this rhetoric. Because
of the hierarchical racial relationship between whites (the supposed
dominant race) and Others, it is especially threatening to the viabil-
ity of the culture when the women date white men as the virility and
strength of non-white men are questioned. For example, some black
male leaders attempt to enforce patriarchy within the African American community by drawing on mainstream depictions of gender roles
within African cultures. These leaders often accuse black feminists,
who expose patriarchy and sexism within the African American community, of weakening the race. However, as bell hooks states, "If the
black thing is really a dick thing in disguise, we're in serious trouble!"
because community cannot be achieved if gender oppression persists
(quoted in Riggs 1995). Yet this sexist rhetoric continues. Similarly,
in the above post, women who do not conform to the ideals of the
group (e.g., Asian women who date outside their race) are labeled as
traitors: "I also see Asian females bleaching their hair color, getting
their eyes rounded, and trying to act white. Why are Asians so des-
perately seeking ***WHITE WASH** treatment? I think Asian women are
selling themselves to white men because they are ashamed of their
culture. They think marrying white will get them one step closer to
being white by having half-white kids. How in the world did they
turned out this way. I mean Asians are thought to have such strong
family values but I guess this stereotype is wrong."
In this section, Jonathan equates the females who bought into the

white standard of beauty with those in relationships with white males. It has been argued that women who go through plastic surgery to achieve the white standard of beauty have internalized racism (Kim 1982). Thus, in equating these two groups of Asian women, Jonathan has established that Asian women who date white males also have internalized racism. Although there may be an overlap in some cases, he does not leave room for the possibility that there may be women involved with white males who are proud of their race and/or ethnic group.

Jonathan also alludes to the racial hierarchy by arguing that Asian women in these relationships are trying to "pass" off as belonging to the dominant racial group, whites. This parallels the discourse on interracial dating in African American communities (Davis 1991). In suggesting that they are trying to pass off as whites, Jonathan again emphasizes these women's self-hate and their participation in the demise of their own culture. In addition, Jonathan implies that only Asian women who marry within the race have strong family values because he believes that women enter interracial relationships by selling themselves, not for any other reasons. Eventually, stereotypes of people involved in interracial white male/Asian female relationships were cross-posted on all the Asian soc.culture groups. For example, the "Asiaphile" and "Whiggie" letters were letters cross-posted to several "Asian" newsgroups, such as soc.culture.japan, soc.culture.hongkong, and soc.culture.singapore, to name a few.

The "Asiaphile" thread contains stereotypes of white men who date Asian women. This particular post generated 138 responses from several different newsgroups; 97 of the responses came from self-defined white males from the United States: "The ASIAPHILE a brief profile of men afflicted with 'yellow fever.' ORIGINS: Asiaphiles are typically found residing in major U.S. and European cities, although increasing numbers have been venturing overseas in their quest to 'get an oree-enul woman.' NOT TO BE CONFUSED WITH: Intelligent, nonracist and socially-functional men who are free of fetishes and racial bias."

The participant's decision to frame this post in the form of a profile or definition is significant because the use of these genres implies an authoritative tone. Even though this post clearly contains the author's opinion, the format and the author's decision to remove himself from the post (there are no first-person pronouns in the post) changed the nature of the debates largely because it came off as an attempt to officially classify a certain subset of people.

In the beginning of this post, it is already clear that the person who wrote the post intended to insult, and hopefully ostracize from the newsgroups, Western men who believe in the stereotypes of Asian ("Oriental") women. The participant's use of the term "yellow fever" alerts readers to the existence of a social problem, while the "oree-enul" indicates not only the Asiaphile's ignorance of the negative connotation of the term "Oriental" but also the Asiaphile's low social status through his inability to speak "proper" English.

"CHARACTER TRAITS: —Poorly developed masculine identities, pathetically uncomfortable with themselves, inept at romance with women of their own race. —Insatiable appetite for Asian cultural trivia, which is used to camouflage/legitimate their underlying fetish (a superficial knowledge of Asian art impresses the shit outta the babes). . . . Resentment of white females—assertive, strong-willed personality traits (whether real or perceived). . . . —Ignorant and narrow minded, eager to adopt fallacious Western media stereotypes of Asian women" In this next section, the participant not only defines the Asiaphile, he defines white and Asian women as well, thereby maintaining Orientalism. The participant demasculinizes the Asiaphile in two ways: (1) by stating that he cannot find a date within his own race and, therefore, has lost control of the race and (2) by reifying the stereotype of white women as "assertive, strong-willed" *in relation* to these males. Interestingly, he accuses the Asiaphile of believing the stereotypes of Asian women, while proclaiming a blanket statement about Asian women: that we would be impressed by the Asiaphile's "superficial knowledge of Asian art." By referring to the Asiaphile's inability to enter relationships with "assertive, strong-willed" white women and his ability to (or belief that he can) "impress the shit out of [Asian] babes" through trivial knowledge, he reified the stereotype of the strong independent white woman as opposed to weak, shallow Asian women discussed in the beginning of this chapter. In addition, referring to women as a "fetish" and not referring to any other personality traits strips Asian women of agency. Inconsistencies run rampant, however, in this and the corresponding Whiggie post. "—Unable to accept non-whites or women as equals. Insistent racial stereotypes. Chauvinistic. . . . —Disdains ethnic studies; regards it as a waste of taxpayer's money and an ultimate threat to white male privilege and cultural hegemony. . . . —Thinks that the poverty, prostitution and white cultural imperialism in certain Asian countries is a good deal while it lasts. Favorite holiday destination: Bangkok. . . . —Believes that racism does not exist because

he, as a WM [white man], has never experienced it first hand. . . .
—Denial of all the above."

In this last part of the post, the description of the Asiaphile as
not only Western (from the United States and major European cities)
but undoubtedly *white* is twice reified. The particular subject-position
"Western white male" is significant because in the last part of this post
the participant states that the Asiaphile is also a white supremacist.

This post does not explicitly state it is against Asian women/white
male relationships in general. However, because the topic of interracial relationships caused such alarm in soc.culture.filipino and because
the participants had already been embroiled in a heated discussion
about the perceived inequities involved in Filipino female/white male
relationships and what they represent, this post caused great alarm
on the newsgroup. Ninety-seven responses to this post were from white
males protesting the stereotyping. Many of them tried to defend their
relationships and their characters. But the person who wrote this post
(and his/her supporters) just pointed to the last characteristic ("Denial of all the above") and accused the detractors of being Asiaphiles.
It became especially difficult for any white male to defend being in a
relationship with a Filipino women, even if the relationship did not
involve the sex tourist industry in any way. In some of the responses,
however, another part of the Orientalist discourse emerged: that of the
sensitive, caring white male versus the unemotional, hypercontrolling
Asian male. David, a white American male, uses this rhetorical more
to defend white males against two self-defined Filipino males who
extolled the author of the Asiaphile stereotype:

> A shame it never occurred to y'all to get up off your knuck-
> les, belay the macho posturing and behave like civilized men.
> If you did, you might be pleasantly surprised at the change
> in the way women (Asian and otherwise) look at you. . . .
>
> Women don't like whiners. . . . And over and above that,
> you don't like women. Of course you "want" women, in the
> same way that you want a cup of coffee or another 16 megs
> of ram, but you don't "like" them. You don't care a fill of beans
> for them as people, and couldn't give a rats ass what they like
> or don't. You want them because they're decorative and so you
> can have sex with them, period.

As we can see, David took advantage of the impersonal, "objective" tone of the Asiaphile profile and the description of Asian women as fetishes and acquisitions to accuse the Asiaphile author (who he assumed to be male) of being sexist. This rhetorical move is common; Orientalism is dependent on characterizing not only Asian and white females, but also the males. As stated earlier, the sensitive, all-knowing white male character has emerged in recent years as a counterpart to the hypermasculine, sexist male characters shown in numerous films. Interestingly, in this particular thread, David did not explicitly mention race; yet, in his previous posts, he always established that his posts were from a "white male perspective." All of a sudden, he switched from being one voice among many (i.e., the white male perspective in a Filipino newsgroup) to the generalized "voice of reason": "The problem is that you consider women a commodity, and by and large women don't find that very flattering. If given the choice between associating with a man who likes her as person and one who considers her a possession, most women will opt for the former. Surprise, surprise."

Here, whether he intended to or not, David reified the images in the media of white males as "civilized" and sensitive to women's needs and, by extension, of Asian males as uncivilized and hypercontrolling (Espiritu 1997). Because David is a white male addressing two Asian males, some read that post as a white versus Asian male letter, as we will see in the following response. It appeared that David also accused Asian males of commodifying women, an interesting rhetorical move given that many newsgroup participants blamed white males for the commodification of Asian women. Subsequent posts from white men to the newsgroup were largely read the same way—as an attempt to differentiate Asian men from white men. This prompted Daniel, a Filipino American male, to post: "Well for those white postees who believe themselves to be such intellectuals I have one question: are you not aware of the societal advantages whites have over other minority groups? As a student lucky enough to have an Ethnic Studies Program I have learned so many things that is absolutely impossible to learn about unless you take these classes."

Here, Daniel established authority by stating that he is a college student taking ethnic studies classes; thus, his assessment of the situation was presumably academic and objective. Asking the white participants if they were aware of the social power attributed to them because of their race was a powerful move because he asserted that there is a racial hierarchy between Asians and whites, an observation which is absent in most of the posts. However, as we will see, he, too, simplified the reasons Asian women enter interracial relationships: "Anyway, with whites having such enormous social power you have a major advantage in acquiring a woman of any minority. That's just how it is apparently, women marry up to men with a higher social status."

In framing his argument this way, he left out any other reasons Asian women enter interracial relationships. In this sense, he reinforced the stereotype that women in relationships with white males do so only because they are overly conscious of social status and want to marry whites in hopes of climbing the social ladder. But, as we will see, Daniel's use of the phrase "acquiring a woman" takes the emphasis away from the fact that a racial hierarchy does exist. His use of this phrase still objectifies the women involved in interracial relationships. In subsequent posts, people unfortunately focus on this phrase. Daniel continues, "White men with a minority woman is a very common equation (except for maybe black women which they do not find attractive . . . stats back me up). With Asians making up just 3% of the population of course us college students are going to be threatened from what's going on. Not only are there white college students only attracted to young Asian women, but middle-aged white men as well."

Here Daniel re-emphasized his authority by invoking the all-powerful voice of statistics. He then argued that Asian males are upset by the high number of interracial relationships because, as members of a minority racial group, they cannot compete with the white males on campus (especially, he argues, since women would rather marry people in a higher status group). Of course, he did not allow that there may be other reasons for increasing interracial relationships besides "status," nor did he invoke the statistic that Filipino male/non-Filipino female relationships are also increasing (Espiritu 1997). He then attempted to justify the Asiaphile post: "So what if we crack jokes. They certainly aren't racist because we are not talking about all white men. If you think some postees are sophomoric, then why shouldn't it be, we're college students. These jokes are harmless."

This part of the post is a bit ironic because the white males who responded to the author were often accused of being racist against Asians even if they did not implicate outright all Asian males. His second defense is interesting because he spent much of the post establishing his authority as a college student taking ethnic studies classes. Now, at the end, those who support the Asiaphile post are just "sophomoric college students," thus the Asiaphile profile is only a harmless joke.

When David responded to Daniel, he focused on the phrase "acquiring a woman," and also dismissed Daniel's argument that race matters. This simultaneously erases discussions of racism and reifies the racial imagery of white and Filipino males.

> *Daniel:* Well for those white postees who believe themselves to be: such intellectuals I have one question: are you not aware of the societal advantages whites have over other minority groups?
>
> *David:* Sure are. So what?
>
> *Daniel:* Anyway, with whites having such enormous social power you have a major advantage in acquiring a woman of any minority.
>
> *David:* If you assume that a woman is a mindless commodity, sure. But, then if you're inclined to make that sort of assumption you've damaged your own chances of "acquiring a woman."

Exchanges like this continued for months. Interestingly, of the 138 posters who responded, only 2 were women, and they directly addressed the contents of neither the original post nor the white/Asian male distinction. In fact, their responses did not even address interracial dating or gender relations at all; they posted at a time when the thread began to morph into another subject matter. As in other heated debates, they signaled that they wished to close the debate by posting a non-response as a response, causing the thread to morph into another subject. What is interesting is that their responses did not close the debates at all. In fact, the Asiaphile debates increased. This may partially be because the Asiaphile responses were cross-listed across multiple soc.culture groups. But, I believe that the primary reason the posts did not decrease on soc.culture.filipino is because Filipino males' masculinity as well as Filipino culture itself was at stake. Like in other once-colonized and/or subordinate racial groups, Filipino males' control of women's bodies serves to "protect" the culture from outside influences (Anthias and Yuval-Davis 1994). And, here in soc.culture.filipino, this was most apparent. That is, it was apparent until agency was attributed to the females.

Unfortunately, as the Asiaphile debates increased, the original poster created another profile: the Whiggie. According to this person, a "Whiggie" (short for "White guy groupie") is the Asiaphile's counterpart. There were only thirty responses to the post and, as we will see, they mirrored the Asiaphile post. I discuss both the original post and some responses in this section.

A Whiggie Profile 2.3: The following profile contains HU-MOR. . . .

Whiggies are a subset of women of Asian ethnicity, usu-ally found residing in major U.S. cities, although they have been known to appear overseas occasionally. Closely related to their cousins, Yellow Cabs (Japan), Gwei-Po's (Hong Kong), Sarong Partu Girls (Singapore), Twinkies and Bananas [yel-low on the outside, White on the inside].

CHARACTER TRAITS:

—Poorly developed self-identity, pathetically uncomfort-able with themselves and their ethnicity. . . .

—Brainwashed into believing that they, as AF's[Asian fe-males], are more desirable than other women in an exotic kinda way. Perception of Western media sexual stereotypes of AF's as a marketing advantage; willingness to exploit this to the max. . . .

—Thoroughly whitewashed. Desperate need to fit into what they perceive as "mainstream" (i.e., white) society and to distance themselves from their Asian heritage.

In this part of the profile, the poster reiterated the stereotypes of Asian women in interracial relationships with white males that had emerged through discussions of mail-order brides. That is, Asian women in relationships with white males are gold-digging opportun-ists and race traitors. According to this profile, they disdain their cul-ture, have internalized racism, and are willing to use cultural stereotypes of Asian women to climb the social ladder: "—Has lost count of how many WMs [white males] she's done this month. . . . —Fundamentally insecure, utterly confused, lacking in self-respect. Basically clueless. . . . —Denial of all the above. . . . MEDIA REPRESENTA-TION/ROLE MODELS: Connie Chung, Amy Tan, Margaret Cho . . . any of the Joy Luck Club protagonists (except the one who married the Asian dude)."

This post undeniably shows that Asian women who date white men are stereotyped as promiscuous sellouts. As in the Asiaphile post, any woman who would deny any of the listed traits could automati-cally be accused of being a Whiggie. But what sets this post apart from the Asiaphile profile are the "media representation/role models" that

the poster listed. This anonymous poster and other participants spo-
radically mentioned their distaste of "women in news" because some
Asian newscasters try too hard to look and act white. This, without a
doubt, shows the influence of American racial classification systems
and racial experiences in the characterization of all Asian women
worldwide and Asian women's behaviors (i.e., dating patterns, speech
patterns, and even consumer tastes, as we will see below). They are
heavily scrutinized by Filipino and other Asian men. This, in conjunction with their responses to the Asiaphile post, also illustrates the desire
to control "their" women. This is reflected in the following response
to this Whiggie profile: a Filipino male stated,

> Why are Asian-American women so ashamed of their culture?
> They seem very quick to sell out. They will even degrade and
> mock Asian men and paint them as weak and sexually infe-
> rior for their white masters.
>
> Everytime I go to the USA I see Asian women reading the
> news acting soooooooo white, Do American men like to have
> their news "served" to them by an Asian chicky poo?
>
> They are very taken in by corporate propaganda and spend
> most of their sad lives telling white Americans "Look at me
> in my GAP shirt, Calvin Klein's, see I white too" or "Me a white
> girl now totally radddd fur shure, see, see I white, I white like
> you."

In this short post, the image of an unequal racial and gender hierarchical relationship emerged. The participant's referral to white males
as "masters" as well as the image of Asian woman "serving" American (white) men point to this. In addition, while Connie Chung is married to a white male, this post's focus on Asian American newscasters'
communication skills suggests that Asian women who evince any Western characteristics (in this case, the ability to speak unbroken English)
are selling out their race. Posts that center on "acting white" in conjunction with images of the ideal Filipino woman contributed to the
confusion of Filipino American's identity *as* Filipino women in this
newsgroup. In defining what is *not* a Filipino woman, these posts also
contribute to the image of "real" Filipino women. Also, the last part
of the post reifies Orientalism in that the participant places a boundary between Asian and American. Although Connie Chung, Amy Tan,
Margaret Cho, and all of the Joy Luck Club protagonists are Americans of Asian descent, he assumes otherwise by equating the use of

broken English as an Asian characteristic and the use of proper English by a woman of Asian descent as trying to act white.

What is incredibly interesting about this post, however, is that it does not implicate Asian males who engage in similar behavior. In soc.culture.filipino, not one poster commented on the fact that there are Filipino males worldwide who engage in conspicuous consumption and purchase American goods for various reasons including to show off their buying power. In addition, there was no discussion about Filipino males' dating patterns in the years I studied soc.culture. filipino. This, however, is not surprising; as stated before, women are the gender markers between nations, culture, and/or races (Anthias and Yuval-Davis 1994; hooks 1994; McClintock 1997). And though many of the participants generally warn of "colonial mentality" and "selling out" (see chapter 3), the only behavior Filipino male participants were heavily criticized for was emigrating from the Philippines, especially if they left for the United States.

Although there were far fewer responses to the Whiggie profile, the responses mirrored those of the Asiaphile profile. The same participants even replied to the post. David simply wrote, "The following profile contains HUMOR. No it doesn't [contain humor]. It simply contains the bitter maunderings of a benighted racist fool." To this Arthur replied, "Are you one of those asianophiles?"

At this point, respondents moved away from the content of the Whiggie profile and began to argue about the difference between Asian and white men again. As with the Asiaphile post, men posted most of the responses. Only one woman responded, and, as with the Asiaphile responses, she did not address the contents of the Whiggie profile or the Asian/white male dichotomy. Their silence tells us much about inequality: the establishment of a forum that promotes the discussion of multiple narratives and the decentering of voices does not necessarily lend itself to egalitarianism. However, this does not mean that Filipino women were absent altogether. In the next section, I discuss the few responses women did contribute.

Responses by Filipino Women: Understanding the Importance of Location and Gender

Filipino women, generally, contributed heavily to the conversations on soc.culture.filipino. In discussions about emigration and Filipino values, for example, Filipino women around the world

would contribute to discussions about life in their host countries, contribute nostalgic descriptions of life in the Philippines (whether lived
experiences or not), and, as Norma did, voice their concerns about the
economic and political state of the Philippines. It was in this discussion about the characteristics of Filipino women that they were largely
silent. The reason for this silence is unknown, as I did not individu-
ally e-mail and ask any of the female participants on the newsgroup
why they were silent. However, I believe that the threat of being known
as a "race traitor" silenced many women.

It is difficult to assess numerically how many and in what ways
Filipino women were affected because, as in other communities, not
many women joined the conversation. While it is apparent that most
of the participants on soc.culture.filipino are male, this fact in and of
itself does not explain why Filipino women did not participate in this
particular conversation. On other mundane threads with topics such
as "the cheapest way to call the Philippines," many women posted. I
also did not post responses to any of these posts. Part of the reason I
chose not to do so was because I was afraid that if I posted first, I would
somehow "taint" the discussion. And, so I waited to see what would
happen.

Given that the level of participation by female Filipino participants
was low, I believe that the use of the Filipino woman as a gender marker
between the United States and the Philippines discursively marginalized Filipino women participants who did fit the criteria. While
it is possible that the reason most of the regular female posters did
not participate is because they believed this discussion was somewhat
"beneath" them, these discussions led at least one participant (whose
posts I discuss below) to redefine her identity.

With respect to interracial dating, Filipino women who stated that
they were happy in interracial relationships (especially with white
males) were derided mainly because of the belief that yellow fever runs
through all Kanos. All participants in Asian woman/white male relationships were criticized and stereotyped. One Filipino American
woman in particular complained of the conflation of mail-order bride
relationships with all interracial relationships. She began, "I've always
been opposed to [mail-order] brides. It gives relationships between
Filipinas and American men a stereotype that basically disgusts me."

Then she tried to counter two stereotypes: (1) that all white males
enter interracial relationships with Filipino women because of some
stereotypes associated with "Filipinas" and (2) that Filipino women

enter relationships for financial security. "My beau fell in love with me not because I'm Filipina. . . . But because he could see me as an equal intellectually. At least that was the start. My parents are wealthy back home so there is no need to worry about offering financial help. Still, I hate getting stared at!!! I'm not sure whether it's because I'm tall (I'm 5' 10", which is unusual for Filipino women) or because my beau is White!!! Grrrrrr!"

But not all Filipino women responded this way. Interestingly, those who stated that they were Filipino nationalists (both men and women) also tended to portray Filipino women as "good wives," while at the same time fighting against the exploitation of Filipino women. According to L. West (1992), Filipino feminist nationalists often do not confront the traditional social stricture or male authority. Belinda Aquino, a Filipino feminist nationalist, has similarly stated that "the female self concept is less individualistic and is defined by a more complex set of institutions that do not necessarily emphasize abstract notions of self-help, equality, independence, justice and control over one's life" (quoted in L. West 1992). In a similar vein, Aquino argues that a commitment to solidarity, cooperation, and the family or kin group define Filipino women's behavior. In her words, "family solidarity is still the norm."

Certainly, many participants did not question the stereotype of Filipino women as good (i.e., devoted, non-divorcing) wives but vehemently fought against stereotypes of Filipino women as prostitutes. The following post was written by a Filipino woman in Singapore: "Filipina women are usually very caring to their white husbands and are very obedient. We learn to be satisfied less. That is why white men like Filipinas . . . not because we are loose."

Yen Le Espiritu's (1997) work in the San Diego area and Chang and Groves's (1997) study in Hong Kong show that many Filipino women in communities outside the newsgroup embrace the stereotype of Filipino women as good wives. L. West (1992) and Espiritu (1997), among others, have argued that this occurs because some Filipino women still want to differentiate themselves from American women.

Although most posts concerning Asian or Filipino females have been written by self-defined males, many self-defined Filipino American females (including myself) expressed opinions in just a few threads. One particular debate occurred when a Filipino American feminist woman (Janet) attempted to reason with a man who posted this: "I have been to about 17 countries and have met people from all corners of the world. Filipina women seem to be the most perfect women for any man to have as a friend, wife, companion, lover etc. . . . They are beautiful, they speak English, are moral and friendly but not promiscuous. Why would anybody ever want to look for a woman from another country?"

In contrast to the Filipino women in Singapore, the woman respondent warned against accepting the stereotype of Filipino women as good wives. Instead, she wished to get rid of all stereotypes. "You seem to suggest to me that all Filipinas are beautiful, english speaking, moral, friendly and not promiscuous. I can think of specific Filipinas who do not possess one or more of the traits you so prize. Does that make them any less Filipina?"

In this post, she offered counterexamples to undermine the essentialism and, at the end of her post, almost dared participants to characterize Filipino women who are not "beautiful, english speaking, moral, friendly, and not promiscuous" as not Filipino. Interestingly, no one publicly addressed her post. This, however, does not mean that she "won." What happened was that the other participants simply ignored this post, which, in turn, caused this thread (and, therefore, Janet's voice) to die.

Meanwhile, the stereotyping of Filipino women did not cease after her letter. Despite this, Janet continued to reply to posts that contained essentialist images of Filipino women. In the following exchange, she attempted to reason with a man who posted a personal ad. As in the last post, she warned against accepting the stereotype of Filipino women as good wives: "Well, I wish you luck in finding true love. Caveat emptor: not all Filipinas are as you describe. Make sure you get to know your future wife for an extended period of time before you marry her, don't just jump into marriage. What's worse: a bad marriage or divorce? The third time is a charm, especially if you make an honest effort to find out whether the person you're marrying is the right one for you. When you find the right person, no matter what her nationality, you shouldn't have to worry about divorce."

Despite her warning against stereotyping Filipino women, a participant, Scott, chose to stereotype Janet based on her statements about divorce:

> You see what I mean, Janet. If I were a betting man, I would bet it all that you are a Filipina. You are bright, sincere, concerned and caring for the future of a man and woman that you

don't even know. You really feel that there is no need to worry about divorce, I do not believe that you would consider that as an option going into a marriage. I know a young, beautiful, intelligent american girl that talks with me about things from time to time. Just a couple of days ago, I was talking to her about marrying her boyfriend which she plans to do. Her comment was: I hope, I hope it will be for the rest of my life. I pray we won't divorce. This is a wonderful girl, but do you see my point? She is going into marriage "hoping" there will be no divorce, but knowing it is a very distinct possibility. You will not even consider the possibility when you marry, of divorce. You will commit for life. Am I wrong?

Thus, Janet's warnings against stereotyping Filipino women were ignored, while her general statements about divorce were used to accentuate the differences between American and Filipino women. Janet replied to Scott's bet that she is a Filipino by stating, "Close. My parents are from the homeland; I was born and raised in the United States."

This part is interesting in and of itself because Janet, in all of her other posts, referred to herself either as a "Filipina" or a "Pilipina." Although, in her previous posts, she frequently told the newsgroup that she was raised in the United States, she always made sure to refer to herself as a "*Filipina* raised in the United States" (my emphasis). Her response to Scott, however, signaled a change in the way she identified herself. With the above statement, she differentiated herself from Filipino women located in the Philippines and, interestingly, did not use "Philippine," "Filipino," or "Filipina" to refer to herself at all. This is significant because her most recent description emphasized her affiliation with the United States whereas, previously, she equalized her affiliation with the Philippines and the United States, which, I argue, is at least partially due to the discourse surrounding Filipino women on this newsgroup. She then responded to Scott's question about whether she would ever divorce: "I will commit for life. However, if I find myself stuck in a bad marriage, I will be far from passive about it."

Here, she attempted to argue against the stereotype of Filipino women as good (dependent) wives by showing that she would not put up with a bad marriage. Her choice of words at the end is important because in stating that she, a Filipino woman, would be "far from passive," she attempts to invalidate the stereotype of Filipino women as submissive. However, by proclaiming that she is not a "Filipina" in the first part of her post and highlighting that she was born in the United States, she unintentionally allowed subsequent posters to "de-Filipinize" her and highlight her Western ways. One poster quoted her and responded to her comments: "'I will commit for life. However, if I find myself stuck in a bad marriage, I will be *far* from passive about it.' . . . That's why I wouldn't marry a Westernized filipina. they're as bad as most White american women. Feel sorry for your boyfriend but that's his problem."

In the previous posts that I presented, participants accused Filipino and Asian women in general who chose to date white males as "whitewashed" women who were so ashamed of their culture that they were willing to sell out the race. But in this post, the person characterized Westernized Filipino women in general. All Westernized Filipino women (regardless of their dating patterns) are to be avoided as they are just like white U.S. women. But, since the stereotype of Filipino women as good was initially created and is continually used to differentiate white U.S. women from Filipinas, Westernized Filipino women were marginalized from Filipinos (i.e., members of the culture), not just from "Filipinas."

Some participants were not as kind. Janet told the group that, unfortunately, she has been called a "feminazi" and "a White girl trapped inside a Filipina's body" because of her opposition to the "good wife" stereotype (and the other stereotypes). She contends that the most hostile responses have been from Filipino men because she's too independent and refuses to play along with the stereotype that Filipino women are good wives who would never divorce their husbands.

Again, the dichotomy between the United States and the Philippines is highlighted. "Filipina" serves as a marker between the two cultures, and Filipinas who fall between these cultures are not "real" Filipinas. In other words, Janet and other Filipino women who fight against all stereotypes (including stereotypes that differentiate them from American women) are marginalized and forced to ask whether they are Filipino women.

Approaches to Combat Stereotyping

The focus on creating a unique cultural identity has created much confusion among the participants, especially Filipino American women. I argue that this strategic essentializing of Filipino women has troubling implications because the participants fixed "Filipino woman" in one political position. For example, many took an anticolonialism stance, but that occluded possibilities of interracial relationships.

In the struggle against the commodification of Filipino women, the participants on the newsgroup first had to decide on a definition of a Filipino woman. As participants contested the characteristics of Filipino womanhood, I just lurked. I depended largely on Janet—the woman accused of being a "feminazi"—to defend Filipino Americans. I know this is unfair, and I suspect other Filipino American women were doing the same.

What can we learn? It is true that, in this forum, the stories of male and female participants from various nations could be read, the overall picture was not completely decentered, and the stories were not necessarily fragmented. This is not to say that different stories were not told; indeed, different viewpoints were often discussed. However, we must remember that the sheer proliferation of stories in cyberspace and elsewhere does not necessarily reflect a dismantling of traditional narratives.

In the struggle against the stereotyping and commodification of Filipino women, we need to take into account the positions of those expressing their opinions. Just because the participants joined the virtual Filipino community and/or consciously wanted to form a Filipino coalition does not mean that they had not socialized essentialist characterizations of races, genders, and cultures. In addition, since the participants (one hopes) spend most of their time engaging in real-life issues, we cannot expect them to leave their issues behind when they travel onto cyberspace. Anticolonialism, though not explicitly discussed, affected the participants' definitions of "Filipino." Here, as elsewhere, defining Filipino in opposition to American marginalized Filipino American women and upheld the gender hierarchy.

The promising thing about discussing issues like this on the Internet, however, is that the problems with using essentialist descriptions were somewhat exposed. Though there weren't many posts that discredited the sexist, essentialist descriptions of Filipino women, it is technically very easy to propose an alternative position. Also, the lack of moderation of most newsgroups ensures that alternative voices can be heard. Even in this newsgroup, for a while, it became very clear that a diasporic Filipino identity could not be formed using the old formula of dichotomizing two cultures. Partially because of this discussion on gender and another on the importance of citizenship in defining

Filipino identity, as we will see in the next chapter, participants tried to devise a classification system that would include Filipinos from around the world. Through these discussions, we all became more cognizant of the fact that Filipinos aren't all within the Philippines, cultural values aren't genetic, and culture isn't static. As postcolonial theorists have stated, we discovered (though temporarily) that to avoid marginalization, "Filipino" (and "Kano," for that matter) needs to be redefined in such a way that it both transcends national and racial boundaries and remains fluid. However, because of high turnover and the continuing proliferation of personal ads, the discourse revolving around Filipino women continued to be discussed using essentialist characterizations.

Identity is always in flux and created in relation to several political issues. When discussing identity in a transnational location, we can see the many inherent contradictions. Some participants (male and female), many of whom were interested in emphasizing the difference between the Philippines and America, did not view the "good wife" stereotype as problematic because it was used against the image of overly independent white Western women. For many of them, the Westernization of the Philippines is the most pressing problem, and, therefore, Filipinos should focus on retaining their culture and/or protecting Filipino women from Western males. This goal clashed with the desire of others who wished to challenge essentialist images and who dismissed the distinction between Filipino and American women that the former group wished to establish.

While both groups struggled against the commodification of Filipino women to some degree, the latter group (to which I belong) believes that all essentialisms must be eliminated because stereotypes are used to commodify Filipino women. How can we reconcile these different discourses and fight against the commodification of women together? On a more general level, can the American/Filipino national dichotomy—or any dichotomy and essentialist rhetoric—be transcended on the Internet? If we can shake the fear of being reprimanded in "real life" by people who hold dominant viewpoints, could discussions on the Internet lead to a stronger coalition among those who belong to subordinated groups? On the Internet, it is now even easier to post anonymously and to hide one's real-life identity—such as race, ethnicity, and gender (Danet 1998)—than it was when I did my participant observation. Because of this, I believe that it is currently psychologically easier to post counter-narratives than it was when I was studying this newsgroup. Even though people can preserve the grand narrative simply by ignoring alternative viewpoints, the voices would still be present in the forums (provided the group is unmoderated), thereby exposing all participants to different worldviews.

In addition, scholars and antiracist activists have shown that some efforts at identity politics have gained strength because of the Internet. White supremacist groups, for example, have grown internationally in number and size, recruiting members through the proliferation of Web sites and the distribution of their music on the Internet (Center for New Community 2000). As a result, for example, white supremacist groups are much more organized now than they were even fifteen years ago. As I write this, we are not sure to what extent Internet sites affect people's attitudes about race and racism, nor do we know how they affect people's actions. However, given that the Internet is able to organize some groups so effectively, it is imperative that we continue to examine how racial/ethnic/gender/national identities are formed, maintained, and/or transcended on the Internet, as well as how the Internet will affect race, gender, ethnic, and global relations in general.

Emphasizing the fluidity of identities does not mean that we should not examine the power relationship between the United States and the Philippines. Cultural and economic colonialism are the root of various issues, including the commodification and stereotyping of Filipino women. However, as many feminists of color have stated oppressions are linked, not hierarchical. Thus, we cannot choose between "women's issues" and "anticolonialism," but must address both simultaneously, as well as globalization, and other issues. As Lorde has eloquently stated, "The master's tools" will never dismantle the master's house (1984b, 112). Nor can we dismantle the master's house by remaining silent.

During the height of the "What is Filipino/a?" debates, participants began to dialogue. As we will see in the next chapter, in light of the debates over Filipino identity, they attempted to create an identity using jokes that they believe all Filipinos should understand, but which did not include references to racial, national, or even gendered boundaries. A closer look at these jokes shows that this process and form follows other general classification schemes.

As we have seen throughout this book, the process of stereotyping and social oppression always defines two or more groups of people. Through analyzing the Asiaphile and Whiggie threads, we also learn that oppressions are linked (that is, that race is gendered and gender is raced). Thus, diasporic Filipinos cannot form a community by using the old formula of dichotomizing two cultures or, in general, relying on old categorical concepts for definitional purposes. By analyzing the underlying rhetorical moves within these arguments, we can expose more efficiently the marriage between articulation ("the form of connections that *can* make a unity of two elements") and resistance (Hall 1996). That is, it is easier for us to see (1) which ideologies and ideas work with one another to further oppression, which could tell us (2) how to *dislocate* that articulation, so that we can best resist oppression. In this chapter, we see the oppressive ideologies of Orientalism, patriarchy, colonialism, and sexism upheld by proponents for radical change on the newsgroup. Specifically, their conversations and descriptions of white male/Filipino (Asian) females show the importation of oppressive ideologies in so-called tactics of resistance.

To avoid this trap, we must redefine both "Filipino" and "Kano" (i.e., American) in such a way that they transcend both national and racial boundaries while continuing to examine the power relationship between the United States and the Philippines. I argue that it is very important for scholars to analyze the effects of cultural and economic colonialism so we can understand better various issues, including the commodification and stereotyping of Filipino women.

In the next chapter, we see the participants' efforts to transcend these categories and avoid the traps of essentialization and oppression.

5 | Laughter in the Rain
Jokes as Membership and Resistance

In this forum designed to articulate "what Filipino culture really is and what it is rumored to be," participants of soc.culture.filipino debated hundreds of questions, including the following: Are Filipino values rooted in the Philippines or can they be taught in other parts of the world? Do we want to teach our kids Filipino values? Do we even know what they are? Can Filipinos in the diaspora, especially Filipinos naturalized in the United States, be "as Filipino" as those in the Philippines? Or, did they give up their Filipinoness when they became citizens of another country? If naturalized citizens of the United States lost their Filipinoness, what are Filipino Americans who were born and raised in the United States? Are they more American than their parents? But Kanos are white, aren't they? Does this mean that all Filipino Americans are "whitewashed"? Should all Filipino Americans or all second generation Filipino kids refer to themselves as "born of Filipino parents" as Janet (see chapter 4) did? If so, then what do third or later generation immigrants call themselves?

We've learned that Tagalog isn't really an authentic language, but was created—partially by the Filipinos, but also partially by the Spaniards, a colonial power. Does that mean that the board was right in changing the alphabet to reflect colonial influences? In asserting national pride and independence, shouldn't we try our best to abstract colonial influences? Isn't that one way of getting rid of "colonial

113

mentality"? These questions upset many members of the newsgroup, particularly those who wished to discover or describe an authentic Filipino culture.

In the following sections, I show how jokes were used to ease that pain and simultaneously create a sense of community and, thus, a Filipino group identity.

Mourning and Laughter: Using Closure to Temporarily Deflect Pain

Scholars have shown that humor is often used to ease pain; it is essential to the psychological well-being of people (see Rafael 1997; Mulkay 1998). Mulkay states that jokes offer an "enjoyable release from the restrictions of serious discourse, and also in the sense that it helps them to deal effectively with certain kinds of recurrent interactional difficulty" (1998, 153; see also Alampay 1995).

In the past two decades, Filipinos have had to deal with intense political corruption, martial law, the assassination of a well-loved expatriate (Benigno Aquiño), and the plundering of the country's wealth (the Marcos regime). News of abused overseas contract workers and mail-order brides were made even more apparent with the execution of Flor Contemplacion. Yet with each tragedy a proliferation of jokes erupted.

On the newsgroup, jokes were used as a tool to decrease the tension that arose when various aspects of Filipino identity were debated. Participants used jokes in two ways: to close a heated debate and, more importantly, to determine membership within the Filipino community. When debates about Filipino identity became so profuse that people started questioning the very possibility of attaining a group ethnic identity as well as the unification of Filipinos, jokes were offered to show us that we Filipinos can and do share a common bond with one another.

On many occasions, participants offered jokes to ease their pain from having to debate seemingly endless issues that they felt did not need to be debated in the first place. In addition, they were also used to show us that Filipinos can unify in the face of any disaster. Many participants have argued that using humor to ease the pain is *itself* a "Filipino trait." One participant stated, "Jokes have always been an integral part of the Filipino culture. We are a people who have always been able to laugh at ourselves. This is one of the ways Pinoys are able to face great adversity and hardships. . . . By turning otherwise unfortunate events into something light and funny, we are able to deal with life's hardships easier."

Another participant illustrates the importance of redefining unfortunate events. He recalls that after the assassination of Senator Benigno Aquiño (an expatriate and archenemy of former President Ferdinand Marcos), the collective mood in the Philippines and among members of the Filipino diaspora "became stale . . . one could really feel it. As if the whole heart and soul of the Filipino people just stopped beating, stopped existing. But right after . . . oh well . . . there was a proliferation of Ninoy Aquiño and Rolando Galman (the purported assassin) jokes. . . . Some of which were pretty inane, but some were very sarcastic and true. And funny too."

The pain suffered by members of this newsgroup due to the endless debates seems trivial compared to the above tragedy. But as I stated above, participants believe that "knowing one's culture makes one rich," and dismantling their images of the Filipino culture was confusing and painful. Yet interestingly, many of the most heated debates were temporarily closed through the use of jokes. For example, jokes temporarily ended a debate that centered around the use of *f* in the Philippine language. In this debate, several common beliefs about Tagolog were contested, such as the fact that the traditional Abakada was not wholly constructed by indigenous Filipinos. Thus, those who wanted to ground Filipino identity by finding an authentic Filipino tradition and language lost an important tool. The debate about language incorporated references to assimilation and colonial mentality, two topics that often were geared toward diasporic Filipinos, particularly those in the United States, more than Filipinos back home. Then one day, a participant posted the following: "As long as we fronounce our f's froferly, I think there's no froblem with that."

At this point, the conversation shifted from a heated debate to a lighthearted conversation as subsequent letters revolved completely around this post. Here is an example of the types of replies to this post: "Iksyusmi," "Did yu jas sey 'ep'?? [Did you just say *f*?]," and "Ang 'P' ay ipo-pronawns mo as 'PEE'; ang 'F' naman 'EFF'—Did you get my foint? [You should pronounce 'P' as 'PEE' and 'F' as 'EFF'—Did you get my point?]."

Throughout this interchange, it is obvious that the participants knew the difference between *p* and *f* and knew exactly where *p*'s and *f*'s should be used, and they were careful to pick words that began with *p* or *f* to make this point. The significance of this particular post is in its timing. The context in which the joke is told is very important. For example, the second person's use of "Filipinized" English ("Did yu jas sey 'ep'?") did not cause a stir at all at this point in time because of the fiery debates that had preceded this letter. Since it was told in a context where participants pointed out that Filipinos do know how to speak English "properly," and was posted after a very lengthy debate about whether *f* should be used in the Filipino language, it was only seen as funny. However, when posts using "Filipinized" English were written after the language debate had long since subsided, another intense and hostile debate erupted, this time regarding the arrogance of Filipinos who critique those who transpose *p*'s and *f*'s. What had months earlier united the newsgroup community divided it later.

The transposition of *p*'s and *f*'s is not a completely "innocent" gesture. Instead, I argue, it points to something more significant—the imposition of the Tagalog structure over English. This, in addition to some participants' pride in the "Filipino way" of pronouncing English words, shows subtle forms of resistance against full assimilation to American culture and colonial mentality.

Participants often put naturalized Filipinos in America on the spot because "Filipino" is usually defined against the Filipino/United States dichotomy. Because of this, Filipino Americans occupy a marginal space more than other Filipinos in the diaspora. Furthermore, Rafael (1997) has shown that *balikbayans* (or Filipinos naturalized in the host country who visit the motherland) are viewed with suspicion by Filipinos in the Philippines, as they seem aloof and arrogant, willing to come back home as tourists but not willing to give back to the country. Especially when juxtaposed against the image of overseas contract workers, they are perceived to be only sentimental toward but not really concerned about the homeland.

The "You might be a Filipino if" thread of 1995 was a major thread which began in the midst of debates about Filipino identity, colonial mentality, naturalization, and degrees of Filipinoness. This thread began in April, only three weeks after Flor Contemplacion was executed in Singapore, and as members of soc.culture.filipino and soc.culture.singapore declared a cease-fire on the flame war. A Filipino American began the thread, and although Filipinos from around the world contributed to the thread, a majority of the responses came from Filipinos in the United States. I believe the reason for the Filipino American domination in this thread is not merely because they were greater in number, but rather because much of the discussions revolved around the dubiousness of Filipino Americans' loyalty to the Philippines. Filipino Americans needed to ground their Filipino identity in *something*. Thus, they created this list of jokes.

Jokes as Genre

Jokes are a specific form of "speech genre." Bakhtin (1986) has argued that we should not only study their functions in general, but examine why particular genres are used at a specific point in time. Participants began and continued the "You might be —— if" genre as a tactical move toward unity. The jokes they put forth did not have to be stated within this particular genre. They could have just sent out stand-alone jokes. In fact, from 1995 to 1996, there were several jokes that were sent independently which, if understood, would determine one's membership as a Filipino as well as demarcate different boundaries around the community. Being able to understand most of these jokes would already establish one's membership in the Filipino community, as they usually contained a reference to a Filipino dish, custom, word, historical event, or stereotype. But, the "You might be —— if" genre itself implies that the goal itself is the establishment of membership. It is comprised of a list of characteristics or codes that you must comprehend or perform to fit in. The idea is that if you understand the joke, you affirm your membership as a Filipino. In addition, if most of these characteristics apply to you, then you are Filipino. Therefore, the use of this particular genre ("You might be Filipino if") signals both the need for membership and the need for boundary making.

These lists of jokes were put forth not only to ease pain and create a temporary community, but also to create an identity that addressed the structural relationship between the United States and the Philippines and transcended the American/Filipino dichotomy. This was done not to justify colonial mentality, but to show that the incorporation of colonial words or customs does not necessarily mean that they have sold out. As we will see, the incorporation is often resistive in that it mimics the dominant culture, but is distinctly Filipino. As previously stated, this was needed especially at this time, since the debates were more numerous than in previous years. There was enough divisiveness; now it's time to unite.

In this chapter, I will show that this list of jokes both addressed debates about colonial mentality and transcended the boundaries participants had erected between Filipinos in the Philippines and diasporic

Filipinos, particularly those in the United States. I will also show that
many of these rhetorical moves echo the attempts of other diasporas
to form a strong, united community.

Mimicry, Sly Civility, and the Refusal to Assimilate: Taglish as Resistance

"Sly civility" emphasizes the vulnerability of colonized peoples and focuses on their status as "victims," sly civility
emphasizes their ability to resist assimilation into the dominant culture by intentionally appropriating the colonists' cultural norms
(Bhabha 1994). Therefore, their civility is sly because they do not simply mirror the colonial power's culture, but *mimic* or appropriate colonists' culture, while simultaneously translating it into their own
(Bhabha 1994). They are "almost the same, *but not quite*," a state which
irritates the "teacher" and empowers the "student." Fanon (1967) addresses the argument that learning and speaking the colonizers' language attains colonial mentality (in his words, "becomes whiter"), an
argument echoed by many participants on the newsgroup. He argues,
"To speak means to be in a position to use a certain syntax, to grasp
the morphology of this or that language, but it means above all to assume a culture, to support the weight of a civilization" (Fanon 1967,
17–18). However, mastering the colonizer's language is not completely
disempowering (Bhabha 1994; Smith quoted in Lippard 1990; Rafael
1993). Smith argues that retaining sentence structure and accents of
the "lost" language when speaking the colonizer's language are ways
to retain control of one's identity. Mimicking a language allows colonized people to subvert full assimilation and maintain their culture.

Participants who contributed to the list of jokes showed the sly
civility of Filipinos and their ability to mimic and appropriate the dominant culture. I have divided these jokes into three categories: (1) Taglish,
(2) unique pronunciation, and (3) intentional hybridity.[1] I believe that
this especially served Filipino American members as these jokes show
that incorporating American words and customs does not necessarily
point to colonial mentality (or, as one participant said, "evidence that
[we live in a] 'mental colony'").

Rafael (1995b) has shown that Taglish has the potential to be a
lingua franca for Filipinos in the Philippines. He argued that Taglish
is powerful because it both invokes and *collapses* the hierarchical relationship among English, Spanish, and Tagolog. With respect to the

jokes that the participants told, many highlight the appropriation of American English into the Filipino language. Here are some examples: "You refer to the refrigerator as the 'ref' or 'pridyider' [frigidaire]." "You refer to your VCR as a 'beytamax' [Betamax]." "You refer to season-ings and all other forms of monosodium glutamate as 'Ajinomoto' [Japa-nese influence is established]."

Here we have English words that are given new nicknames ("ref") or new spellings altogether (as in "beytamax" or "pridyider"). The last joke even reflects the incorporation of a Japanese word into Tagalog, invoking Japanese Occupation during World War II. Changing the spell-ing and creating new nicknames make these English (and Japanese) words *Filipino*, and thus in a way reverses the assimilation process and counters accusations of false consciousness and colonial mentality.

Other jokes emphasized a subtle refusal to assimilate through mim-icry. As stated before, mimicry is powerful because being "almost the same, but not quite" points to the failure of teachers, and the silent victory for the subordinate group. The following jokes are examples of mimicry:

> You pronounce F's like P's and P's like F's.
> You say "he" when you mean "she" and vice versa.
> *Bonus question*: You understand this joke (make sure you read
> the punchline with a Filipino accent!): How many bears
> were in the car with Goldilocks?
> Four—the momma bear, the poppa bear, the baby bear, and
> the driver [pronounced "dri-bear"].

As stated before, the *p* versus *f* debate refers to the imposition of English letters on the Tagalog (Abakada) alphabet. The bonus ques-tion refers to the same debate. *v* was not originally part of the Tagalog alphabet, which alludes to the substitution of the *b* sound to the *v* words or syllables. The he/she nondistinction refers to the fact that Tagalog (and other dialects, such as Cebuano) have only one gender-neutral pronoun (*siya*).

Though not militant behaviors, these jokes are resistive because the structure of Tagalog is used even when English is spoken. The speakers, in framing these pronunciations within the "You might be Filipino if" genre, show that Filipinos use these pronunciations or structures not out of ignorance or the inability to speak proper En-glish, but presumably because it is the Filipino way of doing things. In so doing, these jokes are examples of mimicry and how Filipinos have kept their heritage despite colonization and, thus, show how charges of full assimilation, appropriation, and colonial mentality are unfounded.

Unique Pronunciation as Resistance

In a similar vein, some Filipinos on the newsgroup have commented that the particular pronunciation of certain words distinguishes Filipinos from other races and Asian subgroups. This, they argue, should not be a source of shame, but something to celebrate because it sets Filipinos apart from other Asian groups and "Amerikanos" (i.e., white or white-washed Americans). As in the last category, pronouncing English words in a new way is mimicry and resistance, not simply "failed" assimilation. But, it differs from the use of Taglish and jokes, for example:

> If you pronounce "furniture" as "poor-nit-chyur," you might
>   be a Filipino.
> If your plural version of the following words end in "s":
>   jewelry
>   equipment
>   homework
>   furniture
>   then you might be Filipino.
> You are definitely Filipino if the word "Wednesday" has three
>   syllables.
> If you say com-'fort-able instead of 'com-fort-able, then you
>   might be Filipino.

Note that the pronunciation of "furniture" once again alludes to the *p* and *f* debate; the other words, however, are all English. Unlike Taglish, they are not English words that are given new Tagalog spellings (i.e., "jokes" are "dyoks"); each of these words have corresponding Tagalog words. The difference is largely in the pronunciation. Jaune Quick-to-See Smith has argued that although most Native Americans speak English, they retain use of their lost language by using the sentence structure and accents of their languages when speaking English (quoted in Lippard 1990). I argue that the unique pronunciation of the English words listed above is a similar type of resistance against Americanization. These jokes, too, are examples of sly civility and mimicry: English is used, but it is again the "almost the same, but not quite" pronunciation that makes it Filipino. In addition, because they are framed within the "You might be — if" genre, these pronunciations are markers of Filipinoness and understanding the jokes verify one's membership within the community.

Intentional Hybridity

Intentional hybridity—or the creation of new words and new cultural traditions —is the third type of resistance. Here we can see how American things became Filipino:

> You say "comfort room" instead of "bathroom."
> You say "for take out" instead of "to go."
> You "open" or "close" the light.
> You asked for "Colgate" instead of "toothpaste."
> You asked for a "Pentel-pen" or a "ball-pen" instead of just "pen."
> You refer to the refrigerator as the "ref" or "pridyider."
> You own a Mercedes Benz and you call it "chedeng."[2]
> You say "Kodakan" instead of "take a picture."
> You order a "McDonald's" instead of "hamburger" (pronounced ham-boor-jer).
> You say "Cutex" instead of "nail polish."
> You prefer to make acronyms for phrases, such as "OA" for "overacting," or "TNT" for, well, you know.

Using different English words to refer to common objects and places is not unique to Filipinos. But, using this "You might be Filipino if" genre, a person can determine their membership within the community if they either use these phrases or words or if they at least know the significance of these substitutions. As in the section on pronunciations, these English words have been "Filipinized." In the last joke, the reader must know the Filipino definition of the acronym TNT. Though explosive, the definition does not refer to dynamite; instead, it refers to "tago ng tago," or, to put it nicely, a way to extend a friend's visit in your country without wasting government officials' time.

In addition, the use of the product name to refer to common objects reflects Filipino's simultaneous love and hatred of Western products. The proliferation of Western, particularly U.S.-based products in the Philippines serves as a constant reminder of the unequal and codependent U.S./Philippine postcolonial relationship. The love and hatred of their ties to the former colonial power can be found in the language. With the creation of new nicknames, either by using the product's name as a substitute for the common name or by merging the product's name with a Tagalog suffix (i.e., Kodakan), Filipinos have imposed the Tagalog structure over English and thus made these objects distinctly Filipino.

The participants also wanted to show that commonly consumed American items have also been Filipinized: "You put hot dogs in your spaghetti"; "Your Cupboards are full of Spam, Vienna Sausage, Ligo, and Corned Beef, which you refer to as Karne Norte"; "You fry Spam or hot dogs and eat them with rice." As we have seen, one of the major focal points was the appropriation of English words, letters, and phrases into Tagalog. Some have argued that Taglish is a corruption of Tagalog; Teodoro Agoncillo, a nationalist historian, has labeled Taglish a "bastard language" (quoted in Rafael 1995b). The national language, he and other nationalists argue, should incorporate words from the various dialects spoken in the Philippines, not words from the colonizers. The participants who contributed to these jokes, however, did more than just argue that it was okay to use Taglish. Framing these jokes in the "You might be Filipino if" genre, they showed that Filipinos had successfully taken the languages of the colonists, made them Filipino, and so effectively socialized this process that the very *practice* of imposing a Filipino structure on the English language is Filipino. Thus, these jokes, as the other ones, establish membership into the community while demonstrating that intentional hybridity does not necessarily reflect colonial mentality.[3]

Cultural Traits and Artifacts

The jokes in the above section are used to demonstrate that something new is created, not that we are moving toward a homogenous culture. In this section, I show that the participants also asserted that the traditional culture still exists. This move parallels a tactic that members of the Jewish diaspora employ (Boyarin 1994). Boyarin argues that one way for members of the Jewish diaspora to assert their identity is to be practicing Jews in both senses of the term. That is, Jewishness is not only about following the Jewish religion, but about asserting and following what they believe to be cultural traditions. In this way, they are practicing their Jewishness as well as their religion.

Filipinos knowing Tagalog and identifying certain kinds of food and other artifacts are ways to practice Filipinoness. By framing these jokes in the "You might be Filipino if" genre, they magnify the importance of these artifacts and traditions.

Common Language

The first and most obvious way to assess one's Filipinoness is to see if the person can understand bits and pieces of the language. This is not a unique move, as other ethnic groups demonstrate membership using the same tool. For example, Jonathan Boyarin (1994) has argued that speaking and understanding Yiddish allows Jews in the diaspora to practice "thinking in Jewish" and is one avenue they use to articulate their Jewish identity. In addition, some have argued that black English is spoken by many black Americans for the same reason: to strengthen and maintain black identity. One of my African American students explained to my class, "When I speak, I formulate my sentences using black English in my head first before I can articulate myself using English. . . . I have to translate what I'm thinking into English before I say it." The following jokes are an example of this ethnic test. I have placed the translation of the terms in brackets to show that the items that they refer to are rather ordinary. "You bring your baon [boxed lunch] most of the time to work"; "You consider dilis [dried anchovies] the Filipino equivalent to french fries"; "You have a tabo [pitcher] in the bathroom"; "You have two to three pairs of tsinelas [slippers] at your doorstep."

These items could be found in houses occupied by people of any other race and/or ethnicity,[4] but what determines one's membership as a Filipino is the person's ability to translate the terms. In addition, the last two jokes are double coded. The jokes about the *tabo* and the *tsinelas* depend not only on understanding the words, but also on understanding the placement of these items. Having a pitcher in the bathroom and slippers at the doorstep are considered to be Filipino habits, so if you recognize the placement as well as the word, you are definitely Filipino. The tabo in the bathroom is used for personal hygiene. The placement of slippers, of course, is not unique to Filipinos. But the participants' use of the Tagalog word tsinelas makes it Filipino.

Demonstration of behaviors similar to the above shows the continued use of Tagalog and the uniqueness of Filipino artifacts, as the following attests: "You have family member that has a nickname that repeats itself. i.e., 'Deng-Deng,' 'Ling-Ling,' or 'Bing-Bing,' etc."; "You order things like tapsilog, tocilog, or longsilog at restaurants"; "You know how to play pusoy and mah-jong"; "Your other piece of luggage is a Balikbayan box." These jokes refer to items that do not have a corresponding word in English. *Tapsilog, tocilog,* and *longsilog* refer to various kinds of cured meat served with fried rice. They are all contractions of Tagalog words (for example, longsilog refers to *longanisa* [a type of sausage] with *singangag* [fried rice] and *itlog* [eggs]). *Pusoy* and *mah-jong* are games (although they are not limited to the Philippines).

The term *balikbayan* is a little more controversial. Balikbayan boxes are large, standardized cardboard boxes that are used by Filipinos in the United States to carry gifts (*pasalubong*) to their relatives in the Philippines. "Balikbayan" literally means "return to the town (or nation)," and these boxes are significant in that they symbolize the hierarchical relationship between the United States and the Philippines (Rafael 1997). Although, many people of different diasporas routinely return to their homeland to visit, balikbayan connotes more than just a return. Balikbayans are not highly regarded as they appear to flaunt what the United States has and what the Philippines does not have. Balikbayans and those who covet what the balikbayans brought, Rafael states, are often considered to be worse than the colonizers themselves, as they appear to have sold out and betrayed the country (Rafael 1997, 270).

The next two jokes, taken together, reflect stereotypes of balikbayans, those that have colonial mentality and wish to have what the balikbayans have as well as their habits: "You like everything imported or 'state-side'"; "You check the labels on clothes to see where it was made before buying." Yet, despite the negative association with balikbayans, they, the boxes, and their supporters are viewed as strictly Filipino by the Filipinos in the diaspora.

Replacing Words and Knowing Cultural Artifacts
Tagalog References

The next set of jokes refers to the persistent use of Filipino words instead of their English equivalents. Participants show that even though Filipinos know the English counterparts, they continue to use Tagalog words. This continued use of Tagalog by Filipinos signifies the maintenance of Filipino identity: "You say 'Ha?' instead of 'What'"; "You say 'aray' instead of 'ouch'"; "Your sneeze sounds like 'ahh-ching' instead of 'ahh-choo.'"

The next two jokes refer to Filipino brand names. Goldilocks is a confectionery distributor and Jufran and Mafran manufacture banana sauce (Filipino ketchup). "'Goldilocks' means more to you than just a character in a fairytale"; "You gotta have a bottle of Jufran or Mafran handy." Note how these jokes are written. The emphasis is on the capitalized words "Goldilocks," "Jufran," or "Mafran," but unlike many of the other jokes, there is no context that one can use to decipher to what these words may be referring. I argue that the reason these terms are devoid of context (other than "You might be Filipino if") is precisely that if you understand what these terms refer to, you must be Filipino. The word "Goldilocks" should immediately evoke images of *polvoron* (a type of Filipino candy) wrapped in colored plastic wrap with the word "Goldilocks" on each piece. Similarly, the words "Jufran" and "Mafran" should immediately evoke images of ketchup bottles filled with maybe even the taste of the spicy sauce.

Exotifying and De-mystifying Words: On the Power of Connotation

"You think that eating chocolate rice pudding [*samporado*] and dried fish [*dilis*] is a great morning meal"; "You eat purple yam [*ube*] flavored ice cream"; "You think that half-hatched duck eggs [*balot*] are a delicacy"; "You know that 'chocolate meat' is not really made with chocolate."

All of these kinds of food have Tagalog names that are not translated easily into English. What separates this from the above section on the use of Tagalog is the participants' *willingness* to translate these items. Why did they choose to translate these terms? If these terms were left untranslated and one was to explain that they were Tagalog terms, a person would assume automatically that they were Filipino dishes. But that is not as much fun as translating the terms because in leaving the terms untranslated, one cannot show the uniqueness of the food itself. The person just might dismiss the Tagalog word as the translation of a common meal, such as chicken.

The last joke refers to a common description Filipinos use to describe *dinuguan,* a dish made of meat and either beef or pork blood. Filipinos often use this term in front of non-Filipino guests. Is this submission? Not in the way I've seen it used. Toelken (1996) argued that connotation helps form a shared WE; it allows outsiders to stay outsiders. When my friends tell their non-Filipino significant others that dinuguan is "chocolate meat," they do so not only because they want their non-Filipino significant others to try it, but because "it's fun to see their reaction when they find out what it really is. They totally freak!"

Common History

Alluding to a common history is another move used by members of other diasporas (Boyarin 1994; Hall 1990). The imposition of Spanish Catholicism and customs immigration patterns to the United States and the unique agreement between the U.S. military and the Philippine government are all alluded to in the following jokes:

> *Resistance to Colonialism:* "You have a 'Weapons of Moroland' shield hanging in the living room wall."
>
> *The Spanish Influence:* "You hang a Rosary on your car's rear view mirror. You have a shrine of the Santo Ninyo in your living room. You were raised to believe that every Filipino is an aunt, uncle, or cousin."
>
> *U.S.-Philippine Military Bases Agreement of 1947:* "Your dad was in the Navy." "You have a family member or relative that works in the Post Office."
>
> *Establishment of American Medical Schools in the Philippines and the 1965 Immigration Act:* "Your mom or sister or wife is a nurse."

Although the above historical events are not referred to explicitly in these posts, the similarity of household decorations and experiences is now open for question. If participants answer "yes" to these jokes, the next step would be to ask "why." This could potentially open up an entirely different discussion on the "common history" of Filipinos. Although this did not occur as the jokes were posted, the common history and this list of jokes were alluded to in a discussion about Filipino "roots" a few months after the "You might be a Filipino if" thread began. In a debate about finding Filipino roots, Rick, a Filipino American, argued that although Filipinos are diverse and Filipino identity is emerging, they have a common history that links them all as Filipinos. He twice refers to the "You might be Filipino if" jokes as proof that there are many characteristics that "run through nearly all pinoys."

Essentializing and Abstracting

The use of language, artifacts, and common history in these jokes paralleled the topics of the debates discussed on the newsgroup. Filipinized American English showed that cultural traits continue despite the Westernization of the Philippines, and they began a discussion on how Filipinos around the world are affected by common history, two moves that other diasporas have made (Boyarin 1994; Gilroy 1993; Hall 1990). In this sense, they attempted to transcend problems such as dichotomizing nations and cultures, issues that were commonly debated. As we will see, some issues were not addressed at all, particularly the discussions on values and gender. It seems as if the participants felt that these issues could be transcended by *not* addressing them and instead offering new traits upon which to focus.

Essentializing Behavior

In the effort to assert Filipino identity, participants also named behavior that either applies only to a certain set of Filipinos or to anyone. This is a common problem with classifying (Bowker and Star 2000). In attempting to establish criteria to classify people or things, particularities are either overemphasized or are abstracted so much so that the prerequisite means nothing. In this section, I give examples of those two problems.

> You have to kiss your relative on the cheek as soon as you enter the room.
> You consistently arrive thirty minutes late for all events.
> You point with your lips.
> You nod upwards to greet someone.
> You eat using your hands—and have it down to a technique.
> You go to a department store and try to bargain the prices.

None of these behaviors were contested at the time they were posted probably because they were a welcome alternative to the flame wars that dominated the newsgroup. Many of the respondents welcomed these references as evidence of the unique behavior of Filipinos. However, taken outside the context, some of these behaviors were characterized as "crass" or particular to a certain class or region. A few weeks after the jokes were posted on the Internet, the *Philippine News*, a Filipino American newspaper, addressed the jokes and condemned the participants who contributed to it for belittling Filipinos.

Interestingly, class and regional divisions are considered to be major schisms within the Filipino community at home and abroad (see Bonus 1997 and Espiritu 1995 for examples). However, on this newsgroup, although the participants talked about regional and class difference on the newsgroup, these discussions did not last very long or turn into fiery debates. So, addressing Filipino behaviors that were particular to a certain class or region was not problematic. In other words, at this point in time, in this context, newsgroup members ignored a schism deemed so important in "real life."

Abstractions: Common Behaviors, Material Possessions, and 1970s/Kitschy Artifacts

The following characteristics are behaviors and references to things that anyone of any gender, race, or ethnicity could perform or own. When classifying, sometimes particularities are abstracted so much that the characteristics are too general. Based on the jokes below, many people who had never known they were Filipino could actually be Filipino.

Some participants listed various behaviors that were supposed to indicate whether one was Filipino of not. As we can see, some of the behaviors that were listed could apply to anyone else: "You scratch your head when you don't know the answer." "You like bowling." "You hang your clothes out to dry." "You order a 'soft drink' instead of a 'soda.'"

Here, claiming that certain behaviors distinguish people from certain cultures is not the issue. In the section entitled "Essentializing Behavior," I described various behaviors that the participants acknowledged and appropriated as distinctly Filipino actions. What separates the above list of behaviors from the ones described in "Essentializing Behavior" is that they can be immediately recognized by anyone of any race or ethnicity. That is, they are commonly performed by members of various races and ethnicities, so attributing them to Filipinos is puzzling.

Similarly, claiming that Filipinos own certain possessions is not a new move. In many of the sections above, I have shown that knowing and owning various cultural artifacts indicates membership in the Filipino community. But as in the section on behaviors, some of the artifacts are owned by members of all races and ethnicities: "You own a Karaoke System." "You own a piano that no one ever plays." "You have a rose garden." "You have an air freshener in your car." Again, this list contains references to articles that are not uniquely Filipino. The most interesting abstraction, however, is some participants' claims that Filipinos own 1970s artifacts.

This next section was somewhat surprising, but funny, in that it reminded me of my childhood. Many of the jokes that participants listed contained references to 1970s cultural artifacts and/or kitschy things and behaviors that people of various races and ethnicities in the United States own or do: "You own a 'barrel man' (you pull up the barrel and you see something that looks familiar. schwing)." "You own one of those fiber optic flower lamps." "You own a lamp with the oil that drips down the strings." "You have plastic runners to cover the carpets in your house." "Your car horn can make 2 or 3 different sounds." "Your car has curb feelers or curb detectors."

The reference to the barrel man was especially funny because it reminded me of hanging out with my friends at Spencer's, a store at the local mall. As curious eight-year-olds, we had fun playing with this artifact (until, of course, one of our parents yanked us out of the store). In addition, the reference to the car horn reminded me of the Dukes of Hazzard car which played the first twelve notes of Dixieland when pressed. Thus, this list evoked memories of my childhood rather than images of Filipinos in my community. Although funny, these articles and behaviors, like the other lists in this section, are owned and performed by members of different races and ethnicities in the United States and possibly other places in the world. Given that more than half of the Filipinos in the United States immigrated in the 1970s and that many of the participants on the newsgroup are first-, 1.5-, or second-generation Filipinos, this list may, in fact, reflect their Filipino immigration and consumption patterns after the passage of the 1965 Hart Cellar Act.

The emergence of these lists is not surprising, however, given that the participants generated this list at a time when Filipino identity was highly contested. Since "Filipina," cultural values, the degree of Filipinoness, and language were all being debated, the participants wanted to steer away from characteristics that alluded to these hotly debated issues. As we have seen, many of the jokes attempted to transcend racial and national dichotomies. The sections on appropriating English words into Filipino culture addressed the Filipino/American dichotomy head on. However, when classifying, particularities were often ignored or abstracted. In trying to keep this thread light, many participants contributed jokes that were so race-, gender-, culture-free that they could apply to anyone. The result was the above list of behaviors and artifacts. As expected, at the time the jokes were posted, no one disputed the characteristics. Rather, they were a welcome diversion from the plethora of debates that dominated the newsgroup at the time. However, months later, this list of jokes was reproduced outside the newsgroup in a Filipino American newspaper and on a Filipino American's Web page. I discuss the different receptions of these jokes in the different contexts below.

Determining the Degree of Filipinoness

Because these defining characteristics were put forth as jokes, they were viewed as non-threatening, and at the time rarely offended any of the participants. Being a Filipino American myself, I thoroughly enjoyed the thread and printed out some of the jokes so I could share them with my family. However, it is important to note that these jokes were not considered to be controversial at that particular point in time because they were put forth by self-defined Filipinos and because they were created at a time when the number of debates about Filipino identity and discussions of Filipino nationalism (with respect to the Flor Contemplacion tragedy) were at an all-time high. If the jokes were created by non-Filipinos or in a different context, it is likely that the participants on the newsgroup would have considered the jokes demeaning (see Lippard 1990 on the politics of naming). In fact, when a self-defined white American male recently posted a thread entitled "You know you're married to a Filipina" (see Appendix B) a year later, he was burnt to a crisp by the flames largely because of his position of power. In contrast, when a Filipino American male posted the same list a few weeks later, only one participant objected and his objection was politely worded.

This list of jokes temporarily diverted the participants' attention away from the Flor Contemplacion execution, the debates about colonial mentality, the daily problems overseas contract workers face, and the "loss" of Filipino women (and Asian women in general) to white males. In this newsgroup, the game was just to add to the jokes. However, a few months later the list of jokes was actually turned into a quiz that people could take to determine their "Filipinoness." Points were accorded as follows: "3 points if you can relate to the following characteristics yourself; 2 points if it relates to an immediate family member, i.e., mom or dad or sister/brother; 1 point if you know of someone who has the characteristic." At the end, people were to tally their points to see to which category they belonged:

259–327 points: Welcome to America! Judging from your high score, you are obviously transplant from the Philippines.

There is no doubt what your ethnic identity is! You're Filipino, through and through.

173–258 points: Congratulations, you've retained most of Filipino traits and tendencies your family has instilled in you.

172–51: You have OFT (Obvious Filipino Tendencies.) Go with
the flow to reach full Filipino potential. Prepare for assimilation; resistance is futile!

50 and under: You're white, aren't you?

An interesting move was made here. The jokes, taken out of context, were no longer used as a way for Filipinos in the United States
to assert their Filipinoness. Instead, they were taken as Filipino traits
and used to separate Filipinos from whites. In other words, the quiz
was no longer about *asserting* but *assessing* Filipino identity. And, if
you don't have any characteristics, watch out—you might by white
(washed).

In sum, when the list of jokes was taken out of the context in which
it was generated and made into a "quiz," the way the jokes were *used*
changed. This emphasizes the importance of context in understanding the debates in the newsgroup. When the list of jokes was posted
originally, many participants attempted to bridge the Filipino/Ameri-
can gap, hence the proliferation of references to Filipinized English.
However, by the time the jokes turned into the quiz, the gap between
Filipino and American and the conflation of Filipino and white was
once again in the forefront of the debates. As a result, although some
of the participants believed the list of jokes showed the common root
of all Filipinos, it may be of limited use in other contexts.

Conclusion

When this list of jokes was generated, none who
read the newsgroup publicly disputed anything on it. Instead, most
of the responses were positive. The most active participants on the
newsgroup did not publicly complain about the jokes (although some
of the jokes could be interpreted as self-deprecating) because they were
aware that the jokes started to appear at a time when there were numerous debates and arguments concerning the definition of a Filipino.
Instead, this list of jokes represented a new way of characterizing Filipinos that did not depend on a physical link to the "homeland," nor
on the articulation of rigid, "authentic" Filipino cultural values.

However, to those who did not participate in the newsgroup, this list of jokes may have been interpreted less favorably. When someone from the *Philippine News* (a Filipino American newspaper) read the list, he was prompted to denounce the list of jokes as "self-deprecating" and hurtful to the Filipino community. According to Lippard (1990), this is not uncommon. She states that because cultural artifacts (including jokes) are "shared (exhibited), experienced, and relinquished" (Saar quoted in Lippard 1990), they are bound to be interpreted differently from how the artist intended. Thus, the section on "essential" Filipino behaviors may be interpreted by Filipinos outside the newsgroup as badly representing Filipino culture. In this way, the list may not have been as liberating as its proponents hoped it would be.

Of course, whether it is liberating or not depends not only on the context but also on the individuals who read it. And, within the context of this newsgroup, this particular thread provided a positive atmosphere and the promise of unity within diversity.

More importantly, this discussion points to a phenomenon that Internet meeting places can offer that local meeting places cannot—the ability for sustained and efficient dialogue about local and global phenomena, and the possibility for a transnational community among multiple members of a diaspora. It is one thing to learn about local and global social, economic, and political issues and their effects on diasporic members. It is another to experience through sustained communication and fierce debates how seemingly remote and theoretical issues affect us and those with whom we wish to form a community and our relationship with these people. The reason for the turn to jokes occurred because the participants were forced to situate themselves and their local problems within the context of larger, global patterns. Filipino American participants, in particular, had problems reconciling their ideas about race, gender, colonialism, citizenship, nationalism, and the rigidity and authenticity of cultural boundaries. Additionally, the attempt to define authenticity showed them that traditional boundary making and adjudicating membership based on these traditional categories is a problem. These sustained discussions made the participants (including myself) experience and discover for themselves the power and fallibility of social construction. Even though we never articulated it as such, we saw many of our notions of ourselves and Filipinoness crumble with each debate and flame war.

But, simultaneously, we embraced the idea of being able to define ourselves. In many ways, even despite the tallying of points at the end of the thread, these jokes represent much more than just membership boundaries. They show us alternative ways of thinking about culture—as an active articulation and enfolding of issues that pertain to ourselves and others in the diaspora. Through these jokes we learned how members of the diaspora turned (albeit temporarily) the impact of colonialism and globalization on its head through the introduction and frequent use of new words, like "chedeng." Though not structurally changing the position of the Philippines and Filipinos in relation to the world, this linguistic turn places Filipinos at the center of cultural creation instead of merely passively taking in outside influences.

Much like hip-hop culture did, the use of Taglish and new words offers a distinct inside joke for membership. Once commodified, of course, the participants do have a choice whether to bury the word (as the word "def" was literally buried by Rick Rubin, the co-founder of Def Jam records and father figure of hip-hop since it entered Webster's dictionary in the early 1990s).

It may have been possible for this list of jokes to proliferate and become widespread through more traditional means; indeed, this list of jokes was eventually printed in various Filipino newspapers and eventually published in a book (Santa Romana-Cruz 1997). The significance of this list is that it emerged during some very heated debates which were turning our notions of race, gender, ethnicity, culture, and even nation on its head. We began to realize the fragility of these concepts and how global economic, political, and social issues affected us simultaneously yet differently as Filipinos living in different area around the world. It was through this medium, this particular exchange and its proceeding discussions about unity, that we were able to witness the beginnings of transnational community-building, a phenomena often theorized, but rarely seen.

6 | E Pluribus or E Pluribus Unum?

Can There Be Unity in Diversity?

The jokes that I analyzed in the previous chapter temporarily quelled the debates on soc.culture. filipino. However, because real life goes on and because new people drop into the newsgroup all the time, the debates started again only a few weeks after the last jokes were posted. This does not mean that the list of jokes did not have some impact on the participants, however. For the rest of my stay at soc.culture.filipino, whenever someone lamented that Filipinos were too divisive and could not form a unified front, participants would refer to the "You might be Filipino if" jokes.

But questions of unity and diversity continued. One of these debates parallels scholarly debates on identity politics and the politics of identity (Rajchman 1995). In particular, the debate on identity concerns the "death of the Subject" (Laclau 1995). Some scholars, in acknowledging the constructedness of traditional social groups like "gender," "race," "nation," and "culture," have proclaimed the death of the Subject. However, their opponents contend that celebrating the death of the subject is dangerous, as it calls for a suppression of subjects' voices and thus perpetuates the status quo (Benhabib 1989). Instead, scholars and activists must acknowledge that, although these entities are constructed and although there are multiple identities within a group, identity matters. Therefore, as long as people of certain groups are marginalized, scholars and activists must continue to theorize and refer to identities (Hall 1996).

How we describe identity, however, is much debated. Some want to refer to a common history to find out who we are and where we came from (San Juan 1992). However, others argue that we should study how history, language, and culture affect the "process of becoming, not of being" (Hall 1996; see also Gilroy 1993). That is, we should study history to examine how we have been represented so we can better decide how we want to represent ourselves in the future. I will refer to this particular strand of the scholarly debate on identity as I analyze the debate that participants on soc.culture.filipino had about Filipino identity. In this exchange, this first participant (prsn) responds to a Filipino American's request for information about his "roots":

> What roots??
> To make a long story short, a Philippines does not have a single root. The country was essentially a bunch of tribes in different regions before the Muslims exerted their influence. Then came the Spanish. Then came the Americans. So there was no single "Philippine Culture" before colonial influence. So divided among those lines. The North is very different culturally from the South. Then on each island, one must consider the smaller regionalistic differences. The Philippines is much like an onion. Lots of layers, but when you peel them all away, there is no single core.

By pointing out that, prior to Muslim, Spanish, and American influence, the Philippines was comprised of many tribes, this participant indirectly addresses the fact that nations are constructed. To solidify this, the poster refers to the regional divisions to which Filipinos still adhere. Almirol has found that Filipinos are Tagalog, Ilocano, and Bisayan in an "all Filipino audience"; and Filipinos only "act as Filipinos" when they have to define themselves to non-Filipinos (1985, 241). While this is not the only type of diversity found in the Filipino community, it is one that diasporic Filipinos acknowledge as very real and potentially debilitating. This participant appears to lament the lack of roots and the tremendous diversity of Filipino identity. Because of various colonial influences and regional differences, the poster argues, it is impossible to find an authentic Filipino culture. The participant alludes to scholars' proclamation of the "death of the Subject" when declaring that Filipino identity has "lots of layers, but when you peel them away there is no single core."

Rick, another regular Filipino American, concurs, yet he states that it is possible to find unity in diversity: "While it is indeed true that the Philippine population is quite diverse and there are many regionalistic differences and languages . . . There is a thread that binds them all. There are many things that have become common amongst all Filipinos . . . or did you miss that 'You might be a Filipino if' thread— true that thread was intended to be humorous, but it listed behaviors, beliefs, etc., that runs through nearly all Pinoys."

Rick invokes the "You might be Filipino if" thread discussed in chapter 5. While he agrees that there is much diversity within the Filipino community, he argues that a unique Filipino culture (which is somewhat reflected in the list of jokes) has emerged despite colonial influences and regionalistic differences. This echoes Hall's (1990, 1996) argument that identities are constantly shifting and being reconstructed. Rick argues this point more forcefully here:

> And while you may be right about "there was not single Philippine culture," there IS one that has emerged in the modern day and though it may still be an evolving one, it is a cultural thread that runs through all kinds of Pinoy, no matter what region they're from or what dialect they speak.
>
> Diversity is not a lack of roots MR/MS/whatever prsn, diversity itself can be the roots.

This last comment about "diversity being the root" parallels Hall's (1990) definition of diasporic identity. Hall states that membership in diaspora entails recognizing the diversity of an identity and that identity is *characterized* by hybridity and difference. By claiming that diversity is the root and by emphasizing the emergence of a Filipino identity, Rick echoes Hall (1990), Gupta and Ferguson (1997), Radhakrishnan (1996), and other scholars' arguments that scholars and activists must acknowledge that difference *itself* is constructed. Yet as we will see, Rick roots this diversity only in the past, a move that Hall cautions against. But first, here is a debate between "prsn" (his points are marked by sideways carets) and Rick about whether "diversity can be the roots":

> Diversity in terms of numerous languages and regional loyalty can be a root, but it is not a very strong one.

Diversity is where it starts, like the multiple roots of a tree, but then among this diversity are things in common, things going in the same general direction, just as the many roots of a tree later unite at some point to form the trunk. The diversity you've been seeing prsn are merely the many different "branches" of the Filipino people. But if you trace these branches down you will see a common origin, a common history, common experiences, common beliefs, common behaviors, common struggles.

Prsn's doubt in the argument that "diversity" can be a root is similar to some scholars' belief that plurality can only lead to divisiveness and disorganization (see, for example, Ravitch 1993). But Rick again argues that we must simultaneously address the differences and similarities. His tree metaphor, although flawed, gives the readers a visual picture of how he believes a Filipino culture has emerged. The roots represent regional and tribal differences, which through our common history (i.e., colonialism) have turned into a trunk. The branches, he argues, represent Filipino individuals, but when it comes down to it, we still have all these commonalities.

> If there is any common thread that binds all Pinoys, then what is it? The Catholic religion? Not quite, because that is not solely a Philippine characteristic.

That is merely one commonality in Pinoys. It is one strand on the common thread that binds us. The religion may be foreign origin, but we "have" made it own and Filipinized it. And in a way it is a unique characteristic since we're the only country in Asia that is predominantly catholic.

And if you really wanna argue on this point about something not being a common thread because it is not unique to one country or it is of foreign origin . . . let the debates begin.

In claiming that Filipinos "Filipinized" Catholicism, Rick states that colonized peoples are not forever victims and that the incorporation of colonial traditions does not necessarily point to "assimilation" or colonial mentality. As with incorporation of English words and American traditions that were discussed in chapter 3, Filipinized Catholicism points to the ability of Filipinos to resist the dominant culture and empower themselves (Rafael 1993). Mimicry is empowering. Rick continues:

[W]e Filipinos made [Catholicism] our own, added a distinct
Filipino flavor to it, intertwined it with our culture. So now
it acts as one of the binding threads or one of the strands of
the binding thread that unites my people.

The participant then challenges Rick to name unique traits that
most Filipinos share:

> What trait(s) do all Pinoys have that is uniquely theirs
that can be shared with most (or all) Filipinos? My point is
that every a citizen of a country should be able to point to
something in their culture or history that makes them UNIQUE.

Unless this can be established, he says, we cannot claim to have
a Filipino culture. His desire for "uniqueness" reflects the desire of
many ethnic groups for "authenticity." As Hall (1990) argues, one way
people try to define cultural identity is by looking for that unique core,
an essence that members of the group can grasp, point to, and claim
as their own. Diversity is seen as a weakness, a sign that the authentic culture is lost forever. Yet because cultures and differences are created (Gupta and Ferguson 1997; Hall 1990), finding an authentic
essence is an impossible task. What now? Rick answers, "You have
the answer to your question right there in your statement. 'History'—
every country has its own unique history. A common history or heritage is one of the things that makes a group of people a 'race' a nation.'"

Rick roots Filipino identity in a country's history, a move that many
Filipino studies scholars stress. However, Hall (1990) warns against
rooting identity only in the past. Instead, he states that we must see
how current history and power relations contribute to the formation
of cultural identities. Again, differences should not be treated as an
end point because differences have been used to create and maintain
unequal power relations. As Trinh Minh-ha states:

They? Yes, they. But, in the colonial periphery (as in elsewhere), we are often them as well. Colored skins, white masks;
colored masks, white skins. Reversal strategies have reigned
for some time. *They* accept the margins; so do we. For without the margin, there is no center, no heart. . . . The margins,
our sites of survival, become our fighting grounds and their
site for pilgrimage. Thus, while we turn around and reclaim
them as our exclusive territory, they happily approve, for the
division between margin and center should be preserved, and

as clearly demarcated as possible, if the two positions are to return intact in the power relations. Without a certain work of displacement, again, the margins can easily recomfort the center in its goodwill and liberalism; strategies of reversal thereby meet with their own limits. (1991, 16–17)

Rick then refers to the "You might be Filipino if" list to strengthen his argument that Filipinos do have a unique identity and roots: "I leave it to the other Filipinos here to list the other things that make us unique. (Someone 'please' repost that 'You must be a Filipino if' thread!)."

Thus, the list of jokes that I analyzed in chapter 5 was effective not only during the time they were posted, but a few weeks afterwards. Unlike the soc.culture.filipino FAQ (which was last updated in August 1994, eight months before I began my research), it continues to have some staying power partially because it serves to unite the participants on the newsgroup. While flawed, the generation of this list of jokes is evidence of the creation of a common identity. As I stated above, the list of jokes is on numerous Web sites and has recently been turned into a book. As we will see, the characteristics on the "You might be Filipino if" list have been and are continually debated, but for a little while on the newsgroup some of the participants embraced everything on the list, as it reified Filipino identity.

Filipino American: Conclusions and Implications of Studying Filipinoness in Cyberspace
Building Diaspora: Reexamining the Foundations of Diaspora

In this book, I examined how technology affects the construction of national, racial, ethnic, and even gendered identities. Through the utilization of participant observation and the method of instances, I was able to examine how national, racial, and ethnic identity was articulated, reified, and re-created within the soc.culture.filipino newsgroup on the Internet.

Through an extensive analysis of several debates, I witnessed community and identity formation of a diaspora in relation to various political and polemical arguments—mainly neocolonialism, Eurocentrism, Orientalism, and patriarchy. This was important because I was able to see the participants anchor their identity on experiences and cultural artifacts created by past and present socio-historical events, after the attempt to articulate an authentic experience or culture failed. In doing so, I was able to watch participants rearticulate their ideas of community building and witness identity construction which was, as Stuart Hall (1996) described it could be, "subject to the continual play of history, culture, and power."

I do not believe that discussions about identity, culture, or community in other ethnic groups or even within Filipino communities would necessarily be debated in exactly the same way. However, I do believe that this transnational space, the Internet, gives rise to the possibility that images, experiences, political viewpoints, and historical knowledge will come to a head whenever participants wish to construct diasporic identity. And, in doing so, we experience the tenuousness of even the foundational characteristic of diaspora—the idea that there are authentic, unchanging values, images, norms, and behaviors within the homeland that people could run to and hold onto.

In soc.culture.filipino, we saw that real life clashes with both imagined life and virtual life. For example, in chapter 3, we saw that participants from all locations brought images of America, the Philippines, American life and culture, and Philippine life and culture into the discussion. However, those who lived in the United States and those who lived in the Philippines had to negotiate these images, as the colonial relationship between the two countries ended up shaping the conversations. The debate between Norma and Jhun about whether the Philippines has a booming economy was a good example of this. Norma, a 1.5-generation Filipino immigrant to the United States, had to rearticulate and defend her relation to the Philippines and the United States when responding to Jhun. She summoned both her experiences and images of the Philippines to establish her expertise and membership in the Filipino community when responding to Jhun. But, since she lived in the United States (i.e., the colonial power), Jhun was able to undermine Norma's authority. In other words, Jhun and others depended largely on physical location, their images of these locations, and, more importantly, the historical relationship between their two locations (the United States and the Philippines) to argue that they had more authority regarding Filipinos and Filipino identity.

When images of locations were no longer sufficient, images of dichotomous cultures were used to establish who the real members were. This was articulated throughout chapters 3, 4, and 5 via discussions about the authentic language and what characterizes real Filipinos.

While trying to uncover natural differences between cultures, or, more broadly, the East and the West, some tried to bring in their experiences to make their points. However, because experiences are also constructed by prevailing discourses (Scott 1995), in this case, fears of American cultural hegemony and a distrust of the former colonial power ran through all the discussions. And because prolonged discussions about various topics inevitably led back to this desire to build a Filipino versus American dichotomy, the participants were eventually able to reassess the meanings of experiences and link them to local and global histories in this transnational location.

The most painful lesson I learned when studying this newsgroup was that asserting a strong Filipino identity by perpetuating existing dichotomies only marginalized people in the diaspora. In chapter 4, I showed that since "Filipina" was used as a gender marker between the United States (the neocolonial state) and the Philippines, Filipinas, particularly those in the "wrong" location (the United States) were further marginalized.

I had initially thought that women's individualism was only frowned upon in our community. For example, the emphasis on cultural values and Filipina characteristics is very strong. My thirty-five-year-old cousin, a woman who immigrated to the United States when she was ten, and I are constantly told that we are "Kano" when we raise our voices and place individualism over family. Bernie rarely ventures out with her husband. When she explains, "I'm just married to the guy. I'm not attached to him!" someone inevitably remarks, "Ay! Talagang Kano ka na [Oh! You really are American now]." Although her brother says and does the same thing, he is always "talagang Pilipino" (truly Filipino). My friends and I used to joke: "All of our parents were friends, ya know. They all drink the same water. It's gotta be in the water. We gotta write the DuPage County water department about this." But, when I went to college and heard similar stories from Filipino women here, I knew it was a bigger problem. *It's gotta be the water in the State of Illinois. . . . We gotta write the Governor of Illinois.*

But in the newsgroup, I learned that Filipino women everywhere are expected to be passive and that this expectation was held not only by non-Filipinos, but male and female Filipinos as well. I could no longer blame the water (sigh). Many women of different races and ethnicities have written about not being allowed to "talk back" (hooks 1994; Anzaldúa 1987); so, is this "just a gender thing"? Perhaps this is a commonality that many women share. But although this may be a commonality, I argue that the difference is how talking back is *articulated* by certain members of the Filipino community that I grew up around and within the newsgroup I studied. Their objections to women—particularly Filipino *American* women—"talking back" contains elements of their rejection of colonial mentality as well as notions of authentic cultures and stereotypical images of race and gender. It is not only disrespectful to one's elders, it is too individualistic, a sign of not acting like a "real Filipina," a sign of assimilation, of rejecting the Filipino culture, and of being American.

As a Filipino woman in the United States of America, I felt I was thrust into liminal space in this virtual homeland. Once again, I was not at the center. I can only imagine how interracial Filipino Americans (especially those who have a white parent) felt when they read these threads. This prompted me to learn more about the construction of the "Filipino woman" and its uses, a project that I intend to address in the future.

Despite the difficulty of reading and participating in some of these debates, in some instances the participants and I were able to keep our sense of humor. It is through humor that participants attempted to transcend traditional boundaried groups, such as race, gender, nation, and culture. With these jokes, participants were able to imagine a different, hybrid Filipino, one who rearticulates culture and uses this rearticulation as resistance. Instead of dichotomizing Filipino and American cultures, they attempted to collapse the hierarchy into syncretized, but strictly Filipino language and customs. Perhaps scholars should examine all cultural artifacts and language the same way. Maybe then we will learn that our goal should not be merely articulating differences, but recognizing similarity and examining the construction—and uses—of difference.

By examining cultural artifacts and language more closely, we could see that the participants simultaneously articulated hybridity and Filipinoness. It is through these jokes that I saw concrete instances of sly civility and mimicry which characterize colonized and/or oppressed communities. It is also through these jokes that participants were able to articulate that "diversity is the root" of Filipino identity. This hybridity may not appear to be empowering in some sociologists' view, because they say it still doesn't erase the hierarchical structure of cultures nor challenge the economic, political, or economic hegemony of the United States. But in these Filipinos' view at the time they wrote the list of jokes, taking control of the language and being able to turn things around like they did was empowering and not just in a tragic sense. It shows us, just like Bhabha (1992, 1994) and Rafael (1993) said, that they have never completely assimilated, that they are not completely colonized, that they have all along just mimicked the colonial power.

Technology, Authority, and the Promise of Blurring Boundaries

While the diffusion of scholarly articles or books pertaining to one's cultural identity helps many ethnic organizations organize their local community members, it appears to be more difficult to use discussions or sources created and posted on Internet newsgroups to help define an ethnic identity and community for two main reasons: decentralization and the authority of paper.

The Internet does offer participants an efficient, decentralized space which has the potential to allow everyone to join in discussions about various social issues, including ethnic identity and community. However, in the offline world authority is established not only through centralized, hierarchical, peer-reviewed structures, but also through the existence of words *printed on paper*. Though some communities—particularly various political and/or cultural organizations—are becoming more comfortable with the authority of Web sites,[1] the intangibility of digital text and the decentralized nature of newsgroups and/or interactive Web sites is still seen as ephemeral and—due to the increased nature of flaming by anonymous posters—sometimes suspect.

But even though there were these problems, I still maintain that researchers interested in computer-mediated communication and postcolonial studies should continue to do sustained ethnographies on Internet communities. One of the main reasons to do so—particularly for postcolonial, transnational, and/or diaspora scholars—is because one can simultaneously study the effects of local and global politics (like global and local racial classifications) on diasporic members' characterization of ethnic, racial, national, or even gender identity. And, significantly, there is the possibility to study—and, more importantly, show—any efforts at new diasporic identity formations that are based on underlying histories that reflect local and global politics. That is, the process of categorization, whether by race, ethnicity, culture, gender, and/or a combination of all concepts, is based on common sociopolitical issues. In uncovering—and publishing widely—these patterns and underlying histories, there is the possibility that members of different diasporas would recognize the positive and negative effects of common sociopolitical issues upon them. It is my hope that as a result of seeing the impact of these common oppressive practices on members of the Filipino diaspora, people of all races and ethnicities will see and want to continue to research the commonalities each community faces, instead of just focusing on the differences between them.

The next step for all of us, however, is systematically studying how online relationships and conversations regarding all these issues affects people's offline choices and view of the world. Participating in various discussions within this "virtual homeland" and seeing how relatively quickly the participants moved from trying to establish ideas of "authenticity" to talking about the effects of local and global sociopolitical issues on Filipinos around the world gave me hope that this new technology could be used to make some positive changes in the world. It is true that, even now, ten years after I first began this research, we still need to address the national and global "digital divide" (and the globalization policies which exacerbate this divide) which, unfortunately, is leaving many behind by sustaining educational and economic inequality.[2] After all, as one Web master critical of the utopian idea that Internet technology can bring the world closer together stated, "youcantsendbreadasattachments.com." However, even in this study, I was able to see that computer-mediated communication can help members of a diaspora better understand their post- or neocolonial situation, which enables them to use the Internet as a possible site for community formation and broader social or political organizing efforts. This, in addition to the knowledge that Filipinos were able to gather nearly a half million people to an organized protest via phone texting, and on a global level, being able to witness largely successful anti-war organizing efforts via the Internet, is evidence of the perpendicular spaces of offline and online worlds.

In addition, we should also systematically examine not just the disjuncture between these worlds or simply the effects of one world on the other, but the simultaneous transformations of each world and even between the worlds. While this seems small, the transformation of "emoticons" (i.e., a series of keyed characters used in e-mail to indicate an emotion, such as happiness [:-)] or sadness [:-(]) is an example of how the online world changes due to offline needs (i.e., the need to emote while casually conversing with others) and how the offline world changes due to online behaviors (i.e., the word "emoticon" is now in Webster's dictionary, and computer programmers around the world are constructing new animated smiley faces people can use in various instant messaging and/or e-mail programs). With respect to postcoloniality, race, gender, and other issues, it would be very interesting to systematically document the effects of the conversations people have online and off as participants uncover their common histories and discover the divisiveness that ensues when people are ghettoized by essentialist and static notions of race, culture, gender, and even diaspora.

From Oprah to Mills: Reclaiming "The Personal Is Political"and Putting It to Use

Canadian citizenship notwithstanding, through the course of researching and writing this book, I have struggled with, created, and re-created my identity, not only as a Filipino *American* woman but as a scholar, feminist, and even as the girlfriend of a white American male. At the beginning of this book, I showed that growing up with Filipino immigrants taught me that Filipino identity is not stable, but always changing depending on context. When writing the first two chapters on the material effects of the colonial relationship between the United States and the Philippines, I could not help but exorcise the ghosts of my own relationship with the Filipino American community in the Chicago area. The struggles other Filipino Americans in my community and I face mirror the struggles in the newsgroup.

Since I was so confused about what Filipino meant (and people in my community knew it), it was puzzling to many people in my community why I would choose to write about Filipinos. After a while, they calmed down, saying, "It's all 'book oriented'; it's not really about being Filipino." I cannot say that this is completely untrue, I often did draw upon theory particularly when I felt self-conscious of the fact that I had to de-authenticate and de-Filipinize characteristics which everyone else in the newsgroup believed to be authentic. But, while drawing comparisons between patterns of responses to colonialism, racism, sexism, and other oppressions can be comforting (in that they forced me to think of Filipinos and Filipinoness as a subject), this does not mean that there was no pain involved.

When researching and writing this book, I read the debates as a scholar and a person of Filipino descent. I thought about the various occasions in which these debates occurred in my "real life." For example, when I wrote about empowerment through language in chapter

3, I spoke as a member of the Filipino community who sees the smirks on Filipinos' faces as they "correct" each other's use of English phrases and slang, as well as the smiles on their faces as they say, "You say fridge, but we call it ref." Seeing these reactions and knowing full well the importance of membership, I felt the pushes and pulls of we-ness, they-ness, insider- and outsider-ness that accompanied each statement of comparison. As I coded and analyzed this material, I often had doubts as to whether the empirical material and my assessment were of any worth: *Is this just the Filipino talking? Where's the scholarly criticism in that? She's too entrenched in the community to be a good scholar. She's too scholarly to actually appreciate Filipino culture.*

Yet it is precisely this kind of fluidity, not only within one's personal identity, but within each discussion of Filipinoness, that allows us to uncover what policies, practices, and/or laws contribute to the constant renegotiations of identity and community. At the outset, studying the politics of identity may seem "fluffy," and if one belongs to the community they study, it may even appear to be narcissistic. But as Weber ([1920] 1997) argued long ago and as Fanon (1967) and other scholars writing about colonial oppression remind us, identity is essential to maintaining oppression. Once the dominant group is successful at socializing those they have colonized into believing their version of history and culture, assimilation is complete. So for those who come from colonized cultures—especially those like the Philippines, which supposedly went through "benevolent" assimilation—it is imperative that they understand that the hierarchical relationship between them and the colonial power is often implicit in each characterization of both colonized and colonizer socialized into them. Or, as Fanon (1967) put it, "A black man is not. And neither is a white man."

It was in seeing the fluidity of identities that I was able to see the tenuousness of this hierarchical relationship between colonizer and colonized. Day in and day out, I saw evidence that what some people assume is colonial mentality can actually be quite subversive. Seeing bits and pieces of American culture mimicked and turned upside down, particularly in the list of jokes, showed that being "almost, but not quite" allows those in the subordinate group to be at the center in that their creations and re-creations of their selves simultaneously create and re-create the dominant group. And within these creations were included a complex understanding of the political and economic relationship between the United States and the Philippines.

I am a chameleon. Sometimes I fit in the Filipino community; sometimes I don't. When my cousin's husband, my ex-boyfriend, and my aunt's husband—all white males—are around, I'm in the clear; I blend in, and my birthplace is not a problem at all. They are a source of amusement to my family ("Let's see what they'll eat!") and a source of frustration ("We don't have any bread in the house. . . . They're going to have to eat rice."). Richard, though, is particularly amusing because, as my mom says, "He eats anything! Thai food, Japanese food, Indian food, and even Filipino food! He's really strange." Jack, my cousin's husband, has been around long enough to become a Filipino. *"Not that there's anything wrong with that,"* my Filipino American friends and I joke, quoting Jerry Seinfeld. I saw the debates unfold and participated in a few of them, yet I struggled with disclosing them. Was this treason? While analyzing the data on mail-order brides, Asiaphiles, and Whiggies, for example, I struggled with subverting the Filipina and concentrating on being the scholar, but I learned that would never happen. I am always simultaneously both, and I hope this book reflects that.

I am not saying that by being a scholar of Filipino descent, my word on the Filipino community is more "valid" than that of other scholars. I do not advocate ethnic ghettoizing of scholars. Besides, if there is anything that I've learned from the two years I spent in my virtual homeland, it is that we should not, as Chow (1993) states, "submit to our ethnicity." Instead, I believe that we should continue to discover how differences are constructed so we can better assess how power relations work, and thus figure out a better way to empower ourselves. That, I believe, is my task as both Filipino American woman and a scholar.

Appendix A: Studying the Definition of "Filipino"

Subject: studying the definition of "Filipino"
From: Emily Ignacio eignacio@alexia.lis.uiuc.edu
Organization: University of Illinois at Urbana
CC: eignacio@alexia.lis.uiuc.edu
Newsgroups: soc.culture.filipino

Hello!

My name is Emily Ignacio and I am a sociology grad student at the University of Illinois. I am interested in studying the various definitions of "Filipino" that are articulated on this newsgroup.

I will not be using any names or e-mail addresses in my paper, so everything will be kept confidential and everyone will retain their anonymity.

Please e-mail me privately at eignacio@alexia.lis.uiuc.edu if you have any questions or concerns so we don't take up any room on this newsgroup.

=)

Thank you very much!
Emily

Appendix B: You May Be Married to a Filipina If

You May Be Married to a Filipina If:

(written by an American guy who loves his Filipina wife in spite of the following idiosyncrasies)

*Instead of a dowry, you got the whole bill for the wedding and honeymoon.

*Most of the decorations in your house are made of wicker.

*You are expected to be able to read her mind just by watching her eyebrows move up and down and which way her lips are pointed.

*All her relatives think your name is Joe.

*Your in-laws take 10 years to acknowledge your existence and to call you by something other than "that white guy."

*The instant you are married you have 3,000 new close relatives that you can't tell apart.

*Your refrigerator is always full but you cannot find any food that you recognize.

*All the desserts are sticky and all the snacks are salty.

*You throw a party and everyone is fighting to chop the leathery skin off a roast pig.

*All your kids have 4–5 middle names.

*You try to call her up on the phone and someone tells you "for a while," and you want to know "for a while, what?"

*You are trying to go to sleep and she keeps asking for the comFORT'r, and you ain't got a clue what she's talking about.

*Your phone bills are all international and average 3 hours per call.

*She sweeps with something that witches usually fly around on.

*The rice cooker is on 24 hours a day and uses up 50% of your electric and food budget.

*On your first trip to the Philippines, you have 18 giant boxes that weigh 1,000 pounds each and your "carry on" luggage requires a small forklift truck.

*The first time she's pregnant you have to go out at 4:00 in the A.M. for some weird type of greasy sausages.

*You buy a new $500 freezer so she can store 200 pounds of SPAM that was on sale.

*Everything in your house was bought on sale, even if you don't need it as long as it was a "bargain" is all that matters.

*All your postage bills instantly double.

*Her favorite sauce is called "patis," Americans call it turpentine.

*She prefers bistek to beef steak.

*She'll offer you a halo-halo with 2 straws for a romantic dessert.

*You still don't know what's the difference between manong and manok.

*Her homeland has more Megamalls than islands.

*Before every holiday and visit, her sisters fax you a 10 page "bilins" list which says suggestion only.

*Your kitchen table has a merry-go-round in the middle.

*All the vegetables she buys at the Filipino store look like they were grown at Chernobyl.

*Your in law's first visit lasted 6 years.

*Her friends are named Chinky, Girlie, Boy, and Bimbo and you are not allowed to smirk.

*All your place settings have the silverware backwards and there are no knives.

*She's done her best job planning a surprise party for you if she manages not to tell you about it until a week or two before.

*She "cleans" her closet by throwing all the crap into your closet.

*You were married 5 years before she explained to you that "ARAY!" doesn't mean "ohh baby!"

*And last but not least: You are pretty proud of yourself because you think that you snagged up for yourself some unique, rare, tropical goddess type until you go to the Philippines and can't tell her apart from anyone else in the whole country (unless she's taller than 5'1", then it's a bit easier)

Appendix C: Are You Really Filipino?

Are you confused about your ethnic identity? Want to know just how Filipino you are?

Take this less-than-scientific quiz to rate your "Filipinoness."

SCORING

3 points if you can relate to the following characteristics yourself

2 points if it relates to an immediate family member, i.e., Mom or Dad or sister/brother

1 point if you know someone who has the characteristic

MANNERISM AND PERSONALITY TRAITS:

1. You point with your lips.
2. You eat using hands—and have it down to a technique.
3. Your other piece of luggage is a Balikbayan box.
4. You always have at least three other people taking you to the airport.
5. You're standing next to eight big boxes at the airport.
6. You nod upwards to greet someone.
7. You put your foot up on your chair and rest your elbow on your knee while eating.
8. You use a rock to scrub yourself in the shower.
9. You have to kiss your relative on the check as soon as you enter the room.

10. You collect items from hotels or restaurants "for souvenire."
11. You smile for no reason.
12. You flirt by having a foolish grin in your face while raising your eyebrows repeatedly.
13. You go to a department store and try to bargain the prices.
14. You use an umbrella for shade on hot summer days.
15. You scratch your head when you don't know the answer.
16. You never eat the last morsel of food on the table.
17. You like bowling.
18. You know how to play pusoy and mah-jong.
19. You find dried up morsels of rice stuck on your shirt.
20. You prefer to sit in the shade instead of basking in the sun.
21. You add an unwarranted "H" to your name, i.e., "Jhun," "Bhoy," "Rhon."
22. You put your hands together in front of you as if to make a path and say "Excuse, excuse" when you pass between people or in front of the TV.
23. Your middle name is your mother's maiden name.
24. You like everything imported or "state-side."
25. You check the labels on clothes to see where it was made before buying it.
26. You hang your clothes out to dry.
27. You are perfectly comfortable in a squatting position with your elbows resting on your knees.
28. You consistently arrive 30 minutes late for all events.
29. You always offer food to all your visitors.

VOCABULARY:

30. You pronounce F's like P's and P's like F's.
31. You say "comfort room" instead of "bathroom."
32. You say "for take out" instead of "to go."
33. You "open" or "close" the light.
34. You asked for "Colgate" instead of "toothpaste."
35. You asked for a "Pentel-pen" or a "ball-pen" instead of just "pen."
36. You refer to the refrigerator as the "ref" or "pridyider."
37. You say "Kodakan" instead of "take a picture."
38. You order a "McDonald's" instead of "hamburger" (pronounced ham-boor-jer).
39. You say "Ha?" instead of "What."
40. You say "Hoy" to get someone's attention.

41. You answer when someone yells "Hoy."
42. You turn around when someone says "Psst!"
43. You say "Cutex" instead of "nail polish."
44. You say "he" when you mean "she" and vice versa.
45. You say "aray" instead of "ouch."
46. Your sneeze sounds like "ahh-ching" instead of "ahh-choo."
47. You prefer to make acronyms for phrases such as "OA" for over-acting, or "TNT" for, well, you know.
48. You say "air con" instead of "a/c" or air conditioner.
49. You say "brown-out" instead of "black-out."

HOME FURNISHING:

50. You use a "walis ting-ting" or "walis tambo" as opposed to a conventional broom.
51. You have a "Weapons of Moroland" shield hanging in the living room wall.
52. You have a portrait of "The Last Supper" hanging in your dinning room.
53. You own a Karaoke System.
54. You own a piano that no one ever plays.
55. You have a tabo in the bathroom.
56. Your house has too many burloloys.
57. You have two to three pairs of tsinelas at your doorstep.
58. Your house has an ornate wrought iron gate in front of it.
59. You have a rose garden.
60. You have a shrine of the Santo Ninyo in your living room.
61. You own a "barrel man" (you pull up the barrel and you see something that looks familiar, schwing).
62. You cover your living room furniture with bedsheets.
63. Your lamp shades still have the plastic covers on them.
64. You have plastic runners to cover the carpets in your house.
65. You refer to your VCR as a "beytamax."
66. You have a rice dispenser.
67. You own a turbo broiler.
68. You own one of those fiber optic flower lamps.
69. You own a lamp with the oil that drips down the strings.
70. You have a giant wooden fork and spoon hanging somewhere in the dinning room.
71. You have wooden tinikling dancers on the wall.
72. You own capiz shells chandeliers, lamps, or placemats.

AUTOMOBILES:

73. You own a Mercedes Benz and you call it "chedeng."
74. You own a huge van conversion.
75. Your car chirps like a bird or plays a tune when it is in reverse.
76. Your car horn can make 2 or 3 different sounds.
77. Your car has curb feelers or curb detectors.
78. Your car has too many "buroloys" like a Jitneys back in P.I.
79. You hang a Rosary on your car's rear view mirror.
80. You have an air freshener in your car.

FAMILY:

81. You have aunts and uncles named "Baby," "Girlie," or "Boy."
82. You were raised to believe that every Filipino is an aunt, uncle, or cousin.
83. Your dad was in the Navy.
84. You have a family member or relative that works in the Post Office.
85. Your mom or sister or wife is a nurse.
86. Your parents call each other "mommy" and "daddy," or "ma" and "pa."
87. You have a family member that has a nickname that repeats itself, i.e., "Deng-Deng," "Ling Ling," or "Bing Bing." Etc.

FOOD:

88. You put hot dogs in your spaghetti.
89. You consider dilis the Filipino equivalent of French fries.
90. You think that eating chocolate rice pudding and dried fish is a great morning meal.
91. You order things like tapsilog, tocilog, or longsilog at restaurants.
92. You instinctively grab a toothpick after a meal.
93. You order a "soft drink" instead of a "soda."
94. You dip bread in your morning coffee.
95. You refer to seasonings and all other forms of monosodium glutamate as "Ajinomoto."
96. Your cupboards are full of Spam, Vienna Sausage, Ligo, and Corned Beef, which you refer to as Karne Norte.
97. "Goldilocks" means more to you than just a character in a fairytale.
98. You appreciate a fresh pot of rice.
99. You bring your "baon" most of the time to work.

100. Your "baon" is usually something over rice.
101. Your neighbors complain about the smell of tuyo on Sunday mornings.
102. You eat rice for breakfast.
103. You use your fingers to measure the water when cooking rice.
104. You wash and re-use disposable plastic utensils and Styrofoam cups.
105. You have a supply of frozen lumpia in the refrigerator.
106. You have an ice shaver for making a halo-halo.
107. You eat purple yam flavored ice cream.
108. You gotta have a bottle of Jufran or Mafram handy.
109. Your fry Spam or hot dogs and eat them with rice.
110. You think that half-hatched duck eggs are a delicacy.
111. You know that "chocolate meat" is not really made with chocolate.

BONUS QUESTION:

You understand this joke (make sure you read the punch line with a Filipino accent!):

How many bears were in a car with Goldilocks?

Four—the momma bear, the poppa bear, the baby bear, and the driver.

Tally your scores and see what category you belong.

259–327 points:

Welcome to America! Judging from your high score, you are an obvious (something) from the Philippines. There's no doubt what your ethnic identity is! You're a Filipino, through and through.

173–258 points:

Congratulations, you've retained most of the Filipino traits and tendencies your family has instilled in you.

172–151:

You have OFT (Obvious Filipino Tendencies). Go with the flow to (something) Filipino potential. Prepare for assimilation; resistance is futile!

50 and under:

You're white, aren't you?

Notes

PREFACE   WHY FILIPINOS?

1. "Pinoy" is a slang term for Filipino.
2. *The Debut* (2002) is an independent film that captures Filipino Americans' struggles with race, racism, identity, and "the American Dream." Directed by Gene Cagayon, it also is one of the first feature films that contains a predominantly Filipino and Filipino American cast and, as of this writing, is still making its rounds across the United States. What is notable about its continued showing is that it has a limited budget, and thus limited advertising. The continuing success of the debut at the box office has been largely dependent on good reviews in local city newspapers, true to the ongoing power of networking so well documented in Rick Bonus's (2000) *Locating Filipino Americans*.
3. Many of the concepts that I use (such as "authentic," "race," "gender," and "culture") should be enclosed in quotes because they are contested terms. I am very aware that these terms are contested; however, because I frequently use these words, I have left out the quotes.
4. "Lolo" and "Lola" are Filipino terms for "grandfather" and "grandmother," respectively.
5. To protect the identity of the participants on the newsgroup, friends, and other people I conversed with, all names used in this study (aside from my own and "Mom" and "Dad") are pseudonyms.
6. See Anzaldúa (1987) for an illustration of "Latino" identity construction, and Marlon Riggs's (1995) third documentary, *Black Is . . . Black Ain't* for a poignant and reflective look at what it means to be black in the United States.

CHAPTER 1   INTRODUCTION

1. In 2001, as then President Joseph Estrada faced impeachment, an estimated 70 million Filipinos passed a message via texting (i.e., sending text messages

through cell phones) to gather at a religious shrine and demand that Estrada step down from office. Four days later, after intense rallying at this shrine, Estrada stepped down (*Wired*, January 23, 2001).

2. Internet 'zines such as commondreams.org, indymedia.org, and online magazines such as thenation.com and znet.org have been instrumental in organizing anti-globalization and antiwar protests.

3. In the aftermath of September 11, 2001, people of many different ethnicities and races affirmed their national pride by displaying the United States flag at their residences, on their cars, and on many other possessions. For racial minorities, particularly those who have physical characteristics which could be deemed as "Arab looking," the prominent display of the United States flag and other American symbols was particularly important, as the symbols "protected" them from their neighbors' wrath. Even though many of them were well aware that they may be targeted by the government by virtue of their surnames, residential neighborhoods, national origin, and/or their physical features, many felt they could deflect individuals' violence toward them by participating in visible acts of solidarity and patriotism.

4. Scholars who study CMC (computer-mediated communication) are generally concerned with how technology will affect traditional social units such as communities and the self (Baym 1995a, 1995b; Jones 1995; Danet 1998). Thus, they often document either the transcendence and/or erasure of traditional identities, and they express a concern that cultural identities will be homogenized because of the current U.S.-centric nature of the World Wide Web. Both CMC and postcolonial scholars, however, show that the Internet can be an arena in which identity can be radically altered (because it is a constantly changing arena that transcends not only time zones but also traditional political boundaries).

CHAPTER 2 PROBLEMATIZING DIASPORA

1. Interestingly, this love of Spam is widespread across the Pacific Islands (Sacks 1997; Theroux 1993). My friend Janice regards this preponderance of luncheon meat in various Pacific Islands as part of a "Western conspiracy to get rid of yellow and brown people."

2. Why include white rednecks? Because of the idea that if one can make fun of one's own race, then there can't be any racism.

3. Ironically, most Americans still celebrate Thanksgiving, an American holiday premised on the exact opposite image of Native Americans—that without them, all white settlers may have perished—while reincarnations of the American Indian wars in the form of a Cowboys versus Redskins game flicker in the background.

4. Upon hearing of the MSNBC headline, Dad and Mom, the former a U.S. World War II veteran and both avid skating fans, bitterly complained that "the yellow peril hasn't gone away."

5. The term "global ethnoscapes" captures the shifting of "social, territorial, and cultural reproduction of ethnic identity" (Appadurai 1991, 191). "Global ethnoscapes" captures the importance of the images of cultures as well as the migration of people. Appadurai argues that because of migration, diasporas, and technological advances (including print capitalism and television), the definition of ethnicity is contingent upon both lived experience and imagined experience.

6. See Bautista 2002 for a comprehensive discussion of the early Filipino settlers (the Manilamen) in the United States.
7. For more excellent recent works on the Filipino diaspora, see Bonus 2000; Manalansan 2003; Espiritu 2003; Rafael 2000; Okamura 1998.

CHAPTER 3   SELLING OUT ONE'S CULTURE

1. Gupta and Ferguson's (1997) *Culture, Power, Place* is an excellent volume of essays which critically examine how transnational flows, post- and neo-colonial relationships, and mass media affect our understanding of identity, place, power, and resistance.
2. Definitions of diaspora and diasporic identity have traditionally been based on the notions of separate nations and cultures. Diaspora originally referred to the exile and dispersion of Jews from their homeland. It represented a break from their place of origin and yet a continued sense of belonging. Recently, new theories of diaspora have emerged that accommodate those who voluntarily emigrate from their homelands.

   Safran, for example, has extended the definition to include "expatriate minority communities" with six characteristics. (1) The individuals are dispersed from an original homeland to two or more "peripheral" places. (2) They perpetuate a "memory, vision, or myth about the original homeland." (3) They believe that they are not (and may never be) completely accepted by their host countries. (4) They wish to return to their ancestral homeland eventually. (5) They commit themselves to maintaining and/or restoring the homeland. (6) Finally, they define their identity and solidarity against their relationship with their homeland (Safran 1991, 83–84). Although Safran's definition highlights the importance of "memories" and "myths" of the homeland, it still privileges space—the homeland/host country dichotomy—over other important factors in the articulation of identity, such as time and memory (Boyarin 1994). In addition, Safran stipulates a desire for a physical return to the homeland, something expatriates, first-generation immigrants, and 1.5 or later generation members may not desire. The focus on the movement across national boundaries makes it difficult to address the notions of "borderlands," cultural heterogeneity within territories, and shifting cultures using these definitions of diaspora. I believe that concentrating on the movement across territories does not take into account the blurring of boundaries that technology, transnational capitalism, and diaspora itself have caused.

   Some theorists who problematize territorial boundaries continue to reify the notion of cultural boundaries. For example, Rouse (1991) points out that members of the Aguilillan community continually travel from one culture (Michoacán) to another (American). To describe the effects of the movement from one culture to another, he introduces the term "cultural bifocality." This refers to the ability of the Aguilillans to live in a space where "two cultures or two political systems come face to face" (Rouse 1991, 15). Although this may apply to the Michoacáns, I believe that cultural bifocality cannot be applied to the Filipino diaspora because this term is contingent upon juggling two different (and presumably separate) cultures. This does not leave room for instances where the two cultures and the two political systems are already tied to one another, as in the United States and the Philippines. In addition, because it reifies the boundaries between cultures, it does not capture the heterogeneity that may exist within each culture, nor does it explain how this circular migration changes both cultures.

3. Hall (1996) argues that the meaning or definition of an identity is always dependent on an "arbitrary stop" and is not permanent. Because identity cannot be defined without a "relation of difference," the identity of subordinated people necessarily encompasses the dominant culture's power.

4. Pilipino is mostly based on Tagalog, a language spoken most heavily in the northern regions of the Philippines.

5. The Pilipino/Tagalog Abakada alphabet is *a b k d e g h i l m n ng o p r s t u w y.* The new alphabet is *a b c d e f g h i j k l m n ñ ng o p q r s t u v w x y z.*

CHAPTER 4 *"AIN'T I A FILIPINO (WOMAN)?"*

1. Although the word "Filipina" is used widely (as are the gendered nouns "Pinoy" and "Pinay"), I tend to use the term "Filipino woman" instead of "Filipina" because of my family's insistence that there are no gendered words in Tagalog. In this sense, I understand that I am contributing to my own family's idea of what is and what is not authentic.

2. The other two-thirds were news stories about Filipinos and Filipino history and smaller items, such as recipes, jokes, and the least expensive way to fly to the Philippines.

3. Flor Contemplacion was a domestic worker in Singapore who was accused of murdering another domestic helper, Delia Maga, and the son of her employer in 1991. Despite requests for clemency, she was executed for the double murder on March 17, 1995, just before I began studying this newsgroup. Filipinos worldwide condemned the actions of the Singaporean government, but also blamed the Philippine government for not caring about overseas Filipino workers.

4. There are various definitions of "identity politics." Calhoun states that identity politics not only involves seeking recognition but "refusing, diminishing or displacing identities others wish to recognize in individuals" (1994, 21). However, Calhoun also describes new social movements (NSMs) that adopt a "soft relativism," a tendency to "[imply] that everyone is equally endowed with identity, equally entitled to their own identity, and equally entitled to respect for it" (1994, 24). Calhoun argues that this often naturalizes difference rather than examining its construction. It is this type of identity politics that I refer to as "simple identity politics."

5. People get so confused by this statement. The eggplant the poster is referring to is a Chinese eggplant, elongated and skinny in shape.

6. In 1898, the United States "acquired" the Philippines, Cuba, and Puerto Rico from Spain as part of a peace treaty (Treaty of Paris) for $20 million. They also annexed Hawaii and other Pacific islands in 1898 for reasons that will become apparent later in this section. The very-little-known Filipino American War broke out as the United States attempted to establish control of the Philippines. The war lasted over ten years and over six hundred thousand Filipinos died as a result of war, disease, and starvation. Members of soc.culture.filipino often allude to this Filipino resistance, the Katipunan, and urge present-day Filipinos to get rid of their "colonial mentality" and resist the continuing cultural and economic influence of the United States (Ignacio 1998).

CHAPTER 5   LAUGHTER IN THE RAIN

1. Literature on marginal spaces often includes discussions about hybridity (Anzaldúa 1987; Rouse 1991; Young 1995, for a critique). Bakhtin (1981) studied the hybridity within languages and illustrated how pidgin languages fuse two or more languages together. This is what he terms *organic hybridity*, implying that this "naturally" happens when two or more cultures meet in the "contact zone" (Pratt 1992). But according to Bakhtin (1981), there is also another form of hybridity: *intentional hybridity*. This type of hybridity describes the act of appropriating the colonial Other's cultural values and norms and making them their own.

   This is in contrast to the idea of "colonial mentality," where incorporating "foreign" cultural norms is described as evidence of false consciousness, "selling out," and/or the loss of one's culture. The empowerment of colonized peoples is contingent upon finding the one "true" culture and extrapolating and discarding the elements of the colonial culture. In this dichotomous scenario, either you are "in" or "out" of the circle; this essentializes both cultures and thus does not make any room for movement in between or the creation of an in-between or new space. Filipinos on the newsgroup and outside it are concerned that colonial mentality inhibits the creation of a true Filipino consciousness (see interviews in Espiritu 1995; Rafael 1997). Yet, as we have seen in the previous chapters, the division between the Philippines and America is not easily discerned.

2. "Chedeng" is a nickname for Mercedes Benz and cannot be translated into English.

3. For example, the participants could have written, "You are a Filipino if you eat *manok* [chicken]." If their only intent was to just quiz the reader in basic Tagalog, this would have been a good joke. But the game in the above set of jokes is not to be able to recognize and translate Tagalog words into English. By translating these terms, the participants show that Filipinos enjoy totally different kinds or combinations of food than other cultures. You are a Filipino if you recognize these descriptions, and probably even more so if you could translate them into their proper Tagalog terms.

4. Wayne Wang (1985) uses the latter image in his movie *Dim Sum* to symbolize the changing relationship of family members in a Chinese American household.

CHAPTER 6   E PLURIBUS OR E PLURIBUS UNUM?

1. For example, several progressive or liberal scholars, activists, and organizations are quick to name Web sites such as commondreams.org, workingforchange.com, or indymedia.org as places to read "alternative" news, but the authority of even those sites depends on the authority of the contributors and/or the media organizations from which the news was culled (as well it should, in my opinion).

2. Since information technology is currently the commodity which many developing nations "sell" to more developed nations, like the United States, it is imperative that this infrastructure is in place in less-developed countries. However, as many scholars (see especially Joseph Stiglitz 2003; Andrew Barlow 2003) have pointed out, current practices of the International Monetary Fund, the World Bank, the World Trade Organization, as well as globalization policies carried out by more developed countries only exacerbate this digital divide.

References

Abelmann, Nancy, and John Lie. 1995. *Blue dreams.* Cambridge: Harvard University Press.

Alampay, Romy. 1995. Forgive but don't forget. Today-Manila Newspaper, March 29.

Almirol, Edwin B. 1985. *Ethnic identity and social negotiation: A study of a Filipino community in California.* New York: AMS Press.

Anderson, Benedict. 1991. *Imagined communities.* London: Verso.

——. 1995. Cacique democracy in the Philippines: Origins and dreams. In *Discrepant histories: Translocal essays on Filipino cultures,* ed. Vicente L. Rafael, 3–47. Philadelphia: Temple University Press.

Anthias, Floya, and Nira Yuval-Davis. 1994. *Racialized boundaries: Race, nation, gender, colour, and class and the anti-racist struggle.* New York: Routledge.

Anzaldúa, Gloria. 1987. *Borderlands/LaFrontera: The new mestiza.* San Francisco: Aunt Lute.

Appadurai, Arjun. 1991. Global ethnoscapes: Notes and queries for a transnational anthropology. In *Recapturing anthropology: Writing in the present,* ed. R. G. Fox, 191–210. Santa Fe, N.M.: School of American Research Press.

Appiah, Kwame Anthony. 1994. Identity, authenticity, survival: Multicultural societies and social reproduction. In *Multiculturalism,* ed. Amy Gutmann, 149–163. Princeton, N.J.: Princeton University Press.

Aquino, Belinda A. 1987. *Politics of plunder: The Philippines under Marcos.* Quezon City, Philippines: Great Books.

Atkinson, Kevin. 1996. *Usenet info center.* http://sunsite.unc.edu/usenet-i/info.

Azarcon de la Cruz, P. 1985. *Filipinas for sale: An alternative Philippine report on women and tourism.* Manila: Aklat Filipino.

Bakhtin, Mikhail M. 1981. Discourse in the novel. In *The dialogic imagination,* ed. Michael Holquist, 259–422. Austin: University of Texas Press.

————. 1986. *Speech genres and other late essays.* Austin: University of Texas Press.

Barber, Benjamin R., and Andrea Schulz. 1996. *Jihad vs. McWorld: How globalism and tribalism are reshaping the world.* New York: Ballantine.

Barlow, Andrew. 2003. *Between fear and hope: Globalization and race in the United States.* New York: Rowman and Littlefield Publishers.

Bautista,Veltisezar. 2002. *The Filipino Americans (1763–Present): Their history, culture, and traditions.* 2nd ed. Warren, Mich.: Bookhaus Publishers.

Baym, Nancy. 1995a. The emergence of community in computer-mediated communication. In *CyberSociety: Computer-mediated communication and community,* ed. Stephen G. Jones, 138–163. Thousand Oaks, Calif.: Sage.

————. 1995b. From practice to culture on Usenet. In *The cultures of computing,* ed. Susan Leigh Star, 29–52. Oxford: Basil Blackwell.

Bello, M., and V. Reyes. 1986. Filipino Americans and the Marcos overthrow: The transformation of political consciousness. *Amerasia* 13: 73–84.

Benhabib, Seyla. 1989. On contemporary feminist theory. *Dissent* 36 (summer): 366–370.

Berger, Peter L., and Thomas Luckmann. 1966. *The social construction of reality: A treatise in the sociology of knowledge.* New York: Doubleday.

Bhabha, Homi K. 1992. Postcolonial authority and postmodern guilt. In *Cultural studies,* ed. Lawrence Grossberg, Cary Nelson, and Paula A. Treichler, 56–68. New York: Routledge.

————. 1994. *The location of culture.* New York: Routledge.

Bonilla-Silva, Eduardo. 2003. *Racism without racists.* New York: Rowman and Littlefield Publishers.

Bonus, Rick, ed. 1994. *Remapping memory: The politics of timespace.* Minneapolis: University of Minnesota Press.

————. 1997. Homeland memories and media: Filipino images and imaginations in America. In *Filipino Americans: Transformation and identity,* ed. Maria P. P. Root, 208–218. Thousand Oaks, Calif.: Sage Publications.

————. 2000. *Locating Filipino Americans.* Philadelphia: Temple University Press.

Bourdieu, Pierre, and Loic Wacquant. 1993. *An invitation to reflective sociology.* Chicago: University of Chicago Press.

Bowker, Geof, and Susan Leigh Star. 2000. *Sorting things out: Classification and its consequences.* Cambridge, Mass.: MIT Press.

Boyarin, Jonathan, ed. 1994. *Remapping memory: The politics of timespace.* Minneapolis: University of Minnesota Press.

————. 1996. *Thinking in Jewish.* Chicago: University of Chicago Press.

Burayidi, Michael A. 1997. *Multiculturalism in a cross-national perspective.* Lanham, Md.: University Press of America.

Butler, Judith. 1995. Subjection, resistance, resignification: Between Freud and Foucault. In *The identity in question,* ed. John Rajchman, 229–249. New York: Routledge.

Calhoun, Craig, ed. 1994. *Social theory and the politics of identity.* Cambridge, Mass.: Blackwell Press.

Center for New Community. 2000. *Soundtracks to the white revolution: White supremacist assaults on youth music subcultures.* Chicago: Center for New Community.

Chan, Sucheng. 1991. *Asian Americans: An interpretive history.* Boston: Twayne.

Chang, K. A., and Julian M. Groves. 1997. "Saints" and "prostitutes": Sexual discourse in the Filipina domestic worker community in Hong Kong. *Working Papers in the Social Sciences, No. 20,* Hong Kong: Division of Social Science, Hong Kong University of Science and Technology.

Chicago Cultural Studies Group. 1995. Critical multiculturalism. In *Multiculturalism: A critical reader,* ed. David Theo Goldberg, 114–139. London: Blackwell.

Chow, Rey. 1993. *Writing diaspora.* Bloomington: Indiana University Press.

Cicourel, A. V. 1968. The acquisition of social structure: Towards a developmental sociology of language and meaning. In *Cognitive sociology,* by A. V. Cicourel. Harmondsworth: Penguin.

Clifford, James. 1986. Partial truths. In *Writing culture: The poetics and politics of ethnography,* ed. James Clifford and George E. Marcus, 1–26. Berkeley: University of California Press.

———. 1992. Traveling cultures. In *Cultural studies,* ed. Lawrence Grossberg, Cary Nelson, and Paula Treichler, 96–116. New York: Routledge.

———. 1994. Diasporas. *Cultural Anthropology* 9, no. 3: 302–338.

Coll, Steve. 1992. Anatomy of a victory: CIA's covert Afghan war. *Washington Post,* July 19.

Correll, Shelley. 1995. The ethnography of an electronic bar. *Journal of Contemporary Ethnography* 24, no. 3: 270–298.

Danet, Brenda. 1998. Text as mask: Gender, play, and performanace on the Internet. In *Cybersociety 2.0,* ed. Steven G. Jones, 129–158. Thousand Oaks, Calif.: Sage Publications.

Davis, F. J. 1991. *Who is black?* University Park: Penn State University Press.

DejaNews. 1997. http://www.dejanews.com.

Denzin, Norman K. 1992. *Symbolic interactionism and cultural studies: The politics of interpretation.* Oxford, U.K.: Blackwell Publishers.

———. 1998. In search of the inner child: Co-dependency and gender in a cyberspace community. In *Emotions in social life,* ed. Gillian Bendelow and Simon J. Williams, 97–119. London: Routledge.

DuBois, W.E.B. [1903] 1998. *The souls of black folk.* New York: W. W. Norton & Company.

———. 1978. *On sociology and the black community.* Chicago: University of Chicago Press.

Eng, David L. 2000. *Racial castration: Managing masculinity in Asian America.* Durham, N.C.: Duke University Press.

Enloe, Cynthia. 1989. *Bananas, beaches, and bases: Making feminist sense of international politics.* Berkeley: University of California Press.

Espiritu, Yen Le. 1989. *Asian American panethnicity.* Philadelphia: Temple University Press.

———. 1994. The intersection of race, ethnicity, and class: The multiple identities of second-generation Filipinos. *Identities* 1, no. 2–3: 249–273.

———. 1995. *Filipino American lives.* Philadelphia: Temple University Press.

———. 1997. *Asian American women and men.* Thousand Oaks, Calif.: Sage.

———. 2003. *Homebound.* Berkeley: University of California Press.

Fanon, Frantz. 1967. *Black skin, white masks.* New York: Grove Press.

Fiske, John. 1994. Audiencing: Cultural practice and cultural studies. In *Handbook of qualitative research,* ed. Norman K. Denzin and Yvonna S. Lincoln, 189–198. Thousand Oaks, Calif.: Sage.

Flores, Juan. 1993. *Divided borders: Essays on Puerto Rican identity.* Houston, Tex.: Arte Público Press.

Foucault, Michel. 1990. *History of sexuality.* Vol. 1. New York: Knopf Publishing Group.

Frideres, J. S. 1997. Multiculturalism and public policy in Canada. In *Multiculturalism in a cross-national perspective,* ed. Michael A. Burayidi, 87–111. Lanham, Md.: University Press of America.

Gerth, Hans, and C. Wright Mills. 1946. *From Max Weber: Essays in sociology.* New York: Oxford University Press.

Gilroy, Paul. 1987. *There ain't no black in the union jack.* Chicago: University of Chicago Press.

———. 1993. *The black Atlantic: Modernity and double consciousness.* Cambridge: Harvard University Press.

Goldberg, David Theo, ed. 1995. *Multiculturalism: A critical reader.* London: Blackwell.

Gupta, Akhil. 1994. The reincarnation of souls and the rebirth of commodities: Representations of time in "East" and "West." In *Remapping memory: The politics of timespace,* ed. Jonathan Boyarin, 161–183. Minneapolis: University of Minnesota Press.

Gupta, Akhil, and James Ferguson, eds. 1997. *Culture, power, place: Explorations in critical anthropology.* Durham, N.C.: Duke University Press.

Hall, Stuart. 1990. Cultural identity and diaspora. In *Identity: Community, culture, difference,* ed. J. Rutherford, 222–237. London: Lawrence & Wishart.

———. 1996. Introduction: Who needs "identity"? In *Questions of cultural identity,* ed. Stuart Hall and Paul du Gay, 1–17. London: Sage.

Haraway, Donna J. 1991. A cyborg manifesto: Science, technology, and socialist-feminism in the late twentieth century. In *Simians, cyborgs, and women: A reinvention of nature,* 222–237. New York: Routledge.

Hewson, Claire, Peter Yule, Dianna Laurent, and Carl Vogel. 2003. *Internet research methods: A practical guide for the social and behavioural sciences.* Thousand Oaks, Calif.: Sage Publications.

hooks, bell. 1994. Marginality as a site of resistance. in *Out there: Marginalization and contemporary culture,* ed. Russell Ferguson, Martha Gever, Trinh T. Minh-ha, and Cornel West, 341–343. Cambridge: MIT Press.

Hughes, Everett C. [1948] 1971. The study of ethnic relations. In *The sociological eye: Selected papers,* 153–158. Chicago: Aldine Atherton.

Ignacio, Emily Noelle. 1998. The quest for a Filipino identity in a transnational location. Ph.D. dissertation, University of Illinois at Urbana-Champaign.

Joas, Hans. 1987. Symbolic interactionism. In *Social theory today,* ed. Anthony Giddens and Jonathan Turner. Stanford, Calif.: Polity Press.

Jones, Steven G. 1995. Understanding community in the information age. In *CyberSociety: Computer-mediated communication and community,* ed. Steven G. Jones, 10–35. Thousand Oaks, Calif.: Sage Publications.

Kendall, Lori. 1999. Recontextualizing "cyberspace": Methodological considerations for doing on-line research. In *Doing internet research: Critical issues and methods for examining the net,* ed. Steve Jones. Thousand Oaks, Calif.: Sage Publications.

Kim, Elaine. 1982. *Asian American literature: An introduction to the writings and their social context.* Philadelphia: Temple University Press.

Kling, Rob, and Suzi Iacono. 1995. Computerization movements and the mobilization of support for computerization. In *Ecologies of Knowledge,* ed. Susan Leigh Star, 119–153. Albany: State University of New York.

Kolko, Beth E., Gilbert B. Rodman, and Lisa Nakamura, eds. 1999. *Race in cyberspace.* New York: Routledge.

Laclau, Ernesto. 1995. Universalism, particularism, and the question of identity. In *The identity in question,* ed. John Rajchman, 93–108. New York: Routledge.

Lai, Tracy. 1992. Asian American women: Not for sale. In *Race, class, and gender: An anthology,* ed. Margaret Anderson and Patricia Hill Collins, 163–171. Belmont, Calif.: Wadsworth.

Law, Lisa. 1997. A matter of "choice": Discourse on prostitution in the Philippines. In *Sites of desire, economics of pleasure: Sexualities in Asia and the Pacific,* ed. Lenore Manderson and Margaret Jolly, 233–261. Chicago: University of Chicago Press.

Lee, Robert G. 2000. *Orientals: Asian Americans in popular culture.* Philadelphia: Temple University Press.

Lie, John. 1995. From international migration to transnational diaspora. *Contemporary Sociology* 24 (July 4): 303–306.

Lippard, Lucy R. 1990. *Mixed blessings: Art in multicultural America.* New York: Pantheon Books.

Lorde, Audre. 1984a. Age, race, class, and sex: Women redefining difference. In *Sister/outsider,* by Audre Lorde, 114–123. Trumansburg, N.Y.: Freedom Crossing Press.

———. 1984b. The master's tools will never dismantle the master's house. In *Sister/outsider,* by Audre Lorde, 110–113. Trumansburg, N.Y.: Freedom: Crossing Press.

Lott, Eric. 1995. *Love and theft: Blackface minstrelsy and the American working class.* Oxford: Oxford University Press.

Lowe, Lisa, and David Floyd. 1997. *The politics of culture in the shadow of capital.* Durham, N.C.: Duke University Press.

Madsen, Richard. 1993. Global monoculture, multiculture, and polyculture. *Social Research* 60, no. 3: 493–511.

Magubane, Zine. 2002. Black skin, white masks: Black masculinity in the postmodern age. *Men and Masculinities* 4, no. 3: 233–257

———. 2003. *Bringing the empire home: Race, class, and gender in Britain and colonial South Africa.* Chicago: University of Chicago Press.

Malabon, Dawn B. 2001. The making of *The Debut.* In *The Debut: The Making of a Filipino American Film,* ed. Gene Cajayon and John Manal Castro, 1–23. Chicago: Tulitos Press.

Manalansan, Martin, IV. 1995. Speaking of AIDS: Language and the Filipino "gay" experience in America. In *Discrepant histories,* ed. Vicente Rafael, 193–220. Philadelphia: Temple University Press.

———. 2003. *Global divas.* Durham, N.C.: Duke University Press.

Marchetti, G. 1993. *Romance and the "yellow peril": Race, sex, and discursive strategies in Hollywood fiction.* Berkeley: University of California Press.

Marx, Karl, and Frederick Engels. [1848] 1998. *The communist manifesto.* London: Verso.

McClintock, Anne. 1997. "No longer in a future heaven": Gender, race, and nationalism. In *Sites of desire, economics of pleasure: Sexualities in Asia and the Pacific,* ed. Lenore Manderson and Margaret Jolly, 89–112. Chicago: University of Chicago Press.

Michaels, Walter Benn. 1995. Race into culture: A critical genealogy of cultural identity. In *Identities*, ed. Kwame Anthony Appiah and Henry Louis Gates Jr., 32–62. Chicago: University of Chicago.

Mills, C. Wright. 1959. *The sociological imagination.* New York: Oxford University Press.

Minh-ha, Trinh. 1991. *When the moon waxes red.* New York: Routledge.

MSNBC. 1998. http://www.msnbc.com.

Mulkay, Michael. 1998. *On humor.* Oxford: Basil Blackwell.

Mura, David. 1996. How America unsexes the Asian American male. *New York Times,* August 22.

———. 1998. Strangers in the village. In *Multicultural literacy: Opening the American mind,* ed. Rick Simonson and Scott Walker, 135–153. St. Paul, Minn.: Graywolf Press.

Nakamura, Lisa. 2002. *Cybertypes: Race, ethnicity, and identity on the Internet.* New York: Routledge.

Narayan, Uma. 1997. *Dislocating cultures: Identities, cultures and Third-World feminism.* New York: Routledge.

Okamura, Jonathan. 1998. *Imagining the Filipino American diaspora: Transnational relations, identities, and communities.* New York: Taylor & Francis.

Omi, Michael, and Howard Winant. 1994. *Racial formation in the United States: From the 1960s to the 1990s.* 2nd ed. London: Routledge.

Ordoñez, Raquel Z. 1997. Living in the shadows: The undocumented immigrant experience of Filipinos. In *Filipino Americans: Transformation and Identity,* ed. Maria P. Root, 112–142. Thousand Oaks, Calif.: Sage Publications.

Pido, Antonio J. A. 1986. *Pilipinos in America: Macro-micro dimensions of immigration and integration.* New York: Center for Migration Studies.

Pieterse, Jan Nederveen. 1995. *White on black: Images of South Africa and blacks in Western popular culture.* New Haven, Conn.: Yale University Press.

Poster, Mark. 1995. Postmodern virtualities. In *Cyberspace/cyberbodies/cyberpunk: Cultures of technological embodiment,* ed. Mike Featherstone and Roger Burrows, 79–96. Thousand Oaks, Calif.: Sage Publications.

———. 1998. Virtual ethnicity: Tribal identity in an age of global communications. In *Cybersociety 2.0,* ed. Steven G. Jones, 184–211. Thousand Oaks, Calif.: Sage Publications.

Pratt, Mary Louis. 1992. *Imperial eyes: Travel writing and transculturation.* New York: Routledge.

Psthas, George. 1995. *Conversation analysis.* Thousand Oaks, Calif.: Sage Publications.

Radhakrishnan, Rajagopalan. 1996. *Diasporic meditations: Between home and location.* Minneapolis: University of Minnesota Press.

Rafael, Vicente L. 1993. *Contracting colonialism: Translation and Christian conversion in Tagalog society under early Spanish rule.* Durham, N.C.: Duke University Press.

———. 1995a. *Discrepant histories.* Philadelphia: Temple University Press.

———. 1995b. Taglish, or the phantom lingua Franca. *Public Culture* 8, no. 1: 101–126.

———. 1997. "Your grief is our gossip": Overseas Filipinos and other spectral presences. *Public Culture* 9: 267–291.

———. 2000. *White love and other events in Filipino history.* Durham, N.C.: Duke University Press.

Rajchman, John, ed. 1995. *The identity in question.* New York: Routledge.

Ravitch, Diane. 1993. Multiculturalism: E pluribus plures. In *Our times: Readings from recent periodicals,* ed. Robert Atwan, 353–369. Boston: St. Martin's Press.

Reagon, Bernice. 1992. Coalition politics: Turning the century. In *Race, class, and gender: An anthology,* ed. Margaret L. Anderson and Patricia Hill Collins, 503–509. Belmont, Calif.: Wadsworth.

Rheingold, Howard. 1993. *The virtual community.* New York: Harper Perennial.

Riggs, Marlon. 1995. *Black is . . . Black ain't.* San Francisco: California Newsreel.

Riverdance homepage. 1997. http://www.riverdance.com.

Rorty, Richard. 1995. Demonizing the academy. *Harper's* 289 (January): 13–17.

Rosaldo, Renato. 1989. *Culture and truth: The remaking of social analysis.* Boston: Beacon Press.

Rouse, Roger. 1991. Mexican migration and the social space of postmodernism. *Diaspora* 1, no. 1: 8–23.

Sacks, Oliver. 1997. *The island of the colorblind.* New York: Alfred A. Knopf.

Safran, William. 1991. Diasporas in modern societies: Myths of homeland and return. *Diasporas* (spring): 82–99.

San Juan, E., Jr. 1992. *Racial formations/critical transformations: Articulations of power in ethnic and racial studies in the United States.* Atlantic Highlands, N.J.: Humanities Press.

Santa Romana-Cruz, Neni. 1997. *You know you're Filipino if . . .* Manila: Tahanan Books.

Saukko, Paula. 1998. Voice, discourse, and space: Competing/combining methodologies in cultural studies. In *Cultural studies: A research volume,* vol. 3, ed. Norman K. Denzin. London: JAI Press.

Schiller, Nina G., and Christina Szanton Blanc. 1993. *Nations unbound: Transnational projects, postcolonial predicaments, and deterritorialized nation-states.* New York: Gordon & Breach Publishing Group.

Scott, Joan W. 1995. Multiculturalism and the politics of identity. In *The identity in question,* ed. John Rajchman, 3–12. New York: Routledge.

Shibutani, Tomatsu. 1995. Reference groups as perspectives. *American Journal of Sociology* 60: 562–569.

Smith, Zadie. 2000. *White teeth.* New York: Vintage Books.

So, Alvin Y. 1990. *Social change and development: Modernization, dependency, and world-system theories.* Newbury Park, Calif: Sage.

soc.culture.filipino. 1994. List and answers to frequently asked questions. August 28.

Stacks, Carol. 1996. *All our kin: Strategies for survival in the black community.* New York: Basic Books.

Stacy, Margaret. 1969. The myth of community studies. *British Journal of Sociology* 20, no. 2: 134–147.

Stiglitz, Joseph. 2003. *Globalization and its discontents.* New York: W. W. Norton and Company.

Stoler, A. 1997. Educating desire in colonial Southeast Asia: Foucault, Freud, and imperialist sexualities. In *Sites of desire, economics of pleasure: Sexualities in Asia and the Pacific,* ed. Lenore Manderson and Margaret Jolly, 27–47. Chicago: University of Chicago Press.

Stonequist, Everett V. 1961. *The marginal man: A study in personality and culture conflict.* New York: Russell & Russell Publishers.

Strauss, Anselm. 1978. A social world perspective. *Studies in Symbolic Interaction* 1: 119–128.

Sturdevant, S. P., and Brenda Stolzfus. 1992. *Let the good times roll: Prostitution and the U.S. military in Asia.* New York: New Press.

Taylor, Charles. 1994. The politics of recognition. In *Multiculturalism,* ed. Amy Gutmann, 25–73. Princeton, N.J.: Princeton University Press.

Theroux, Paul. 1993. *The happy isles of Oceania: Paddling the Pacific.* New York: Ballantine.

Thomas, William I., and Dorothy Swaine Thomas. 1928. *The child in America.* New York: Knopf.

Toelkin, Barre. 1996. *The dynamics of folklore.* Logan: Utah State University Press.

Tuan, Mia. 1999. *Forever foreigners or honorary whites? The Asian ethnic experience today.* New Brunswick, N.J.: Rutgers University Press.

Turkle, Sherry. 1994. Constructions and reconstructions of self in virtual reality: Playing in the MUDs. *Mind, Culture, and Activity* 1, no. 3: 158–167.

Võ, Linda, and Rick Bonus. 2000. *Contemporary Asian American communities: Intersections and divergences.* Philadelphia: Temple University Press.

Wallace, Michelle. 1995. The search for the "good enough" mammy: Multiculturalism, popular culture, and psychoanalysis. In *Multiculturalism: A critical reader,* ed. David Theo Goldberg, 259–268. London: Blackwell.

Wang, Wayne. 1985. *Dim Sum.* Beverly Hills, Calif.: Pacific Arts Video.

———. 1989. *Chan is missing.* New York: New Yorker Video.

Waters, Mary C. 1990. *Ethnic options: Choosing identities in America.* Berkeley: University of California Press.

———. 1996. Optional ethnicities: For whites only? In *Origins and destinies,* ed. Sylvia Pedraza and Rubén G. Rumbaut, 444–454. Belmont, Calif.: Wadsworth.

Weber, Max. [1920] 1997. *Theory of social and economic organization.* New York: Simon & Schuster Adult Publishing Group.

West, Cornel. 1995. A matter of life and death. In *The identity in question,* ed. John Rajchman, 15–19. New York: Routledge.

West, Lois A. 1992. Feminist nationalist social movements: Beyond universalism and towards a gendered cultural relativism. *Women's Studies International Forum* 15, no. 5–6: 563–579.

Williams, Hywel. 2001. Crusade is a dirty word. *The Guardian,* September 19.

Wired News. 2001. Estrada got the message. http://www.wired.com/news/business/0,1367,41360,00.html.

Wolf, Diane. 1997. Family secrets: Transnational struggles among children of Filipino immigrants. *Sociological Perspectives* 40, no. 3: 455–482.

Young, Robert J. C. 1995. *Colonial desire: Hybridity in theory, culture, and race.* London: Routledge.

Yuval-Davis, Nira, and Floya Anthias, eds. 1989. *Women-nation-state.* Basingstoke, England: Macmillan.

Zhou, Min, and Carl L. Bankston. 1999. *Growing up American: How Vietnamese children adapt to life in the United States.* New York: Russell Sage.

Index

Abakada alphabet, 69, 70, 71, 72, 115, 119, 160n5
African Americans. *See* black Americans
Agoncillo, Teodorno, 122
Aguinaldo, General Emilio, 39, 62, 63
Algiers, 38
Al-Qaeda, 3, 7
American: men, 83, 86–87, 89; women, 85
"Americanness," 22, 29, 47, 75
America Online (AOL), 21
Anderson, Benedict, 3
Anzaldúa, Gloria, 157n6
anticolonialism. *See* colonialism
Anti-Miscegenation Act, 38, 81
Appadurai, Arjun, 8, 45, 158n5
Appiah, Kwame, 25
Aquino, Belinda, 58, 105
Aquino, Benigno (Ninoy), 58, 59, 114, 115
Arab Americans, 2–3
Asian: Americans, 37, 42, 38, 102; Asian American women, 93; immigrants, 37; men, 60, 81–82, 93, 97–99, 103; women, 40–41, 45, 79, 81–82, 84, 90, 93, 94–99, 101–102, 108

Asian American Journalists Association, 37
Asian female/white male relationships. *See* gender
"Asiaphile," 25–26, 79, 95–97, 99–103, 112
Australia, 20, 33
Austria, 20
authenticity: essentialism, 80, 90, 93, 102, 131, 138, 142; of Filipino identity, 25, 40, 79, 115, 127, 131, 135; language, 68, 70, 73, 102, 131, 138, 142; as membership, 53, 62, 64, 76, 132; presumed nonexistence, xviii–xix, 49, 135; quest for, 5–6, 40, 46, 45, 135; uses, 23–25, 47, 54

Bakhtin, Mikhail M., 16, 117, 161n1
balikbayans, 56, 57, 116, 124
barkadas, 57
Bautista, Veltisezar, 159n6
Bello, M. and V. Reyes, 6
Bhabha, Homi K., 30, 143
Bin Laden, Osama, 2–3
Bisayan people, 135
black: Americans, 35, 75, 94–95, 123; identity, 123; men, 94
black English, 123

Black Hills, 37
Black Is . . . Black Ain't, 157n6
Black Skin, White Masks, 35
Bonifacio, Andres, 51
Bonilla-Silva, Eduardo, 13
Bonus, Rick, 157n2, 159n7
Bourdieu, Pierre, 11
Boyarin, Jonathan, 122, 123
Burayidi, Michael A., 34

Cagayon, Gene, 157n2
Calhoun, Craig, 160n4
Canada, 20, 33
capitalism, 23, 24, 26, 32
Catholicism, 89–90, 126, 137
Cebu, 84, 86–87
Cebuano, 119
Cebuanas, 86–87
Chan is Missing, 11–12
Chan, Sucheng, 69
Chang, K.A. and Julian M. Groves, 90, 105
Chin, Vincent, 38
Chinese American community, 12, 161n4
Cho, Margaret, 102
Chow, Rey, 147
Chung, Connie, 102
CIA, 2
citizenship, 24; and Filipino identity, 109–110, 138–139
Clark military base. *See* militarization
classification, 44, 127, 128, 143
coalition politics, 80
coalitions, 4, 25, 27, 80, 100
colonialism: anticolonialism, 51–52, 79, 83, 90, 109, 111; "colonial mentality," xix, 4, 24, 25, 30, 59, 62, 67, 71, 72, 94, 103, 115–118, 120, 124, 137, 142, 146, 160n6, 161n1; colonial projects, 38–39, 112; cultural colonialism, 87–88, 111; diasporic communities, 3, 48; effects of, 4, 5, 8, 26–27, 78, 112; Filipino identity, 41, 50, 79, 94; impact on identity, 23, 87, 132, 139, 146; language, 67; mimicry, 118, 126, 133; neocolonialism, 5, in Philippines, xviii, 48–51, 87–88;

Japanese–Philippine colonial relationship, 50–51; Philippine–Spanish colonial relationship, 49–51, 59, 69, 90, 126, 135; Philippine–U.S. colonial relationship, 15, 23, 40, 50, 59, 68, 69, 81, 83, 87, 89–90, 93, 117, 121, 124, 135, 140, 146, 160n6; racism, 82
color-blind racism. *See* racism
commodification, of Filipino women, 80–81, 84, 86–88, 109–111
community formation, 26
computer-mediated-communication, 7–8, 143, 158n4
Contemplacion, Flor, 78–79, 114, 116, 130, 160n3
Connerly, Ward, 43
Cubans, 49
culture: African, 94; American, xviii, xxi, 24, 58, 84, 116, 140, 146; construction of, 53–54, 134; Filipino, 14, 23, 24, 41, 49, 57, 67, 75, 79, 90, 100, 115, 137–138; hip-hop, 133; homogenization of, 32, 42, 70, 73, 122; Japanese, 72; McDonaldization, 32; multiculturalism, 5, 23, 32, 33–35, 46, 49, 53; racialization of, 23, 24, 27, 32, 40, 52; Western, 81–82, 84, 102

"death of the Subject," 143, 135–136
deconstructionism, 5, 8
Debut, The, xviii, 46, 157n2
Def Jam records, 133
DejaNews, 19
Department of Education, Culture, and Sports of the Philippine, 69
diaspora: colonialism, 3, 48; diasporic communities, 3–5, 7, 10, 47, 55, 127, 132, 133, 140, 159n2; disaporic identities, 45, 55–56, 133, 136, 143, 159n2; Filipino diaspora, 4, 10, 20, 21, 23, 26, 32, 48, 56, 112, 115–116, 124, 135, 141, 144, 159n2; Jewish diaspora, 8–9, 122
digital divide, 10, 144
Dim Sum, 161n4

diversity, 134–138
"double consciousness," 88
DuBois, W.E.B, 13, 88
Dukes of Hazzard, 129

Ebonics, 73
emoticons, 144–145
England, 33, 38
English language, 17, 24, 63, 67–77,
    102–103, 116, 118–122, 125, 137,
    161n3
Enloe, Cynthia, 83–84
Espiritu, Yen Le, *xviii*, 105, 159n7
essentialism, 24, 25, 48, 54, 55, 59,
    61, 72, 79, 81–82, 106, 108–110;
    authenticity, 80, 90, 93, 102, 131,
    138, 142
Estrada, President Joesph, 4, 157–
    158n1
Euro-centrism, 5, 23, 24
Exclusionary Act, 38

Fanon, Frantz, 30, 35, 36, 38, 118,
    146
FBI, 2
feminism, 81–82, 84, 96, 105, 108,
    111
"Filipina," 79, 80, 83, 84, 105, 129,
    160n1
Filipino Americans, xviii, xxi, xxii,
    19, 23, 41, 44, 46, 49–50, 57, 62,
    64, 74–75, 79, 80, 102, 107, 116–
    117, 118, 124, 127, 129, 130, 132,
    157n2; and dichotomy, 26, 65,
    66, 74–75, 89, 92, 108, 110, 116,
    117, 141, 142, first generation
    Filipino Americans, xix, 75, 90,
    129; "1.5" generation, xx, xxi, 75,
    129; second generation, xx, xxii,
    38, 45, 46, 129; third generation,
    22; women, 81, 105, 142
Filipino-American War, 160n6
Filipino culture. *See* culture
Filipino diaspora. *See* diaspora
Filipino identity: articulation of, 5,
    26, 73, 124, 142; authenticity, 25,
    40, 79, 115, 127, 131, 135;
    citizenship, 109–110, 138–139;
    colonialism, 41, 50, 79, 94;
    construction of, 24, 46, 50, 73,
    87, 114, 117, 141; gender, 25, 87–

89, 141; maintenance of, 67, 124,
    139; search for, xviii, 23, 25, 40,
    129–130, 135
Filipino men, 88, 93, 97, 100, 103,
    108, 141
Filipino nationalism, 79, 80, 83, 84,
    105, 122, 130
Filipino women, 15, 25, 78–92, 97,
    102–109, 112, 141, 160n1;
    commodification of, 80–81, 84,
    86–88, 109–111. *See also*
    "Filipina"
"Filipinoness," 22, 29–31, 42, 59,
    62, 74, 116, 122–123, 129, 130–
    131, 132, 142
Filipinos in the Philippines, 64, 66,
    116; Bisayan people, 135; Ilocano
    people, 135; Tagalog people, 135
"flame wars," 14–15, 18, 116, 127,
    130, 132
Flatley, Michael, 34
"Flipbonics," 73–77
France, 68
Francis, Armet, 55
Fu Manchu films. *See* martial arts
    films

Galman, Rolando, 115
gender: Asian female/white male
    relationships, 25, 79, 89, 93, 95,
    97, 104; Asian men, 60, 81–82,
    93, 97–99, 103; Asian women,
    40–41, 45, 79, 81–82, 84, 90, 93,
    94–99, 101–102, 108; *Cebuanas*,
    86–87; feminism, 81–82, 84, 96,
    105, 108, 111 "Filipina," 79, 80,
    83, 84, 105, 129, 160n1; Filipino
    identity, 25, 87–89, 141; Filipino
    men, 88, 93, 97, 100, 103, 108,
    141; Filipino women, 15, 25, 78–
    92, 97, 102–109, 112, 141, 160n1;
    commodification of Filipino
    women, 80–81, 84, 86–88, 109–
    111; Filipino American women,
    81, 105, 142; gendered
    assumptions, 40; Madonna/
    whore dichotomy, 89; Maria
    Clara stereotype, 89–90;
    patriarchy, 5, 8, 25, 26, 79, 82,
    90, 91, 94, 102, 112, 139; sexism,
    5, 91, 94, 98, 109, 12; Western

gender: *(continued)*
    men, 82, 84, 88, 96, 110; Western
    women, 81; Westernized Filipino
    women, 108; Western feminism,
    82, 96; white men, 79, 81–82, 88,
    93, 95, 101–102, 104, 108, 130;
    white women, 41, 85, 90, 96, 98,
    108, 110; women as gender
    markers, 25, 80, 86, 87, 94, 100,
    103–104, 141
Gilroy, Paul, 8
globalization, 4, 24, 45, 59, 111, 133,
    161n2
Goldilocks, 125
Greece, 20
Guam, 49
Gupta, Akhil and James Ferguson,
    136, 159n1

Hall, Stuart, 8, 55, 136, 138, 140,
    160n3
Hart Cellar Act (1965), 129
Hawaiians, 49
hegemony, 29–30, 94, 141
heterogeneity, 55
Hewson, Claire, 11
Hong Kong, 90
homeland concept, 56, 62
Hotmail, 21
Hughes, Everett C., 53
humor, 26, 73, 76, 113–133, 142
hybridity, intentional, 118, 119, 120,
    137, 142

identity, 12, 55, 110–111, 136, 138,
    146, 157n2, 159n2, 160n3; black,
    123; colonialism, 23, 87, 132,
    139, 146; Jewish, 8–9, 122, 123;
    Filipino, xviii, xix, xxiii, 5, 12,
    14, 17, 23, 24, 25, 26, 40, 41, 46,
    50, 67, 73, 79, 87, 89, 94, 109–
    110, 114, 115, 117, 124, 127, 129,
    130, 131, 135, 138–139, 141, 142;
    formation of, 3–4, 5, 14, 17;
    importance of, 6, 134–135;
    politics of, 80, 134, 160n4;
    national, 25
Ilocano people, 135
imagery, 44–45, 48, 54, 60, 115, 140
immigrant labor, 37
incorporation, 117

indentured servitude, 37
India, 43
indymedia.org, 158n2, 161n1
Institutional Review Board (IRB), 19
Internet, xix, 3, 7, 19, 41, 86, 93,
    109–111, 127, 140, 143–144
Internet communities, 9, 11, 132,
    143
interracial relationships, 93–95, 97,
    99, 101, 104, 109
Irish Americans, 34
Islam, 2
Italy, 21

Japanese Americans, 36
Japanese language, 72, 119
Jewish diaspora. *See* diaspora
jokes, 26, 100, 111, 113–133, 134,
    136, 142
Joy Luck Club, The, 102
Jufran, 125

"*Kano,*" 40–41, 89, 92, 104, 110,
    112, 120, 141
Katipunan, 39, 160n6
King, Martin Luther, Jr., 34
Kling, Rob and Suzi Iacono, 20
Koran, The, 2
Kwan, Michelle, 37

language, 67–68, 70, 115, 161n1;
    authenticity, 68, 70, 73, 102, 131,
    138, 142; colonialism, 67
Latinos, 37, 42, 89
Law, Lisa, 84, 92
Lee, Wen Ho, 38
Lippard, 132
Lorde, Audre, 94

Macedo, Edmundo, 37
Madonna/whore dichotomy, 89
Mafran, 125
Maga, Delia, 160n3
mail-order brides, 79, 84, 86–89,
    91–93, 101, 104, 114
Makati, 59
Manalansan, Martin F., 159n7
Manila, 59, 84
Marcos, President Ferdinand, 6, 51,
    59, 84, 92, 114, 115
Maria Clara stereotype, 89–90

martial arts films, 82
Marx, Karl and Frederich Engels, 48
"method of instances," 11, 17
Mexicans, 49
militarization, 51, 59, 83–84, 90,
    126; Clark military base, 83–84;
    Subic Bay military base, 83–84;
    Wallace military base, 83–84
Mills, C. Wright, 11
mimicry, 30, 118, 119, 120, 137,
    142; and colonialism, 118, 126,
    133
Minh-ha, Trinh T., 138–139
"model minority" concept. *See*
    racism
MSNBC, 37, 158n4
Multicultural Act, 33
multiculturalism, 5, 23, 32, 33–35,
    46, 49, 53
Multi-user Dimensions (MUD's), 9
Muslim influence in the
    Philippines, 135

naming, 50, 130
National Agenda for a Multicultural
    Australia, 33
national identity, 25
nations, 1, 3, 9, 33, 47, 68, 80, 87
Native Americans, 36, 120, 150n3
neocolonialism. See colonialism
Nightline, 35
normalization, process of, 38–39,
    88–89, 97
Norplant, 36

objects, as carriers of culture, 31–32,
    53, 123, 128–129
Okamura, Jonathan, 159n7
Omi, Michael and Howard Winant,
    13, 88
Olympic Games, 37
Ordoñez, Raquel Z., 92
Orientalism. *See* racism

Pakistan, 43
Pakistani Intelligence Agency (ISI),
    2
parallel worlds, 9
patriarchy, 5, 8, 25, 26, 79, 82, 90,
    91, 94, 102, 112, 139
perpendicular worlds, 9, 144

personal ads, 79, 86–89, 106, 110
Philippine News, The, 127, 132
Philippines, The, 20, 21, 24, 31, 38,
    39, 46, 49, 49–51, 58, 61, 83, 92,
    104, 110, 115, 117, 121, 122, 126,
    135; and colonialism, xviii, 48–
    51, 87–88
Program for Internet News and Mail
    (PINE), 15
pronunciation, 118, 120
Proposition 209, 43
prostitution, 83–84, 86–87, 92, 93,
    105
postcolonial theorists, 7–8, 110,
    158n4
Poster, Mark, 8–9
protests, 4
Psthas, George, 11
Puerto Ricans, 49

Racial Privacy Act, 43
racial projects, 36, 37, 38, 39–40, 38,
    54, 78
racism, 4, 5, 7, 13, 23, 34–35, 36, 38,
    00, 95, 90–99, 101, 110, 157n2;
    antiracists, 43, 111; colonialism,
    82, color-blind racism, 13, 43;
    essentialism, 24, 25, 48, 54, 55, 59,
    61, 72, 79, 81–82, 106, 108–110;
    Euro-centrism, 5, 23, 24; "model
    minority" concept, 42, 60;
    Orientalism, 5, 23, 26, 36, 75, 81,
    84, 96–98, 102, 112, 139; "reverse
    racism," 35, 43; white supremacy,
    23, 37, 94, 97–98, 111
Radhakrishnan, Rajagopalan, 8, 136
Rafael, Vicente L., 116, 118, 143,
    159n7
Reagon, Bernice, 80
Riggs, Marlon, 157n6
Riverdance, 34
Rizal, José, 51
Rouse, Roger, 159n2
Rubin, Rick, 133

Safran, William, 159n2
Samoa, 49
Saudi Arabia, 2
Saukko, Paula, 11
Schutz, Alfred, 13
sexism, 5, 91, 94, 98, 109

sex tourist industry, 84, 91–92, 97
Singapore, 20, 106, 116, 160n3
slave labor, 37
sly civility. *See* mimicry
Smith, Jaune Quick-to-See, 120
Smith, Zadie, 38, 48, 118
Spain, 49, 160n6
Spanish-American War, 39
Spanish language, 17, 118
speech genre, 117
Spencer's, 129
social constructionist theory, 42–44
sociological methods, 12–13
Steely Dan, 19
sterilization, 36
Sugiyama, Brandon, 37

Sweden, 20
Tagalog, xxii, 17, 24, 47, 63, 68–77,
    115, 116, 119, 120, 122–125,
    160n4, 161n3
Tagalog people, 135
"Taglish," 63, 118, 120, 122, 127,
    133
Tan, Amy, 102
terrorism, 1–2
thenation.com, 158n2
Toelkin, Barre, 125
"traditional" identities, 23, 55, 132.
    See also authenticity
transnational communities, 6, 9, 32,
    49, 54–55, 66, 110, 133, 140
Turkle, Sherry, 9

United States of America, 20, 23, 25,
    33, 34, 35, 38, 46, 49, 61, 68, 83,
    92
University of California, 43
University of Illinois at Urbana-
    Champaign, xx
U.S.-based stereotypes, 42
USSR-Afghanistan War, 2
"us versus them," 2

values, 53–54, 56–62

Wacquant, Loïc, 11
Walker, John, 2
Wallace military base, 83–84
Wang, Wayne, 12, 161n4
Waters, 34
Weber, Max, 13, 146
Webster's Dictionary, 133, 144
West Bank, The, 43
West, Cornell, 94
Western: feminism, 82, 96; media,
    81–82, 90, 102; men, 82, 84, 88,
    96, 110; women, 81
Westernization, 110, 121, 127
Westernized Filipino women, 108
West, Lois, 89, 105
white: Americans, 36, 75, 88, 89,
    130, 158n2; men, 79, 81–82, 88,
    93, 95, 101–102, 104, 108, 130;
    women, 41, 85, 90, 96, 98, 108,
    110
white supremacy. *See* racism
White Teeth, 38
"whitewashing," 41, 51, 92–93, 94,
    108, 131
"Whiggie," 25–26, 79, 95–97, 100–
    103, 112
Williams, Hywel, 1–2, 3
women, as gender markers, 25, 80,
    86, 87, 94, 100, 103–104, 141
workingforchange.com, 161n1
World War II, 36, 37, 119

Year of the Dragon, 82
"yellow fever," 89, 91, 95–96, 104
Yiddish, 123
youth, 57, 60
Yuval-Davis, Nira and Floya
    Anthias, 80, 87

znet.org, 158n2

About the Author

EMILY NOELLE IGNACIO is an assistant professor of sociology at Loyola University Chicago. Her work on the effect of media technologies on communities has appeared in the *Sociological Quarterly, Cultural Studies/Critical Methodologies, Journal of the American Society for Information Science,* and *Library Trends.* She is currently examining the role of "home masses" in the racial and cultural formation processes within the Filipino American community in Chicago.